SAGE was founded in 1965 by Sara Miller McCune to support the dissemination of usable knowledge by publishing innovative and high-quality research and teaching content. Today, we publish over 900 journals, including those of more than 400 learned societies, more than 800 new books per year, and a growing range of library products including archives, data, case studies, reports, and video. SAGE remains majority-owned by our founder, and after Sara's lifetime will become owned by a charitable trust that secures our continued independence.

Los Angeles | London | New Delhi | Singapore | Washington DC | Melbourne

RIGHT TO HEALTH IN INDIA

RIGHT TO HEALTH IN INDIA
Law, Policy and Practice

SOUGATA TALUKDAR

Los Angeles | London | New Delhi
Singapore | Washington DC | Melbourne

First published in 2022 by

SAGE Publications India Pvt Ltd
B1/I-1 Mohan Cooperative Industrial Area
Mathura Road, New Delhi 110 044, India
www.sagepub.in

SAGE Publications Inc
2455 Teller Road
Thousand Oaks, California 91320, USA

SAGE Publications Ltd
1 Oliver's Yard, 55 City Road
London EC1Y 1SP, United Kingdom

SAGE Publications Asia-Pacific Pte Ltd
18 Cross Street #10-10/11/12
China Square Central
Singapore 048423

Published by Vivek Mehra for SAGE Publications India Pvt Ltd. Typeset in 10.5/13 pt Berkeley by AG Infographics, Delhi.

Library of Congress Cataloging-in-Publication Data

Names: Talukdar, Sougata, author.
Title: Right to health in India : law, policy and practice / Sougata Talukdar.
Description: Thousand Oaks, CA : SAGE Publications India Pvt Ltd, 2022. | Includes index. |
Identifiers: LCCN 2021053356 | ISBN 9789354792557 (hardback) | ISBN 9789354792632 (epub) | ISBN 9789354792717 (ebook)
Subjects: LCSH: Right to health–India. | Public health laws–India. | Medical care–Law and legislation–India.
Classification: LCC KNS2111 .T35 2022 | DDC 342.54/085–dc23/eng/20211223
LC record available at https://lccn.loc.gov/2021053356

ISBN: 978-93-5479-255-7 (HB)

SAGE Team: Aarooshi Garg, Syed Husain Naqvi and Rajinder Kaur

To my parents

Mr Salil Kumar Talukdar and Mrs Ila Talukdar

Thank you for choosing a SAGE product!
If you have any comment, observation or feedback,
I would like to personally hear from you.

Please write to me at **contactceo@sagepub.in**

Vivek Mehra, Managing Director and CEO, SAGE India.

Bulk Sales

SAGE India offers special discounts
for purchase of books in bulk.
We also make available special imprints
and excerpts from our books on demand.

For orders and enquiries, write to us at

Marketing Department
SAGE Publications India Pvt Ltd
B1/I-1, Mohan Cooperative Industrial Area
Mathura Road, Post Bag 7
New Delhi 110044, India

E-mail us at **marketing@sagepub.in**

Subscribe to our mailing list

Write to **marketing@sagepub.in**

This book is also available as an e-book.

CONTENTS

PREFACE

Health and human rights are complementary to each other in securing and advancing human well-being. The rights-based concept of health includes healthcare yet goes beyond it to embrace the broader social dimensions and context of individual and population well-being. Since 1948, the promotion and protection of human rights to health have received increased attention from international and national perspectives around the globe. United Nations, World Health Organization and International Labour Organization are playing crucial roles in addressing 'health' concerns within the international human rights norms by casting responsibilities on the state parties to secure the right to health of the people within their domestic law and also to monitor the compliance of the same. The case of India is no different. India secured the right to health of its people by putting the responsibility on the government to promote and protect health through legislative enactments, judicial pronouncements and policy adaptations. In this background, this book endeavours to explore the scope and ambit of constitutional, legislative and policy protection of the right to health in India with special reference to the recent developments in the field of the right to health under international human rights law.

The book is divided into 10 more chapters including the Introduction and Conclusion. Chapter 1 is preliminary discussing theoretical foundations of health, the right to health and its relationship with human rights. Chapter 2 examines the international legal perspective relating to the right to health, whereas Chapter 3 explores the recognition of the right to health under the Indian Constitutional framework. Chapter 4 is devoted to present the recognition of various issues relating to the right to health under the Indian legislative and policy context. Chapters 5 and 6 document the available protection of the right to health of women and children and disabled persons under international human rights law and the Indian legal system. Since the scope and ambit of protection against epidemic diseases are decisive at the current juncture, Chapter 7 deals with the right to health in the context of epidemic diseases under the international and national legal arena. Chapter 8 is devoted to discussing the counter of international human rights law and national legislative schemes that deal with occupational health hazards.

It is fervently hoped that this book will prove immensely useful not only to the law students of undergraduate and postgraduate but also to the researchers, academicians, jurists, lawyers, judges and members of civil society.

ACKNOWLEDGEMENTS

I would like to acknowledge the immense help which I have received from others at the time of conducting the current study on the law relating to the right to health. Obviously, I must start with the recording of acknowledgments that my greatest debt is to my PhD supervisor Professor (Dr) Jatindra Kumar Das, Faculty of Law, University of Calcutta, who has, during the initial stages of current work, suggested the organic modification of the scope of enquiry of the present study, as well as inspired me constantly to pursue this research work.

I would like to express my thanks to Mr Basana Manna, Assistant Professor, Sureswar Dutta Law College, and Mr Subhajyoti Das, Advocate, Calcutta High Court for their cordial help extended to pursue this study. It is my great pleasure to acknowledge the helps that I received during this study from all my colleagues and friends. Finally, I am deeply indebted to my parents, elder brother, elder brother's wife and little Mohita Talukdar for allowing me to conduct this study by releasing day-to-day burden from my shoulder.

Introduction

The word 'health' is an amorphous word that lacks a single definition. It means different things to different people depending upon the
situations under which it has been defined and also upon the various
determinants of health.[1] Mahatma Gandhi validated the wealth nature
of health when he said: 'It is health that is real wealth and not pieces
of gold and silver'.[2] He was alluding to the idea that health is more
important than monetary wealth, and that a society cannot prosper
unless its people are healthy. Health is necessary for productivity
and full enjoyment of life. The traditional medical concept of health
was based on the assumption that health and disease are objective
and observable phenomena. Developments in the areas of anatomy,
bacteriology and physiology contributed to this view. However, with
the development of the human rights regime, the positive definition
of health has evolved under the Constitutional framework of the
World Health Organization. WHO defines health, 'a state of complete
physical, mental and social well-being and not merely the absence of
disease or infirmity'.[3] By adding the psychological and social criteria,
this definition of health by the WHO acknowledged that health and
illness are essentially multi-causal and shifted the focus from a strictly
medical perspective to the social and psychological perspectives.

Recent development in connection with the normative definition
of the right to health includes both healthcare and health conditions.
This right expands to the right to participate in decisions affecting one's

---

[1] Avanish Kumar, Human Right to Health (Satyam Law International 2007).

[2] M. K. Gandhi, Keys to Health (Navjivan Publishing 1948).

[3] Constitution of the WHO, Preamble.

health. Therefore, it links health issues with active social citizenship which ensures equality of access to care and other preconditions for good health and demands elimination of systemic discrimination in the realization of the right to health. All these interconnected rights imply legal obligations to ensure the right to health and its fullest enjoyment by every individual and also identify the right to live with dignity as the foundation of the right to health.[4] In this background, it is important to understand the evolution of the concept of health from early biological definition to recent WHO's measurement-oriented conceptualization.

International human rights instruments like the Universal Declaration of Human Rights (UDHR), International Covenant on Economic, Social and Cultural Rights (ICESCR), Alma Ata Declaration, and others, specifically recognize the fullest enjoyment of the right to health. The UN Commission in Human Rights Resolution of 2002 provides that the right to the enjoyment of the highest attainable standard of physical and mental health is a human right and such a right derives its validity from the inherent dignity of the human being.[5] Moreover, through the Millennium Development Goals and Sustainable Development Goals, the conscience of international society puts harder stress on the realization of the right to health. The State's responsibility to assure this basic right is also guaranteed under international law. Thus, the recent development of the international right to health is a drive toward its 'real-life' implementation for the benefit of individuals, communities and populations, and is a movement to ensure the human right to health.[6]

The Indian approach to secure the right to health to its citizens is evident from numerous legislative enactments, judicial pronouncements and policy orientation. The Constitutional mandate emerges

[4] Audrey Chapman, *The Foundations of a Human Right to Health: Human Rights and Bioethics in Dialogue*, 17(1) HHR 6, 9 (2015).

[5] Commission on Human Rights Resolution 2002/31 on 'The Right of Everyone to the Enjoyment of the Highest Attainable Standard of Physical and Mental Health'.

[6] Paul Hunt, *Interpreting the International Right to Health in a Human Rights-Based Approach to Health*, 18(2) HHR 109, 110 (2016).

from the directive principles of state policy, the philosophy of preamble and other provisions of the Constitution which recognize the right relating to the health of the individual and public at large by casting various responsibilities upon the State and local authorities. However, the judiciary *i.e.*, the Supreme Court and the High Courts have addressed several issues related to the right to health by expanding the periphery of the right to 'life' under Article 21 of the Constitution and thus has acknowledged the right to health as an unenumerated fundamental right enshrined under the Constitution of India. The Parliament has enacted a plethora of legislations that protect the health interests of the people in general. These legislations relating to the right to health can be divided into the following four types: (a) legislations applied to prevent abuse of drugs and their distribution and storage (e.g., Drugs and Cosmetics Act 1940, Drugs Control Act 1950, etc.), (b) legislations applied for maintaining the quality of food and securing nutrition (e.g., Food Safety and Standard Act of 2006, National Food Security Act 2013), (c) legislations applied in case of organ transplantation (e.g., Transplantation of Human Organ Act 1994), and (d) legislations applied to maintain high standards in medical services (e.g., Indian Medical Council Act 1956, Indian Medicine Central Council Act 1970, etc.). Furthermore, the policy orientation is also evident from the adoption of the National Health Policy, National Health Mission, and other Health Programmes. Thus, in general, though there are various initiatives, the implementation of these laws and policies is always under question and is at a tardy pace. Moreover, most of these legislations required specific amendments to make them associated with right-based orientation and to make them appropriate to fulfil the need of the time.

Apart from these general international instruments and domestic approaches under the Indian legal system, specific discussion on right to health of vulnerable sections like women and children, disabled persons is essential for a better understanding of the legal structure relating to the right to health. With regard to the protection of reproductive health of women and child health, along with other international instruments, the Convention on the Elimination of Discrimination against Women 1979 and Convention on the Rights of the Child

1989 play the most significant role under international human rights law. Within the domestic framework in India, reproductive health is protected under the 1971 Medical Termination of Pregnancy Act and the 1994 Pre-Conception and Pre-Natal Diagnostic Techniques (Prohibition of Sex Selection) Act. The 1971 Medical Termination of Pregnancy Act was enacted to combat illegal abortions. However, due to poverty, low social status of women, and lack of awareness and lack of education, there are still cases of illegal abortion reported in India. The 1971 Act is silent on the right of abortion of the unmarried lady, divorcee, and widow. The Act also does not contain any privacy provision which is very much connected with the abortion issues.[7] Further, the 1994 Act was enacted to curb female foeticide and to check the declining ratio of the female population as against the male population. However, the implementation of the 1994 Act depends upon the complaint redressal mechanism. But in most cases, both the service providers and the service seekers operate in agreement to defeat the provisions of the Act and there is no complaint mechanism. Moreover, the lack of evidence and discretionary power of the medical practitioners to allow abortion in case of mental trauma is also causing difficulties in the path of smooth implementation of the Act. The health issues of the Children have been first addressed through the Child Labour (Prohibition and Regulation) Act, 1986, which provides procedures to identify, prosecute and stop child labour in India. The Juvenile Justice (Care and Protection of children) Act 2015 provides specific provisions for the care and protection with a motive to secure and medical attention to the children. The 2015 Act has ignored the concepts of victimology and restorative justice.[8]

Primarily disabled was considered only from the biological aspect. As a result, the element of the welfare of the disabled people, and the recognition and respect of human dignity and self-esteem were completely missing.[9] Later, the human rights model of disability provides

---

[7] P. Chatterjee, *Medical Termination of Pregnancy Act: A Boon or a Bane for a Woman in India - A Critical Analysis*, 5(9) IJSR 236, 238 (2016).

[8] Ved Kumari, *The Juvenile Justice Act 2015: Critical Understanding*, 58(1) JILI 84, 103 (2016).

[9] *National Federation of Blinds v. State of U.P.*, A.I.R. 2000 All 258.

a detailed road map for the development of human-rights-consistent law and policy with regard to the protection of rights of persons with disability and also provides the systems and frameworks for monitoring progress. This new approach stresses the psychological aspect of disability. Under the UN Convention on the Rights of Persons with Disabilities, 2006, the basic right to health and rehabilitation is recognized. Along with the physical disability, the mental disability and disability due to old age also relate to the area under the right to health discourse. The 2016 Rights of Persons with Disabilities Act (PWD Act) is the principal legislation that casts a duty upon the Government and the local authorities to take necessary measures for securing free healthcare, access to all government and private hospitals, and priority in treatment for persons with disability. Thus, the 2016 Act provides a change in the perception with regard to persons with disabilities.[10] However, the Act is silent with respect to private establishments. Further, the duties of the private sector under the Act are voluntary in nature, which bars disabled persons from claiming those benefits as a matter of right. Under the domestic law, Mental Healthcare Act, 2017 provides specific rights-based guidelines for the promotion of health of the person affected with mental illness. However, the 2017 Act mandates that all the establishments have to take licenses for treating mentally ill patients, but this makes a difference with the general healthcare institutions and gives a way to ignore the treatment of the mentally ill person in the general healthcare institutions. Further, if the decision with regard to the advance directive and nominated representative is whimsical or incorrect, there is a better chance of affecting the treatment procedure severely. The Maintenance and Welfare of Parents and Senior Citizens Act, 2007 directs the State Governments to ensure beds for all senior citizens in government hospitals or government-funded hospitals, separate queues for senior citizens, facility for the treatment of chronic, terminal and degenerative diseases. However, there is no provision in this Act about the management and administration of the old age home and in the absence of such provisions, the intent of the legislatures fails to attain the desired result.

---

[10] *Justice Sunanda Bhandare Foundation v. Union of India,* (2017) 14 S.C.C. 1.

Under the current COVID-19 pandemic situation, it is also important to verify the validity of the quarantine rule and the efficiency of the human rights approach to combat epidemic diseases. Under international law, from the early-stage quarantine rules were the primary way of combating epidemic diseases, and these diseases were treated as a by-product of trade and travel. Later on, through the initiatives of WHO and UN General Assembly, the human rights approach has overpowered the isolation approach and inducted new assimilation and curative approach. In India, the 1897 Epidemic Diseases Act was invoked to control communicable diseases. This 1897 Act provides powers to the Central and State Governments to take special measures and formulate regulations that are to be observed by the people to contain the spread of disease. However, this Act was formulated about 124 years ago and thus has major limitations in this era of changing priorities in public health emergency management. This Act is concerned more with sea travel and not related to air travel which is a more recent development in the communication field. Furthermore, it is not in line with the contemporary scientific understanding of outbreak prevention and response, but only reflects the prevailing scientific and legal standards at the time when it was framed.[11] Further, to tackle the emergency that arises out of disaster, the 2005 Disaster Management Act was enacted. However, these initiatives are not sufficient. The recent experience of COVID-19 has made it clear to us.

Moreover, under the present industrial structure, the health right of the workers under the occupational setup is another vital aspect of the right to health paradigm. Within the framework of international law, the scope of occupational health has gradually evolved in response to social, political, technological and economic changes. As a component of occupational health, occupational hygiene focuses on three major areas: (a) recognition of the interrelation between environment and industry, (b) factors of the working environment that may impair the health and well-being of the workers, and (c) the formulation of recommendations for the alleviation of such problems. Thus, ILO considered the workplace wellbeing is an issue connected to the aspects of

---

[11] P. S. Rakesh, *The Epidemic Diseases Act of 1897: Public Health Relevance in the Current Scenario*, 1(3) IJME 156, 157 (2016).

working life, including safety and quality of the working environment, and workers' satisfaction level about their work organization.[12] Within the domestic law, Employees State Insurance Act 1948, Factories Act 1948, Maternity Benefit Act 1961, etc. secure the right to working people relating to health protection and medical care. However, the implementation of these legal frameworks, the social status of the working labours and the lack of awareness among the working people, the tendency of negligence among the employer are major concerns, posing occupational health hazards.

---

[12] Zohreh Molamohamadi & Napsiah Ismail, *The Relationship between Occupational Safety, Health, and Environment, and Sustainable Development: A Review and Critique*, 5(3) IJIMT 198, 199 (2014).

Theoretical Foundation of Health

Health as a concept evolved through various instruments, principles and policy orientation. The journey from the earliest notion of sin and blessings to the modern human rights approach has deducted health under a conceptual framework. With the evolution of socio-economic rights in general and the right to health in particular after the Second World War, the international and national legal systems have made enormous efforts to recognize and realize these rights. As a result, various facets of the right to health like access to healthcare, access to medicine, public health determinants also received their recognition in the international and national legal instruments. In this background, this chapter makes an effort to address these aspects of theoretical foundations of the human right to health.

I. CONCEPTUAL FOUNDATION OF HEALTH

The concept of health is a complex matter that touches on deep and unanswered issues of medicine, ethics and law as its heart lies in the universal and terrifying fact of human vulnerability.[1] Every community has its concepts of health as a part of its culture. As a result, health is not perceived in the same way by medical scientists, social science specialists, health administrators and ecologists and this different point of view gives rise to confusion about the concept of health. To some, 'health is wealth', given that, in the absence of good health, an individual or society cannot attain its full potential. Etymologically, the word 'health' is derived from the word 'hale' which literally means wholeness, being whole, complete and sound. The word 'hale' comes

---

[1] Pavlos Eleftheriadis, *A Right to Health Care*, 40(2) *J. Law Med. Ethics* 268 (2012).

from the phrase *kailo* which has a Proto-Indo-European root and meaning of which is whole, uninjured. The word *kailo* originated from the Proto-Germanic root 'khalbas', which means something divided. However, as per some scholars, the ancient Greek word 'euexia' is the source of the word 'health', which means being in good condition. In ancient Greece, the unity of soul and body, the balance between an individual and the environment, and the natural origin of disease were the backbones for conceptualizing health. A similar concept existed in ancient India and China also. More precisely, in the early days, health was associated not only with physiological functioning but also with mental and moral soundness and spiritual salvation.[2]

The earliest notion of health under the traditional medical concept was a disease-free state of an individual body. The medical concept of health is based on the 'germ theory of disease', which long dominated medical thought.[3] As per *Butterworths Medical Dictionary*, 'health' means 'the normal physical state, i.e. the state of being whole and free from a physical and mental disease or pain, so that the parts of the body can carry on their proper function'.[4] This disease-based definition of health was largely accepted during the first half of the 20th century, mainly by physicians and medical personnel under changing circumstances and scientific development. However, this concept of health defined health in the narrow view and maintaining health became the ultimate goal of medicine. As a consequence, the definition based on the body not affected by the disease has ignored the role of the environmental, social, psychological and cultural determinants of health. It has been argued that a distinction should be made among the concepts of disease, illness and health dealing with physiological impairments, subjective perception of symptoms and social identity, respectively. Thus, there is a requirement to define health in a social context.[5]

[2] Evely Boruchovitch & Birgitte R. Mednick, *The Meaning of Health and Illness: Some Considerations for Health Psychology*, 7(2) Psico-USF 175, 175 (2002).

[3] D.D. Kulpati, *The Basic Concepts of Health*, in *Conference on Health Policy, Ethics as Human Values* C5–C9, C5 (P.C. Bhatia ed, ICMR Secretariat, 1986).

[4] M. Critchley (ed.), Butterworths Medical Dictionary 784 (Butterworths 1978).

[5] B. Hofmann, *On the Triad Disease, Illness and Sickness*, 27(6) J. Med Philos. 651–673 (2002).

However, with the development of human rights after the Second World War, the World Health Organization (WHO) has given the most popular definition of health. As per WHO, health is 'a state of complete physical, mental and social well-being and not merely the absence of disease or infirmity'.[6] It overcame the negative definition of health and conceptualized health in terms of positive qualities. This holistic and more utopian view of health encompasses and expands the ambit of traditional medical view by conceiving health as a positive state of well-being, and it includes social, psychological, physical, economic and political aspects along with physical health.

II. CONCEPTUAL FOUNDATION OF RIGHT TO HEALTH

The right to health is a relatively new concept, borrowed from the aspirational terms of international human rights instruments and evolving philosophies of distributive justice.[7] The right to health is essential for human existence and as a result, it has acquired global significance.[8] Thus, it denotes that health should be regarded as an individual human right. Like other 'postmodern' rights, the asserted individual right to health is a positive claim on the resources of others. Moreover, it is unlimited by corresponding responsibilities and it pertains exclusively to the individual.[9] The fundamental right to health is the combination of social rights, such as the right to a healthy environment, the right to social security, and classic rights such as the right of human equality and autonomy.[10] Probably, the word 'right' is often used in health arguments because the concept of a right is powerful, emotional and implies that there can be no argument against it. Thus, the concept

---

[6] Constitution of the WHO. *See*, L. Breslow, *A Health Promotion Primer for the 1990s*, 9 *Health Aff*. 6, 9 (1990).

[7] Distributive justice refers to normative principles for the allocation of resources and opportunities in a given society and it adopts egalitarian criteria. *See*, John Rawls, *A Theory of Justice* 86–89 (OUP 1999).

[8] Mallika Ramachandran, *The Right to Health and the Indian Constitution*, 1 *Delhi L. Rev.* 1, 2 (2004).

[9] Timothy Goodman, *Is There a Right to Health?* 30 *J. Med. Philos.* 643(2005).

[10] P.A. Molinari, *The Right to Health: From the Solemnity of Declarations to the Challenges of Practice*, 49(1) IDHL 41 (1998).

of the right to health is a positive concept that includes, (a) issues related to preventive measures, (b) issues related to the sufferings period, (c) issues related to after-cure rights, and (d) issues related to diseases freeness.

Though the international efforts to define the right to health or rights-based approach to health and to establish it within a legal framework, have been long-standing[11] but from the second half of the 20th century, the concept of the right to health started to get its specific recognition under the international legal jurisprudence. The right to the highest attainable standard of health as a normative standard was first enunciated in 1946 in the Constitution of the WHO and since then it has been reiterated in several declarations and conventions. The United Nations through the 1948 Universal Declaration of Human Rights (Article 25) asserted health as an integral part of the right to an adequate standard of living. The most prominent recognition of the right to health has come from Article 12 of the International Covenant on Economic, Social and Cultural Rights (ICESCR). It states that 'in the present Covenant, the State parties recognize the right of everyone to the enjoyment of the highest attainable standard of physical and mental health'. Thus, having recognized the right to health as a universal human right, the Covenant placed an obligation on the States to take necessary measures to ensure the highest attainable level of physical and mental health for their citizens.[12]

III. THE CORE CONTENT AND OVERLAPPING ELEMENTS OF RIGHT TO HEALTH

The concept of the right to health does not evolve within the framework of the right to be healthy. It is a right related to several entitlements and underlying determinants of health.[13] Under the international legal

---

[11] Katharine G. Young & Julieta Lemaitre, *The Comparative Fortunes of the Right to Health: Two Tales of Justiciability in Colombia and South Africa*, 26 HHRJ 179–182 (2013).

[12] Paulius Celkis & Egle Venckiene, *Concept of the Right to Health Care*, 18(1) *Jurisprudencia* 269–277(2011).

[13] H.D.C. Roscam Abbing, International Organizations in Europe and the Right to Health Care 104–105 (Kluwer 1979).

sphere, the right to health has evolved as a part of economic, social and cultural rights. According to Aart Hendriks, Professor of Health Law, the essential minimum core content of an economic, social or cultural right 'corresponds with an absolute minimum level of human rights protection, a level of protection which States should always uphold independent of the state of the economy or other disruptive factors in a country'.[14] However, the core content of the right to health encompasses the essence of the right and therefore contains the minimum entitlements related to health.[15] It has been elaborately discussed in General Comment No. 14 of the UN Committee on Economic, Social and Cultural Rights on Article 12 of ICESCR. The Comment includes the following rights: (a) right of access to health facilities, goods and services, (b) right of non-discrimination in enjoying healthcare, (c) right to have essential medicines, (d) right of reproductive, maternal and child health care, (e) right of immunization against important infectious diseases, and (f) right to access the measures of prevention and control epidemic and endemic diseases as core components of the right to health. However, the sole realization of these core contents of the right to health is not sufficient. The core contents only provide minimum essential requirements as 'an expanding floor' and not as 'a fixed ceiling'.[16]

More importantly, the concept of the right to health consists of various elements that overlap with other human rights also. Thus, the right to health is not only protected by those provisions which are explicitly directed to it but also safeguarded by other provisions which are part of the entitlements and determinants of the right to health. Any violation of these connected human rights may also result in ill-health and can thereby affect the right to health of an individual.[17] For example, the civil and political right to life eminently prohibits the

---

[14] Aart Hendriks, *The Right to Health in National and International Jurisprudence*, 5(4) *Eur. J. Health Law 389–394 (1998)*.

[15] Brigit Toebes, The Right to Health as a Human Right in International Law 244 (Intersentia 1999).

[16] Maite San Giorgi, The Human Right to Equal Access to Health Care 17 (Intersentia 2012).

[17] WHO, 25 Questions and Answers on Health and Human Rights 8 (WHO 2002).

deprivation of life and protects against malnutrition and epidemics. Further, the right to physical and mental integrity prohibits torture, inhuman and degrading treatment and includes the right to privacy. This right protects all individuals against deprivation of medical treatment, food, water, adequate sanitary systems, and mental sickness. Moreover, it explicitly prohibits medical experimentation without the free consent of the person involved, which can lead to cruel, inhuman or degrading treatment. Therefore, the right to health is closely related to and is dependent on the realization of other human rights.[18] The extent of these dependants is not well defined in any legal jurisprudence and it creates confusion in the case of practical implementation of the right to health.

IV. INTERRELATIONSHIP BETWEEN HUMAN RIGHT AND RIGHT TO HEALTH

Good health and secured human rights are universal aspirations, particularly when in jeopardy. However, other human rights and their association with the right to health is always a debatable issue under the human rights legal framework. The major volatileness remains in the nature of their relationships, with regard to how they interact, and their value to medicine and public health practice. But the importance of health rights and human rights, cannot be ignored in the path of human development and human wellbeing. However, the implicit question behind the modern human rights movement remains : what are the societal and particularly governmental roles and responsibilities to help promote individual and collective wellbeing? By studying the recognition to health right under the 1948 UDHR, 1966 ICESCR and other contemporary human rights instruments, it is evident that human rights offer a set of principles that are particularly valuable to setting state obligations in health as well as other dimensions of human development. Human rights do so by providing a framework for policy analysis, policy formulation, international cooperation and adding, at least theoretically if not in practice, a level of enforceability to the health commitments expressed by States in the international human rights forums, concerning what they do and do not do for their

---

[18] GIORGI, *supra* note 17, at 18–19.

people and the international community at large. Human rights also provide guidelines for the assessment of the standard of performance whereby accountability of governments can be enhanced by applying legal obligations as replicated in international human rights instruments. In respect to this, the right to health is recognized as one of the socio-economic rights for which many States have accepted an obligation under international human rights law.[19] In similar terms, Fidler stated that[20]:

> [T]he right to health is an international human right because it appears in treaties, but the right is so broad that it lacks coherent meaning and is qualified by the principle of progressive realization.

Thus, the main difference and relations between health and human rights exist in the dimensions of (a) the positive and negative effects on the health of promotion, neglect, or violation of human rights, (b) the effect of health on the delivery of human rights, and (c) the effects of public health policies and programmes on human rights.[21] The first dimension presumes that the promotion and protection of human rights and promotion and protection of health are closely linked and they share overlapping approaches. The second dimension is considered in a negative sense. It evaluates the impact of human rights violations on health. It admits that all severe widespread violations of human rights endangered human health, which must be recognized and determined. Similarly, the opposite view of restricting the enjoyment of human rights on the ground of public health is a matter of concern. These two views should be balanced for the proper promotion of health and human rights. The third proposition evaluates the linkage by focusing on the State's power in securing the right to health to its people. Thus, the State's failure to acknowledge health issues that affect the marginalized and vulnerable sections may lead to the violation of the right to non-discrimination and other allied rights.[22] All of

---

[19] Tony Evans, *'A Human Right to Health?'* 23(2) TWQ 197 (2002).

[20] D.P. Fidler, International Law and Infectious Diseases 197 (OUP, 1999).

[21] Jonathan M. Mann et al., *Health and Human Rights*, 1(1) HHR 6 (1994).

[22] Jonathan M. Mann et al., *Health and Human Rights*, in Health and Human Rights in a Changing World 16–27, 24 (Michael Groin et al., eds, Routledge 2013).

these rights can be secured affirmatively, under the normative human rights jurisprudence through the states' obligations to respect rights (i.e., to refrain from violating rights), to protect rights (i.e., to ensure that non-state actors do not violate rights), and to fulfil rights (i.e., to ensure that there are laws, structures, mechanisms, and resources to secure rights).[23]

V. SOCIAL INDICATORS OF HEALTH

Social indicators or social determinants can be defined as statistical measures that describe social trends and conditions having an impact on human well-being. Generally, social indicators perform one or more of three functions:

1. providing information for decision-making,
2. monitoring and evaluating policies, and
3. searching for a common good and deciding how to achieve it.

When social indicators are implemented in the health sector, they can also be known as Health indicators. Therefore, health indicators are measures that contain relevant information on particular health status attributes and dimensions as well as the performance of the Healthcare System. In combination, such indicators should reflect the health status of a population and serve in the surveillance of health conditions. The emergence of social determinants of health has added conceptual clarity to the understanding of social inequalities in health. It includes the conditions in which people are born, people grow, live and work. In addition, it contains factors like socioeconomic status, education, neighbourhood and physical environment, employment, and social support networks, as well as access to health care. In 2008 the Commission on Social Determinants of Health of WHO defined social determinants of Health as the impacts of conditions 'in which people are born, they grow, live, work and age' on health status.[24]

---

[23] A. Eide, *Economic, Social and Cultural Rights as Human Rights*, in Economic, Social and Cultural Rights: A Textbook 9–28 (A. Eide et al., eds, Martinus Nijhoff 1995).

[24] CSDH, Closing the Gap in a Generation: Health Equity through Action on the Social Determinants of Health (WHO 2008).

WHO further states that these circumstances are shaped by the distribution of money, power and resources at global, national and local levels. Therefore, inequalities in these subjects/levels are inextricably linked to health preconditions. The socially constructed inequities in access and exposure to the key determinants, make them significant for health. Moreover, these determinants vary from more upstream factors, such as inclusion in political processes to more downstream factors, such as access to clean water and sanitation. Thus, this broad definition of social determinants of health as given by the Commission on Social Determinants of Health encompasses a web of factors that interact with each other in multiple and complex ways and also impact health in a direct or indirect way.[25]

VI. THEORETICAL FOUNDATION TO THE CONCEPT OF HEALTH

The definition of health has travelled a long way as the concept exists from the very existence of humanity. Majorly six opinions concerning the concept of health are prominent in recent times: (a) the medical model, (b) the WHO model, (c) the wellness model, (d) the normative and descriptive accounts of health, (e) the ecological Model and (f) the WHO's new Operational Model. Many scholars prefer to accept only the first two models as the concept of health and the last one as an indicator of health. Now the question arises: How far these definitional approaches are correct and on what ground each is advancing the concept of health? A detailed deliberation of these concepts will provide answers to these questions.

A. Biological Model of Health and Medicalization of Society

The earliest theoretical conceptualization of health was based on the 'germ theory of disease', which evolved from the American Medical Science expertise. However, the phrase 'germ theory of disease'

---

[25] Krycia Cowling et al., 'Social Determinants of Health in India: Progress and Inequities across States', 13 *Int. J. Equity Health* 88–89 (2014).

emerged during the 1860s, though it had no fixed meaning, rather the concept started to shape through a complex process of scientific debate, especially in the period from 1870 to 1885 CE.[26] By utilizing this 'germ theory' a large number of specific microorganisms were identified in the aetiology of different infectious diseases, and several attempts were made to develop immunization against those diseases. Moreover, under the quantitative definition of health in a disease-ridden society, health becomes measurable when the level of disease or illness is determinable. Hippocrates, in the 4th Century BC, viewed health as a harmonious blend of humour in the body-blood, phlegm, black bile, and yellow bile-from four organs in the body: the heart, brain, liver, and spleen, respectively.[27]

Pindar (5th Century BC) by emphasizing the physical dimension, defined health as the 'harmonious functioning of the organs' accompanied by the feeling of comfort and absence of pain.[28] This definition is important as it shows the prerequisite for overall health and wellness even under this advanced jurisprudence. Aristotle, the 'father of Western philosophy' depicted that the human body consists of four elements: earth, air, fire and water. However, Aristotle did not define health as such but stated that any kind of extremes in the bodily condition should be avoided and that maintaining a proper balance is a virtue. Thus, in the early days, health was regarded as the proper balance between the respective primary qualities of a particular human body. On the other hand, a disease is defined as a disruption in such balance. According to Aristotle, there can be four possible deviations from the ideal temperament. These deviations include the dominance of pairs of an active and a passive quality, such as (a) cold and wet, (b) hot and wet, (c) cold and dry, and (d) hot and dry.[29] In a similar vein, Galen, a Greek philosopher (129 CE)

[26] Nancy J. Tomes, *American Attitudes toward the Germ Theory of Disease: Phyllis Allen Richmond Revisited*, 52 J. Hist. Med. Allied Sci. 17–21 (1997).

[27] J. Clarke, Health, Illness and Medicine in Canada (McClelland and Stewart 1990).

[28] Anna Lydia Svalastog et al., *Concepts and Definitions of Health and Health-related Values in the Knowledge Landscapes of the Digital Society*, 58(6) CMJ 431 (2017).

[29] Lennart Nordenfelt, *An Analytic Theory of Health: The Biostatistical Theory (BST)*, in Philosophy and Medicine 15–33, 15 (*On the Nature of Health*, H. Tristram Engelhardt

defined health as the balance between the primary elements of the body.[30] Similarly, in respect of the definition of disease, Galen added that there might be simple dis-temperaments also. These consist of the predominance of one quality combined with a balance between two other qualities. A mixture can thus be merely hot, while there is a balance between the wet and the dry.[31] Therefore, any imbalance among these primary elements denotes an individual as an unhealthy one. This disease-based definition of health was largely accepted till the first half of the 20th century.

The major pitfalls of this concept of health were as follows: (a) it conceptualized health only by emphasizing illness, (b) it neglected the individual as a whole by overemphasizing specific diseases and parts of the body, and (c) it assumed that there is a dichotomy between health and illness which may not always be correct. Here, the proponents of this model use the term 'disease' to mean all states where there are departures from health, including those that might more naturally be termed injuries or disabilities. This disease-based model also causes the medicalization of society. Another issue is the difficulty of adapting this definition to emotional and psychiatric disorders. It also deemphasizes preventive medicine and its impact on health.

B. Social Well-being Model and WHO

i. WHO's Definition of Health and Its Expansion

According to WHO, health is 'a state of complete physical, mental and social wellbeing and not merely the absence of disease or infirmity'. Thus, WHO's Constitution states that the objective of the organization is to attain the highest possible standard of health for all. Notably, this definition was visionary at the time of its creation as it focuses on wellbeing across the physical, mental and social spheres by predating the influential bio-psychosocial model. It was proposed by Dr Andrija

& Stuart F. Spicker eds, Springer 1987).

[30] *Ibid.* at 19.

[31] P.G. OTTOSSON, SCHOLASTIC MEDICINE AND PHILOSOPHY, A STUDY OF COMMENTARIES ON GALEN'S TEGNI 127–135 (Bibliopolis 1984).

Stampar, a prominent Croatian scholar in the field of social medicine and public health and one of the founders of the WHO. At that time of its formulation, it was ground-breaking because of its widespread nature and ambition. This definition included social welfare as an integral element of health because health is closely linked to the social environment and living and working conditions of every individual.[32] The phrasing of this definition shows that the formulators were aware of the tendency of seeing health as state dependent on the presence or absence of diseases which was the pillar of the biological definition of health. Thus, they added in the second portion of the WHO's definition that an individual if he is to be considered healthy should not suffer from any disease. However, through the first portion of this definition, it does not limit 'health' only to the 'individual health', rather it extends to the individual's relationship with the surrounding world. Moreover, WHO's definition was supposed to provide a transformative vision of 'health for all' that went beyond the prevailing negative conception of health based on an 'absence' of any disease.

The WHO's definition of 'health' majorly has three components: (a) physiological or biological component, (b) mental or psychological component, and (c) social components. The physiological or biological component implies the maintenance of homeostasis in the human body. This is often used to infer the soundness of the body. Most often, a disease represents the malfunction of a part of the body system or an intrusion of harmful organisms, such as a virus or parasite. This may cause a breakdown of the affected individual. Therefore, physical wholesomeness is important to the maintenance of health. The mental or psychological component specifies the psychological, emotional and mental status of the individual. Emotional apathy, fixation, and maladjusted personality constitute a part of the manifestation of health in general and illness in particular. The social components signify the behavioural aspect of human health. Being a member of society, it is necessary for a human being to be in the network of social interaction and to be able to fulfil social roles and expectations.[33] Thus, Larson

---

[32] Svalastog, *supra* note 29, at 432.

[33] JIMOH AMZAT & OLIVER RAZUM, MEDICAL SOCIOLOGY IN AFRICA 22 (Springer 2014).

correctly mentioned that since the WHO's definition of health, medicine has treated individuals as social beings whose health is affected by social behaviour and interaction.[34]

The width of this definition can be characterized as (a) health goes beyond physical considerations, (b) health is viewed enough in its psycho-somatic entirety, (c) health is not limited to the person as an individual but is also expressed in the person's relationship with the surrounding world, (d) health is more than the absence of disease, and (e) health is understood in terms of wellbeing.[35] Thus, various scholars like Benjamin Mason Meier described this positive definition as a result of the emerging focus on 'social medicine' in the 1940s.[36] The definition is broad and it incorporates elements of personality, sociability and social skills, and it also partly reflects the norms of the society in which the individual finds himself.

ii. Drawbacks in WHO's Definition

The definition of health as provided by WHO is not absolutely correct and acceptable in all respect. It is noteworthy that the WHO's definition has been the target of criticism since its first appearance in the WHO's Constitution in 1948. Generally, the WHO's definition is criticized as idealistic and subjective. The American bioethicist Daniel Callahan, one of the pioneering critics of this definition, described that 'one of the grandest games' in the field of medicine 'is that version of king-of-the-hill where all players aim to upset the WHO definition of "health"'.[37] In a general sense, the WHO's definition has been criticized on the following grounds: (a) the static nature of the definition, i.e. health as a state, (b) the operationalization of the definition, and

---

[34] James S. Larson, *The Conceptualization of Health*, 56(2) MED. CARE RES. REV. 123 (1999).

[35] Matthias Flatscher & Torsten Liem, *What is Health? What is Disease? Thoughts on a Complex Issue*, 21(4) OPHTHALMOLOGY 27 (2011).

[36] Benjamin Mason Meier, *Global Health Governance and the Contentious Politics of Human Rights: Mainstreaming the Right to Health for Public Health Advancement*, 46(1) SJIL1 6 (2010).

[37] Daniel Callahan, *The WHO Definition of 'Health'*, 1(3) HASTINGS CENT. REP. 77, 77 (1973).

(c) the changing patterns of morbidity. Although the definition has been criticized over the past 72 years, it has never been adopted or accepted by the WHO.

a. Completeness in WHO's Definition

The most important critique concerning the WHO's definition is the requirement of a complete state of wellbeing that portraits an idea of a complete perfect state that is unrealistic and unreachable. Hence, this definition is too broad and signifies a state so extreme that it is nearly impossible to achieve. It generally suffers from difficulties common to maximizing principles. This broad goal of this definition could mean different things to different people at different times in different places, which may hamper the process of achieving informed and active international health cooperation. The absoluteness of the phraseology 'complete wellbeing' in relation to human health denotes most of us unhealthy and thus it forces us to medicalize society. Thus, WHO's ecstatic mode of defining health as a state of complete wellbeing is readily falsified and is invalid for most of us. Since, by this definition, most of the world's population must require care and attention, the WHO has simply written itself into existence for eternity, without considering the practical attainability.[38] The persistent emphasis on complete physical wellbeing could lead to higher levels of medical dependency. The tendency of practitioners in medicine has been 'to approach health through pathology' and to 'deprecate the WHO concept as "wholly" and not subject to scientific application'.[39] This argument of medical practitioners is flawed under modern medical science.

As the WHO's definition is equipped with the highest good, it fails to provide a means of enabling a successful personal life plan. If the definition can be followed, the personal life of an individual will be a concern for healthcare, rather than the person himself. Thus, WHO put forward a static concept of health and denied a dynamic and

---

[38] L. Garner, The NHS: Your Money or Your Life 14 (Penguin 1979).

[39] L. Breslow, *A Quantitative Approach to the World Health Organization Definition of Health: Physical, Mental and Social Wellbeing*, 1(4) Int. J. Epidemiol. 347, 348 (1972).

process-based definition of health.[40] It is also considered too broad for the policymakers charged with the responsibility for a nation's health care.[41] Another difficulty lies with the measurement of 'completeness' within each of the parameters of wellbeing. The WHO's definition does not indicate whether we should understand the precondition of completeness as a measure of individual potential or as an intersubjective measure dealing with the social and psychological determinants but in either case, it immediately runs into problems. The problem is more so in the case of physical wellbeing as it leads to a huge number of unnecessary medications. Hence, the basic question lies with its possibility of achievement which leads to the further question: whether is it even possible for a person to be without any physical, mental or social challenges? Besides, this completeness also increases the tendency to mark a person with minor ailments, mild and well-managed chronic conditions or minor disabilities as ill. Unfortunately, thus, this definition of health does little more than serve as a useful catchphrase for those who wish to emphasize health rather than disease.[42] Hence, this defect in the definitional scheme has made it unrealistic.[43]

b. Operationalization of WHO's Definition

The definition of 'health' in operational and working terms is vital for creating policies and programmes for maintaining and improving health conditions and for understanding the very notion that health simply means the absence of disease. As the definition highlights the positive attitude towards health, it fails to define the qualities of wellbeing and wellness that are required for the attainment of the highest possible standard of health. However, the WHO has developed several systems to classify diseases and describe aspects of health, disability, and quality of life. Yet because of the reference to a complete state, the definition remains 'impracticable' and is neither operational nor

---

[40] Flatscher & Liem, *supra* note 35, at 28.

[41] Eleanor D. Kinney & Brian Alexander Clark, *Provisions for Health and Health Care in the Constitutions of the Countries of the World*, 37(2) CORNELL INT. LAW J. 285, 289 (2004).

[42] J. Stokes et al., *Definition of Terms and Concepts Applicable t) Clinical Preventive Medicine*, 8(1) J. COMMUNITY HEALTH 33, 33(1982).

[43] Boruchovitch & Mednick, *supra* note 2, at 176.

measurable. Thus, the WHO's definition sets out aspirational and universal goals without much guidance on how these goals could be realized. It is not clear, how governments should plan the 'adequate health and social measures' to improve population health, and how the difference in requirements of each country can be addressed under the singular definitional scheme.[44] Further, the judgement of improvement is a relative one. Hence, to achieve WHO's definition to its fullest extent, the assessment instrument needs to be more detailed than a descriptive one, and a monitoring instrument, in addition, must be sensitive to change.

c. Change of Disease Patterns

The third defect lies in the fact that since 1948 the demography of populations and the nature of diseases have changed considerably due to the change of society, industrial evolution, and technological growth. In 1948 acute diseases presented the main burden of illness whereas chronic diseases led to early death. In that context WHO articulated a helpful ambition. Disease patterns and their impact on the human body have changed, with the change of public health measures such as improved nutrition, hygiene, availability of potable drinking water and sanitation and more powerful healthcare interventions. As a result, life expectancy slowly and steadily increased during the 20th century. Ageing with chronic illnesses has become the norm. This has been the consequence of the reduction of infant and early childhood mortality and the control of major infectious diseases around the world health system. Further, under modern medical science, the fear of dying has been replaced by the dedication to survival, health and production, which has evolved as a basic outcome of healthcare progress. Scientific and technological developments have contributed much to creating this pattern of thinking.[45] These changes in the population's age and the pattern of illnesses

---

[44] Johannes Bircher & Shyama Kuruvilla, *Defining Health by Addressing Individual, Social, and Environmental Determinants: New Opportunities for Health Care and Public Health*, 35(3) J. PUBLIC HEALTH POLICY 363, 364 (2014).

[45] A. Horwitz, *Changing Concepts of Health and Health Services: New Opportunities for Nutrition Promotion*, 17(1) PAJPH 61, 61 (1983).

denote the WHO's definition as counterproductive.[46] Further, this epidemiological transition in health and disease is closely associated with the demographic and socio-economic transition, which also nullify the WHO's definition of health.[47] Thus, these lifestyle changes have led to changes in factors threatening health, which WHO's seventy years old definition fails to address.[48]

d. Social Well-being: A Confusion Exists

Another attack comes from the social well-being point of view. The WHO's definition of health fails to define the term 'social wellbeing'. The debate lies with the question: whether social wellbeing is the environment of society or the functional status of individuals? In addition, the recognition of social determinants as an integral part of the definition of health also raises doubt about its applicability. It is evident from the empirical work of John E. Ware, Robert H. Brook, Allyson R. Davies, and Kathleen N. Lohr that social circumstances or determinants are probably best viewed as influences on health, rather than as an integral component of the definition of health.[49] Thus, it was concluded that many physical and mental diseases have strong associations with social factors but they are not considered as such within themselves. Further, among the scholars, there is the widespread unanimity that physically and psychologically oriented health care should ideally seek to restore patients into a healthy position, rather than the point as to how social ills should be corrected.[50] However, the former view is narrow and individual-centric in the real sense. Thus, there is a fundamental difference between the normative goals of physical and

---

[46] Machteld Huber et al., *How Should We Define Health?* 343(2) BMJ 4163 (2011).

[47] AILIANA SANTOSA, WHERE ARE THE WORLD'S DISEASE PATTERNS HEADING? 2 (Umea University Press 2015).

[48] Mohammad Karim Bahadori et al., *Disease Prevention with an Emphasis on the Lifestyle of Military Personnel According to the Social Determinants of Health*, 2(2) IJMR 261, 261 (2015).

[49] John E. Ware et al., *Choosing Measures of Health Status for Individuals in General Populations*, 71(6) AM. J. PUBLIC HEALTH 620, 621–622 (1981).

[50] 3 Georges Canguilhem, *Disease, Cure, Health*, in ON THE NORMAL AND THE PATHOLOGICAL 105 (Robert S. Cohen ed, Reidel 1978).

mental health care as compared to efforts to improve social health. It is noteworthy that the proposition of this criticism is not to downplay the importance of the social determinants of health, rather to include it as influential aid to health. Hence, interventions to improve health must take social determinants into account.

C. Bio-statistical and Welfare Model of Health: A Strict Departure from Social Well-being

A major shift can be seen in the definition of 'health' as deliberated by the WHO, with the development of the Bio-Statistical Model of Health by Christopher Boorse in the mid-1970s.[51] Initially, his concern was to reject normativism in health, especially in the characterization of mental health and in particular rejection of the WHO's definition. He also explicitly aligned himself with the ancient medical tradition that was pioneered by Galen. To support this view, he quotes the medical historian Temkin[52]:

> Such a concept of health and disease rests on a teleologically conceived biology. All parts of the body are built and function so as to allow a man to lead a good life and to preserve his kind. Health is a state according to Nature, disease is contrary to Nature.

Boorse stated that health is normal functioning, where the normality is statistical and the functions are biological.[53] He did so in terms of the conceptual difference between a disease and an illness and by giving practical importance to Engelhardt's statement that 'choosing to call a set of phenomena a disease involves a commitment to medical intervention'.[54] Boorse argued that biological functions can be fully

---

[51] Christopher Boorse, *On the Distinction Between Disease and Illness*, 5(1) PHILOS. PUBLIC AFF. 49 (1975).

[52] 2 Owsei Temkin, *Health and Disease*, in DICTIONARY OF THE HISTORY OF IDEAS 395–407, 398 (Philip P. Wiener ed, Scribners 1973).

[53] Christopher Boorse, *Health as a Theoretical Concept*, 44(4) PHILOS. SCI. 542, 542 (1977).

[54] H.T. Engelhardt, *The Concepts of Health and Disease*, in EVALUATION AND EXPLANATION IN THE BIOMEDICAL SCIENCES 125–141, 137 (Engelhardt and Spicker eds, Reidel 1975).

described in terms of a hierarchy of goals ascribable to different levels of organisms: cells have metabolism functions, organs have body level functions such as blood circulation, whole organisms are eaten and moving around functions, and all of these functions causally contribute to the species-typical goals of survival and reproduction.[55] Boorse admits that the highest-level goals of organisms are somewhat indeterminable and these goals are individual survival, individual reproductive ability, the survival of the species, the survival of the genes, and ecological equilibrium. However, the behaviour of organisms seems to contribute to different and independent goals simultaneously.[56] Thus, as per Boorse, health is determined by the statistically normal state of the population.[57] If a particular genetic defect is universal or at least statistically normal, then that defect cannot be counted as a disease.[58] So, the health of an organism is dependent on the functional normality of that organism. Further, by emphasizing this theoretical aspect of health, Lennart Nordenfelt has given a prescriptive approach to health conceptualization, by arguing that health cannot be understood philosophically unless and until it is clear why it is valuable. Health is not merely a biological norm, it is an ideal. This prescriptive approach to health is known as the Welfare Model of Health. According to Nordenfelt, health should be defined positively as the ability to achieve the vital goals that are necessary and sufficient for one's minimal happiness,[59] which may be a level far below of complete health as urged by the WHO. Nordenfelt quoted that[60]:

A is healthy if, and only if, A has the ability, given standard circumstances, to realize his vital goals, i.e. the set of goals which are necessary and jointly sufficient for his minimal happiness.

---

[55] Christopher Boorse, *Wright on Functions*, 85(1) Philos. Rev. 70 (1976).

[56] Nordenfelt, *supra* note 29, at 18.

[57] 16 Christopher Boorse, *Concepts of Health and Disease*, in Philosophy of Medicine 13–64 (F. Gifford ed, Elsevier 2011).

[58] Nordenfelt, *supra* note 29, at 19.

[59] L. Nordenfelt, On the Nature of Health: An Action-Theoretic Approach ix (Reidel 1987).

[60] *Ibid.* at 90.

Nordenfelt deemed it 'holistic' because it focuses on 'the human being as a whole' and because it uses social and humanistic concepts.[61] In addition to this, Nordenfelt categorized 'given standard circumstances' to determine the content of vital goals. Though this seems descriptively accurate, it overemphasises the importance of local cultural norms or social practices as significant determinants of vital goals related to health. In reply to this, Nordenfelt argued:

> I have not intended that there should be a conceptual connection between standard circumstances and vital goals at all. Besides, I wonder how any ability-based theory of health can avoid a notion similar to my standard or reasonable circumstances. When one assesses that a person has a certain ability one cannot do that in a vacuum, one must presuppose some background.[62]

Nevertheless, Nordenfelt further contended that 'If diseases are potential causes of illnesses, illness is the logically prior concept. The concept of illness determines the concept of disease'.[63] Thus, Nordenfelt figured out that illness though conceptually exists, it should not be used for defining health in a broader sense. However, like Boorse, Nordenfelt begins with the WHO definition of health, but he is more sympathetic to it and hoped to preserve it by crafting a philosophically sophisticated version.

Like the WHO's definition of health, these Biostatistical and Welfare models of health also faced criticism from various corners. Boorse's tendency to overemphasize the biological aspect of health has resulted in backward movement with regard to the definition of health. Nordenfelt gave his theory on the basis of minimal happiness but failed to determine the criteria to measure happiness and the dimensions which can change the quantity of minimalness. Furthermore, Nordenfelt failed to give a scheme regarding what it is for individuals

---

[61] *Ibid.* at 12.

[62] Lennart Nordenfelt, *Standard Circumstances and Vital Goals: Comments on Venkatapuram's Critique*, 27(5) BIOETHICS 280, 281 (2013).

[63] Lennart Nordenfelt, *An Evolutionary Concept of Health: Health as Natural Function*, in DIMENSIONS OF HEALTH AND HEALTH PROMOTION 37–54 (Lennart Nordenfelt and P.E. Liss eds, Rodopi 2003).

to lead their lives as full persons[64] and what it is that is required in order that their lives may flourish.[65] Nordenfelt makes vital goals relative to each community or context and significantly reflective of personal preferences and thus, made the measuring of health a more complex phenomenon. By doing so, Nordenfelt's conception of health faces problems with both socially relative concepts of health and subjectively defined wellbeing. This order of the evaluative and the scientific conceptualization of health leads to implausible results. It is also argued that Nordenfelt's conceptualization includes too many phenomena under the umbrella of ill health and thus the conception of health under Nordenfelt's definition is in danger of supporting medicalization again like WHO's definition of health.

D. Wellness Model of Health: Expanding Approach

The Wellness Model of Health intends to conceptualize health from the aspect of how a person is leading his life and its impact on human health. The original sources of wellness ideas can be found in history, which intended to sophisticate health care systems that respected and aimed for a balance of human body, mind and spirit and perceived human health from its holistic perspective. The American philosopher and psychologist William James said that human beings tend to live too far within self-imposed limits. These limits may recede if we respect more fully the natural drive of the human mind and body toward perfectibility and regeneration.[66] Primarily, wellness can be defined as an approach to personal health that emphasises individual responsibility for wellbeing through the practice of health-promoting lifestyle behaviours.[67] Later on, Professor Charles B. Corbin and his fellow researchers defined wellness as a multidimensional state of being which describes the existence of positive health in an individual

---

[64] M. Ignatieff, The Needs of Strangers (Chatto and Windus 1984).

[65] G. Harman, *Human Flourishing, Ethics and Liberty*, 12(4) Philos. Public Aff. 307 (1983).

[66] N. Cousins, Anatomy of an Illness as Perceived by the Patient (Norton 1979).

[67] Petrus A. Botha & Hein Brand, *Development of a Holistic Wellness Model for Managers in Tertiary Institutions*, 7(1) SAJHRM 166 (2009).

as exemplified by quality of life and a sense of wellbeing.[68] Further, from the words of the American National Wellness Institute in 2018, it is more clear that wellness is the active process of becoming aware of and making choices toward a more successful existence.[69] Thus, it is a continuous process of identifying aspects of one's life that can be improved,[70] then choosing to actively strive toward enhancing that particular deficit in one's life.[71] Based on these dimensions, majorly three thoughts prevail in the wellness model of health (a) Halbert Louis Dunn's High-level Wellness Model, (b) Bill Hettler's Holistic Wellness Model, and (c) Witmer and Sweeney's Wheel of Wellness and Prevention Model.

Halbert Dunn's high-level wellness refers to disease and health on a graduated scale, which is known as the 'health grid'. This is made up of a health axis and an environmental axis. While, the environmental axis includes physical, biological and socioeconomic dimensions affecting the health of the individual, the health axis ranges from death on one spectrum to peak wellness or absence of disease on the other.[72] To justify the use of the 'grid' in defining wellness, he argued that it is essential to shift from considering sickness and wellness as a dichotomy toward thinking of disease and health as a graduated scale.[73] Morley, to satisfy the variation of wellness, Dunn states that 'wellness is more absorbing than sickness'. Thus, this high-level wellness model to some extent is the successor of the traditional Medical Model of Health. Dunn, further, demonstrates that 'the state of being well is not just a drab, rather an static one'.

---

[68] Charles B. Corbin et al., *Definitions: Health, Fitness and Physical Activity*, 3(9) Pres. Counc. Phys. Fit. Sports Res. Dig. 3–4 (2000).

[69] Michael D. Oliver et al., *Health to Wellness: A Review of Wellness Models and Transitioning Back to Health*, 9(1) IJHWS 41 (2018).

[70] For example, physical fitness, food habit, consumption of sufficient water etc.

[71] For example, regular physical activity, timely consumption of quality food, consumption of water from time to time.

[72] Halbert Louis Dunn, High-Level Wellness: A Collection of Twenty-Nine Short Talks on Different Aspects of the Theme 'High-Level Wellness for Man and Society' 1–7 (R. W. Beatty Ltd. 1971).

[73] Halbert Louis Dunn, *High-Level Wellness for Man and Society*, 49(6) AJPH 786–787 (1959).

Bill Hettler propounded the Holistic Wellness Model of health. He defined wellness as 'an active process through which people become aware of, and make choices toward, a more successful existence'.[74] Hettler incorporated a holistic interdependent approach in which all aspects of wellness are seen to work together to contribute to a healthy lifestyle. Hettler's holistic wellness model broadens WHO's definition of health and firmly acknowledges health as a more comprehensive concept.[75] Therefore, according to Hettler, wellness is an 'active' process of self-enrichment by appropriate decision-making. Along with these, Hettler specifically emphasized emotional wellness which implies the ability to express emotions appropriately, adjust to change, healthily cope with stress, and enjoy life despite its occasional ups and downs. Thus, in the research on physiological dimensions of wellness, the holistic wellness model of health always stands as a forwarding step.[76]

The Wheel of Wellness and Prevention Model is the newest one among the wellness models. Witmer and Sweeney considered a multi-disciplinarian approach that included specific character traits of individuals who were healthy and had a high quality of life. The characteristics of wellness are expressed through the five life tasks of spirituality, self-regulation, work, love and friendship and these tasks should be engaged in one's striving for well-being. Further, Sweeney correlated these tasks positively with healthy living, quality of life, and longevity.[77] The main aim of this model was to surround the individual with the Wheel of Wellness, which are life forces that affect personal wellness.[78] Further, the tasks of self-direction were seen as functioning much like the spokes in a wheel and provided the self-management as

---

[74] Bill Hettler, *Wellness: Encouraging a Lifetime Pursuit of Excellence*, 8(4) HEALTH VALUES 13, 13 (1984).

[75] C.E. Thoresen, *Spirituality and Health: Is There a Relationship?* 4(3) J. HEALTH PSYCHOL. 291 (1999).

[76] D.A. Hermon & R.J. Hazler, *Adherence to a Wellness Model and Perceptions of Psychological Well-being*, 77(3) J. COUNS. DEV. 339, 339 (1999).

[77] THOMAS J. SWEENEY, ADLERIAN COUNSELLING: A PRACTITIONERS APPROACH (Taylor and Francis 1998).

[78] Jane E. Myers & Thomas J. Sweeney, *The Indivisible Self: An Evidence-Based Model of Wellness*, 60(3) J. INDIVID. PSYCHOL. 234, 244 (2004).

necessary to meet successfully the other life task. All these models of wellness can be, hence, understood as a multidimensional construct with practical and therapeutic benefits deriving from the unity of the body, mind, and spirit.

E. The Ecological Model of Health: Behavioural Approach

The ecological or relative notions of health emerged in the late 1960s and early 1970s[79] as a result of the modern environmental movement in Western Countries.[80] The ecological model has a long history as it emerged from developments in many disciplines and fields like public health, social science, biology, psychology, which in turn formed the ecological and behavioural foundations to the conceptualization of health.[81] As per the origination, the ecological model is based on the 'Ecological Systems Theory' of psychologist Urie Bronfenbrenner, which explains how human development is influenced by different types of environmental systems.[82] It is important to note that the word 'ecological' has also been used in epidemiology to characterize a largely descriptive approach to population health that is based on associations between the cause of health issues and the result of the same. The American Institute of Medicine defined the ecological model as a model of health that emphasizes the linkages and relationships among various social and environmental determinants affecting health.[83] Among the popular approach of the ecological model, Urie Bronfenbrenner viewed the 'behaviour' as being affected by and affecting, multiple levels of influence.

---

[79] Boruchovitch & Mednick, *supra* note 2, at 176.

[80] Ben Purvis et al., *Three Pillars of Sustainability: In Search of Conceptual Origins*, 14(3) SUSTAIN SCI. 681–683 (2019).

[81] L.W. Green et al., *Ecological Foundation of Health Promotion*, 10(4) AJHP 270 (1996).

[82] Andrea Vest Ettekal & Joseph L. Mahoney, *Ecological Systems Theory*, in THE SAGE ENCYCLOPEDIA OF OUT-OF-SCHOOL LEARNING 239–241, 239 (Kylie Peppler ed, SAGE Publications 2017).

[83] K. GEBBIE et al., WHO WILL KEEP THE PUBLIC HEALTHY? EDUCATING PUBLIC HEALTH PROFESSIONALS FOR THE 21ST CENTURY 1 (National Academic Press 2003).

By using this Bronfenbrenner model, Professor Jackson has developed a behavioural-environmental model of health that can be applied to health promotion issues.[84] Further, Wylie defined health as the perfect, continuing adjustment of an organism to its environment.[85] In similar terms, Purola looked at health as a state of adjustment and harmony between an individual and his surrounding systems, ecological and sociological.[86] This ecological concept of health also presents certain difficulties and drawbacks. Majorly the ecological concepts lack sufficient specificity to guide conceptualization of a specific problem or to identify appropriate interventions.[87] Further, individuals may adequately adapt but the distinctions between healthy adaptation and unhealthy adaptation are not clear. Moreover, the process of adaptation and its successful enjoyment generally differs from society to society. As a result, it can be easily concluded that what is considered healthy in one social context might not be in another. Thus, the ecological model advanced a concept of biological adaptation with environmental determinants to denote the concept of health.

F. WHO's New Approach to Health: A Measurement Orientation

After passing through all these years and all these new approaches, the major question arises what makes health a good thing and whether it is the only human good or just an especially or uniquely important one. To answer these questions, WHO has taken a step to conceptualize health 'for measurement purposes' by upgrading its Constitutional approach. The World Health Report 2000 proposed that the health system should include all actors, institutions and resources that

---

[84] Terri Jackson, *On the Limitations of Health Promotion*, 9(1) Cmty. Health Studies 1 (1985).

[85] C.M. Wylie, *The Definition and Measurement of Health and Disease*, 85(2) Public Health Rep. 100 (1971).

[86] T. Purola, *A Systems Approach to Health and Health Policy*, 10(5) Med. Care 373 (1972).

[87] Kenneth R. McLeroy et al., *An Ecological Perspective on Health Promotion Programs*, 15(4) Health Educ. Q. 351–355 (1988).

undertake health actions, *i.e.* all actions whose primary intent is to improve health.[88] The approach to defining health, as broadly as wellbeing, would imply that the health system includes all areas of human activity such as education, industry, tourism and agriculture, among others.[89] It is evident from the prior models of health that without measuring the health it is not possible to compare health over time between individuals, and across populations. Thus, without measurement, there is no proper science of health. Many scholars like Goldsmith and Bergner have specifically stated that health should be measured in terms of standardized health indicators, such as incidence of chronic illnesses, infant mortality rates, or population survivorship rates.[90] Thus, from the ongoing debates about the scope of health, several basic consensus points have emerged such as:

1. health is a separate concept from well-being, and is of intrinsic value to human beings as well as being instrumental for other components of wellbeing;
2. health is comprised of states or conditions of functioning of the human body and mind, and therefore any attempts to measure health must include measures of body and mind function; and
3. health is an attribute of an individual person, although aggregate measures of health may be used to describe populations.[91]

One of the most critical implications of these three consensus outcomes is that there is a clear distinction between health itself as a concept and its determinants and their impact upon health. Among these, the second consensus outcome is the essence of the new approach of WHO to health which postulates the concept of health as 'an intrinsic, multidimensional attribute of individuals' with

[88] WHO, The World Health Report 2000: Health Systems: Improving Performance (WHO 2000).

[89] WHO, Proposed Strategies for Health System Performance Assessment (WHO 2002).

[90] M. Bergner, *Measurement of Health Status*, 23 Med. Care 696 (1985); S. Goldsmith, *The Status of Health Status Indicators*, 87 Health Survey Rep. 212 (1972).

[91] J.A. Salomon et al., *Quantifying Individual Levels of Health: Definitions, Concepts, and Measurement Issues*, in Health Systems Performance Assessment: Debates, Measures and Empiricism 301–318, 303 (C.J.L. Murray & D.B. Evans eds, WHO 2003).

universal, cross-population, cross-cultural and cross-boundary valid-ity. By relying on this approach, Bircher defines health as 'a dynamic state of well-being characterized by a physical and mental potential, which satisfies the demands of life commensurate with age, culture, and personal responsibility'.[92] Thus, this approach is universal simply because it is grounded on the functioning of the human body and mind. These initiatives to measure health will also help us to find out the drawbacks of the present system of healthcare and will secure the rights-based approach to the individual as well as public health in this technological era.

---

[92] J. Bircher, *Towards a Dynamic Definition of Health and Disease, Medicine*, 8(3) HEALTH CARE PHILOS. 335 (2005).

Right to Health

International Legal
Perspective

The evolution of the right to health is a continuously changing process that is generally affected by increased global wealth, economic
activity, substantial gains in life expectancy, eradication of diseases,
etc. Over time, the right to health was not simply seen as a noble
aspiration but there was a constant effort to link this right with other
economic and social rights.[1] Notably, the international cooperation on
the control of global risk to human health began in the 19th century[2]
which indicated that health and other human rights are interdependent.[3] As a result, the recognition and realization of the right to health
under international law and its normative clarification has significant
conceptual and practical implications in framing the national legal
framework relating to the right to health in India. Therefore, before
examining the scope and ambit of the right to health under the Indian
legal framework, it is necessary to examine the recognition of the
right to health under various international instruments. This chapter
is primarily devoted to the aforementioned aspect.

I. RIGHT TO HEALTH UNDER THE CONSTITUTION OF WHO

A. Historical Development of WHO's Constitution

In the 20th century, the Second World War was one of the major
transformative events as large amounts of physical capital were

---

[1] Brigit Toebes, *The Right to Health*, in Economic, Social and Cultural Rights: A Textbook
169–190, 184 (Eide Krause & Rosas eds, Martinus Nijhoff 2001).

[2] D.P. Fidler, *The Globalization of Public Health: The First 100 Years of International
Health Diplomacy*, 79(9) BWHO 842 (2001).

[3] P.K. Rana, *Right to Health Care for All - Is It a Distant Dream in India?* 12(1) Naya
Deep 55, 56 (2011).

destroyed through six years of ground battles and bombings. After this massive war, the previous organizations and conferences started to lose their relevance and a newly formed right-based approach got its recognition in the field of international cooperation. As a result, with the adoption of the United Nations Charter, the United Nations Organization came into existence on 24 October 1945. This United Nations Charter promises to protect human rights including the right to health as one of the principal objects of the organization and to secure respect for, and observance of, human rights and fundamental freedoms for all.[4] Moreover, the WHO was established as a specialized agency of the United Nations (UN) to protect the right to health in 1946.[5] The WHO was established as a normative agency endowed with unprecedented constitutional powers. This WHO's Constitution provides a 'soft normative standard' emphasizing the importance of science, ethics and human rights. Although the WHO's Constitution is not a binding instrument, this 'soft norm' is influential to national legal systems where these norms can be incorporated into national legislation, regulations or guidelines.[6]

B. Protection of Right to Health under WHO's Constitution

The WHO's Constitution created an institution with extraordinary powers. The Constitution approves the role of the WHO as director and advocate of international health.[7] Further, the Constitution enunciates the object of the institution as 'the attainment of the highest possible level of health'.[8] The basic philosophy of WHO about the

---

[4] UN Charter 1945, Preamble.

[5] The WHO's Constitution was approved by the International Health Conference on 22 July 1946 and came into force in 7 April 1948. Eric Mack, *The World Health Organization's New International Health Regulations: Incursion on State Sovereignty and Ill-Fated Response to Global Health Issues*, 7(1) CHI. J. INT'L L. 365, 367 (2006).

[6] L.O. Gostin et al., *The Normative Authority of the World Health Organization*, 30 PUBLIC HEALTH 1, 2 (2015).

[7] Alison Lakin, *The Legal Powers of the World Health Organization*, 3(1) MED. LAW INT. 23, 23 (1997).

[8] WHO's CONST., art. 1.

protection of health is underlying in its Constitution. The Preamble to the WHO's Constitution, *inter alia*, provides thus: (a) the enjoyment of the highest standards of health is one of the fundamental rights of every human being without discrimination on the ground of race, religion, political belief, social and economic condition, (b) the health of all people is fundamental to the attainment of peace and security and is dependent upon the fullest cooperation of individuals and states, (c) the achievement of any state in the promotion and protection of health is of value to all, (d) unequal development in the promotion of health and control of communicable disease is a common danger, (e) healthy development of the child is of basic importance, (f) the ability to live harmoniously in a changing environment is essential to such development, (g) the extension of the benefits of medical, psychological and related knowledge to all people is essential for attaining highest possible level of health, (h) informed opinion and active cooperation on the part of the public are of utmost importance in the improvement of the health of the people and (i) governments have a responsibility to provide adequate health and social measures to their people.[9] Hence, the Constitution of WHO represented the broadest and most liberal concept of international responsibility for the promotion of health and encompassed the aspirations of the medical community to build a healthy world out of the ashes of the Second World War.[10]

The Constitution also provides certain path-breaking alternations in international health cooperation. It gives a direction to invite non-governmental organizations to participate in the Health Assembly[11] and other arrangements for consultation and cooperation with non-governmental organizations.[12] The Health Assembly is authorized to adopt conventions or agreements,[13] regulations,[14] and

---

[9] Charles E. Allen, *World Health and World Politics*, 4(1) INT. ORGAN. 27, 30 (1950).

[10] Benjamin Mason Meier & W. Onzivu, *The Evolution of Human Rights in World Health Organization Policy and the Future of Human Rights through Global Health Governance*, 30 PUBLIC HEALTH 1, 2 (2013).

[11] WHO'S CONST., art. 18.

[12] *Ibid*. art. 71.

[13] *Ibid*. art. 19.

[14] *Ibid*. art. 21.

recommendations[15] to establish a regional organization to meet the special needs of such areas[16] and to make these regional organizations integral parts of the WHO.[17] It also casts obligations on members to report to the organization relating to the action taken and progress achieved in improving the health of its people,[18] important laws, regulations, official reports,[19] statistical and epidemiological reports.[20] Though, the authority and scope of actions of the WHO depend upon the political will of the member States,[21] the Constitution of WHO made a clear attempt to ensure the organized efforts of the member States for achieving its aim.

II. RIGHT TO HEALTH UNDER THE 1948 UDHR

The adoption of the 1948 Universal Declaration of Human Rights (UDHR)[22] by the UN General Assembly brought human rights revolution in the world, thereby marking the ushering of a new era in mankind's struggle for freedom and human dignity.[23]As the UDHR is the product of the aftermath of World War II and its incredible atrocities, it always emphasizes on State's responsibility and international cooperation. The UDHR restrains the State from denying citizens their basic economic and civil rights.[24] The Declaration states that 'All human beings are born free and equal in dignity and rights. They

---

[15] *Ibid.* art. 23.

[16] *Ibid.* art 44.

[17] *Ibid.* arts. 45–54.

[18] *Ibid.* art. 61.

[19] *Ibid.* art. 63.

[20] *Ibid.* art. 64.

[21] Yves Beigbeder, The World Health Organization 14 (Martinus Nijhoff 1998).

[22] The UDHR was proclaimed by the United Nations General Assembly in Paris on 10 December 1948.

[23] B. Errabbi, *The Right to Health Care: Need for Its Convention into a Statutorily Enforceable Basic Human Need - An Indian Perspective*, 20 Delhi L. Rev. 51, 54 (1998).

[24] Asbjorn Eide et al., *The Universal Declaration of Human Rights: A Commentary*, 17(2) HRQ 398, 400 (1995).

are endowed with reason and conscience and should act towards one another in a spirit of brotherhood'.[25] To achieve this goal founded upon the non-derogable right to life,[26] Article 25 reads:

1. Everyone has the right to a standard of living adequate for the health and well-being of himself and of his family, including food, clothing, and housing and medical care and necessary social services, and the right to security in the event of unemployment, sickness, disability, widowhood, old age or other lack of livelihood in circumstances beyond his control.
2. Motherhood and childhood are entitled to special care and assistance. All children, whether born in or out of wedlock, shall enjoy the same social protection.

A bare reading of the Article clarifies that access to health care, both in the form of public health provision in urban and rural areas and in terms of disease and epidemic control, along with the availability of personal health care resources is essential to secure by the State parties and must be recognized explicitly as rights.[27] Further, this Article ensures the right to a standard of adequate living for the health and well-being of an individual including housing and medical care and the right to security in the event of sickness, disability, etc.[28] This was the first time when important issues related to the right to health such as food, clothing and housing got their recognition under international law. It is, further, evident from the analysis of this Article with other relevant Articles of the UDHR that the declaration does not make holders of rights alone responsible for the quality of his life, since it explicitly recognizes in Article 22 the right of social security, thereby constituting a responsibility on the society of which the holder is a member.[29] Along with this,

---

[25] UDHR 1948, Article 1.

[26] *Ibid.* art. 3. It states: 'Everyone has the right to life, liberty and the security of person'.

[27] GLOBAL CITIZENSHIP COMMISSION, THE UNIVERSAL DECLARATION OF HUMAN RIGHTS IN THE 21ST CENTURY: A LIVING DOCUMENT IN A CHANGING WORLD 55 (NYU Global Institute for Advanced Study 2016).

[28] *Court on its Own Motion v. Union of India*, 2012 (12) SCALE 307.

[29] Bismi Gopalakrishnan, *Right to Health and Resultant Obligation*, 29 (1 and 2) ACADEMY L. REV. 205, 207(2005).

the State has the responsibility to ensure the necessities like food, nutrition, medical assistance, hygiene, etc., and contribute to the improvement of health.[30]

III. RIGHT TO HEALTH UNDER THE 1966 ICESCR

A. Recognition under Article 12 of ICESR

To make a binding law on economic social and cultural rights in 1966 the International Covenant on Economic Social and Cultural Rights (ICESCR)[31] was adopted. The ICESCR is positive in character and imposes affirmative obligations on the State parties. The right to health was specifically included in the ICESCR. The Covenant casts a duty upon the State parties to protect and provide assistance to all children and young persons and to prevent their employment in work harmful to their morals or health or dangerous to life or likely to hamper their normal development by enacting laws to that effect.[32] The ICESCR also recognizes the right of every individual to an adequate standard of living for himself and his family, including adequate clothing, food, housing, and continuous improvement of living conditions as these are prerequisite for achieving the right to health.[33] Article 12 of the 1966 ICESCR, *inter alia*, states that:

1. The States Parties to the present Covenant recognize the right of everyone to the enjoyment of the highest attainable standard of physical and mental health.
2. The steps to be taken by the States Parties to the present Covenant to achieve the full realization of this right shall include those necessary for: (a) The provision for the reduction of the stillbirth-rate and of infant mortality and for the healthy development of the child; (b) The improvement of all aspects of environmental and industrial hygiene; (c) The prevention, treatment and control of epidemic, endemic, occupational

---

[30] *Union of India v. Mool Chand Khairati Ram Trust*, A.I.R. 2018 S.C. 5426.

[31] ICESCR was adopted by the GA Resolution 2200 A (XXI) of 16 December 1966. *See,* UN Doc. A/6316(1966). It came into force on 3 January 1976. It opened for signature 16 December 1966. India acceded ICESCR on 26 March 1979 a˙ ⋅d deposited with the UN on 10 April 1979.

[32] ICESCR 1966, art. 10(3).

[33] *Ibid.* art. 11.

and other diseases; (d) The creation of conditions which would assure to all medical service and medical attention in the event of sickness.

Thus, this is the first time when the international document enumerated recognizes every person's right to the highest attainable standard of health and casts duties on the State Parties to take necessary measures for ensuring the highest attainable level of physical and mental health for their citizens.[34] By imposing all these responsibilities, the ICESCR calls upon State parties to 'respect, protect and fulfilled' their citizens' right to health. While, 'respecting' the right to health means that the Government must refrain from taking actions that inhibit or interfere with people's ability to enjoy their rights,[35] the phrase 'protecting' the right to health means that the State must seek to protect the people from having their rights infringed by third parties, such as healthcare providers, private industry, pharmaceutical companies, researchers or vendors.[36] In addition to this, 'fulfilling' the right to health means that the Government is required to take positive action to implement the right to health by adopting policies that allocate public resources to correct deficiencies in health facilities, goods and services.[37] The Covenant provides the preconditions such as safe drinking water or diet, measures ensuring a healthy working environment and living conditions, and learning of healthy life for the attainment of the highest possible standard of health. On the other hand, the abovementioned Article directs that the member States must ensure the availability of sufficient quality of health care services to all citizens according to the needs and status of the most vulnerable groups.[38]

It is pertinent to note that under Article 12 of the ICESCR right to health is not to be understood as a right to be healthy. The right to

---

[34] Celkis & Egle Venckiene, *Concept of the Right to Health Care*, 18(1) JURISPRUDENCEA 269, 277 (2011).

[35] JUDITH ASHER, THE RIGHT TO HEALTH: A RESOURCE MANUAL FOR NGOs 35–37 (Commonwealth Medical Trust 2004).

[36] Michael J. Dennis & David P. Stewart, *Justiciability of Economic Social and Cultural Rights: Should There be an International Complaint Mechanism to Adjudicate the Rights to Food, Water, Housing and Health?* 98 AJIL 462, 490–491 (2004).

[37] Patricia C. Kuszler, *Global Health and the Human Rights Imperative*, 2(1) ASIAN J. WTO INT. HEALTH LAW POLICY 99, 111 (2007).

[38] S. Gevers, *The Right to Health Care*, 11(1) EUR. J. HEALTH LAW 29 (2004).

health contains both freedoms and entitlements. Freedom includes the right to control one's health and body, including sexual reproductive freedom, and the right to be free from interference, such as the right to be free from torture, non-consensual medical treatment and experimentation. By contrast, the entitlements include the right to a system of health protection, which provides equality of opportunity for people to enjoy the highest attainable level of health.[39] It further prescribes any discrimination in access to health care and underlying determinants of health, as well as to means and entitlements for their procurement, on the ground of race, colour, sex, language, religion, political or other opinions, national or social origin, property, birth, physical or mental disability, health status including HIV/AIDS, sexual orientation and civil, political, social or other status, which has the intention or effect of nullifying or impairing the equal enjoyment or exercise of the right to health has to be denoted as a violation of this provision. Clause (2) of Article 12 of ICESCR is unusual in comparison to other international documents as it identifies relatively specific fields of endeavour in which steps are to be taken to achieve the highest standard of health. The list has not described the right to health itself; rather it lists some of the fields in which efforts are to be made to ensure the enjoyment of the right to health.[40] However, these listed measures constitute certain goals rather than the actions that member nations must take,[41] and thus the Covenant's language provides little guidance as to the specific scope of States' obligations under the right to health.

B. Interpretation of Right to Health by the UN Committee on Economic, Social and Cultural Rights

The Committee on Economic, Social and Cultural Rights (CESCR) was established to carry out the monitoring functions assigned to the United Nations Economic and Social Council (ECOSOC) in the

---

[39] *Nallagonda Rama Gopal v. Government of Andhra Pradesh*, 2020 (3) A.L.D. 235.

[40] Steven D. Jamar, *The International Human Right to Health*, 22(1) SOUTHERN UNIV. L. REV. 1, 22 (1994).

[41] Allyn L. Taylor, *Making the World Health Organization Work*, 18(4) AJLM 301, 327(1992).

ICESCR[42]; it also has responsibility for the promotion, implementation, and enforcement of the covenant.[43] In its General Comment Number 14, 'The Right to the Highest Attainable Standard of Health (Article 12)'[44] in the year 2000 the CESCR Committee has revised Article 12 of the 1966 ICESCR in the context of changes that happened in the various issues related to right to health and admitted that[45]:

> Since the adoption of the two International Covenants in 1966, the world health situation has changed dramatically and the notion of health has undergone substantial changes and has also widened in scope. More determinants of health are being taken into consideration, such as resource distribution and gender differences... Moreover, formerly unknown diseases, such as human immunodeficiency virus and acquired immunodeficiency syndrome (HIV/AIDS), and others that have become more widespread, such as cancer, as well as the rapid growth of the world population, have created new obstacles for the realization of the right to health which need to be taken into account when interpreting Article 12.

In this comment, the CESCR Committee has interpreted the right to health as

> an inclusive right extending not only to timely and appropriate health care but also to the underlying determinants of health, such as access to safe and potable water and adequate sanitation, inadequate supply of safe food nutrition and housing, healthy occupational and environmental conditions and access to health-related education and information, including sexual and reproductive health.[46]

Thus, General Comment, Number 14 highlights health as a fundamental human right and suggests certain ways for the realization of that right.[47] It states that the concept of the right to health is not to be

---

[42] ECOSOC Resolution 1985/17 of 28 May 1985.

[43] Eleanor D. Kinney, *The International Human Right to Health: What Does This Mean for Our Nation and World?* 34(1457) Indiana L. Rev. 1457, 1460 (2001).

[44] Adopted at the Twenty-second Session of the Committee on Economic, Social and Cultural Rights, on 11 August 2000. Contained in Document E/C.12/200./4.

[45] CESCR General Comment No. 14, Paragraph 10.

[46] *Ibid.* Paragraph 11.

[47] *Ibid.* Paragraph 1.

understood as the 'right to be healthy' as it includes both freedoms and entitlements. According to this comment, freedoms include (a) the right to control one's health and body, including sexual and reproductive freedom, (b) the right to be free from interference, such as the right to be free from torture, non-consensual medical treatment and experimentation. Thus, in another way, freedoms include the right to control one's health and body, including sexual and reproductive freedom, and the right to be free from interference.[48]

The entitlements include the right to access a system of health protection that provides equal opportunity for all to enjoy the highest attainable level of health.[49] Moreover, the right to health must be understood as a right to the enjoyment of a variety of facilities, goods, services and conditions necessary for the realization of the highest attainable standard of health.[50] This broad concept of the right to health also includes the promotion of social determinants of good health, such as environmental safety, education, economic development and gender equity, as well as the creation of a system for urgent medical care in cases of accidents, epidemics, the provision of disaster relief and humanitarian assistance in emergencies.[51] Therefore, as a whole, the Comment puts stress on equality of healthcare and casts the duty upon the State to secure the same.[52]

The CESCR Committee also points out the impertinence of participation of the people in all health-related decision making at the community, national and international levels and interprets that States' obligation of progressive realization, *i.e.*, a specific and continuing obligation to move as expeditiously and effectively as possible towards the full realization of Article 12[53] should be the way forward. By specifying the State obligation, the Comment declares that like all other human rights, the right to health imposes three types or levels

---

[48] *Laxmi Mandal v. Deen Dayal Harinagar Hospital*, 172 (2010) D.L.T. 9.

[49] CESCR General Comment No. 14, Paragraph 8.

[50] *Ibid.* Paragraph 9.

[51] *Ibid.* Paragraph 16.

[52] *Ibid.* Paragraph 19.

[53] *Ibid.* Paragraph 31.

of obligations on State parties *i.e.*, the obligations to respect, protect and fulfil. The obligation to respect requires State parties to refrain from interfering directly or indirectly with the enjoyment of the right to health, the obligation to protect requires States to take measures that prevent third parties from interfering with Article 12 guarantees, and the obligation to fulfil contains obligations to provide facilities and promote healthcare services. It requires States to adopt appropriate legislative, administrative, budgetary, judicial, promotional and other measures towards the full realization of the right to health.[54] Thus, Comment Number 14 widened the scope of health and directs the States to take concrete steps to ensure the availability and accessibility of quality health care services.[55]

C. Limburg Principles on the ICESCR

Since the inception of the ICESCR in 1976, international policymakers and scholars have analysed how ICESCR can be implemented effectively. An important landmark in this evolution is the assertion of the Limburg Principles on the ICESR by the UN Committee on Economic, Social and Cultural Rights in 1987.[56] The Limburg Principles is the result of the meeting of a group of distinguished experts in international law, convened by the International Commission of Jurists, the Faculty of Law of the University of Limburg (Maastricht, the Netherlands) and the Urban Morgan Institute for Human Rights, University of Cincinnati (Ohio, United States of America), in Maastricht from 2 to 6 June 1986 to consider the nature and scope of the obligations of States parties under the ICESCR.[57] The Limburg principles set out views on the interpretation of key provisions of the ICESCR. They provide a comprehensive framework for understanding the legal nature of the rules found in the ICESCR. The Limburg Principles on the Implementation

---

[54] *Ibid.* Paragraph 33.

[55] A. Ely Yamin, *Not Just a Tragedy: Access to Medications as a Right Under International Law*, 21(2) B.U. INT'L L.J. 325, 337 (2003).

[56] *Ibid.* at 393.

[57] UNITED NATIONS, ECONOMIC, SOCIAL AND CULTURAL RIGHTS: HANDBOOK FOR NATIONAL HUMAN RIGHTS INSTITUTIONS 125 (UN 2005).

of the International Covenant on Economic, Social and Cultural Rights contend that under international law 'States Parties are obliged, regardless of the level of economic development, to ensure respect for minimum subsistence rights for all'.[58]

In addition to articulating the status of economic, social, and cultural rights as equal to political and civil rights, the Limburg Principles declare these economic, social, and cultural rights as indispensable to the realization of these later rights. Specifically, the Limburg Principles state that 'Legislative measures alone are not sufficient to fulfil the obligations of the Covenant'[59] and that 'States parties shall provide for effective remedies including, where appropriate, judicial remedies'.[60] The appropriateness of the means to be applied in a particular State shall be determined by that State Party and shall be subject to review by the United Nations Economic and Social Council in assistance with the CESCR.[61] The Limburg Principles also utter the meaning of Article 2(1) of ICESCR on the obligation to take steps towards 'full realization of the rights' by stating that all States parties have the obligation to begin immediately to take steps to fulfil their obligations under the Covenant and under no circumstances States have the right to defer from it.[62]

D. Progressive Realization versus Minimum Standards: Way of Entitlements and Implementation of Article 12

Individuals have human rights, for example, the right to health, but unless the required resources are put in place to access health care, no one can enjoy these rights. Thus, Professor Henry Shue explains[63]:

---

[58] United Nations, The Limburg Principles on the Implementation of the International Covenant on Economic, Social and Cultural Rights [UN Doc. E/CN.4/1987/17], Paragraph 25.

[59] *Ibid.* Paragraph 18.

[60] *Ibid.* Paragraph 19.

[61] *Ibid.* Paragraph 20.

[62] *Ibid.* Paragraph 21.

[63] Henry Shue, Basic Rights: Subsistence, Affluence, and U.S. Foreign Policy 15 (Princeton University Press 1996).

A proclamation of a right is not the fulfilment of a right, any more than an airplane schedule is a flight. A proclamation [an example of which would be the domestic legal enactment of an international human right] may or may not be an initial step toward the fulfilment of the rights listed. It is frequently the substitute of the promise in place of the fulfilment.

When a right is fulfilled, it means the rights-holder 'is enjoying the substance of the right'.[64] Thus, for fulfilment and realization of human rights, the ICESCR sets out that[65]:

Each State Party to the present Covenant undertakes to take steps, individually and through international assistance and co-operation, especially economic and technical, to the maximum of its available resources, with a view to achieving progressively the full realization of the rights recognized in the present Covenant by all appropriate means, including particularly the adoption of legislative measures.

This imperative notion is also true in the realization of the right to health. Moreover, entitlements forge an essential link between human rights and its effort to realize the same under international law. Amartya Sen defines the entitlements of any individual as resulting from a specification of the rights structure and the resources and opportunities that enable an individual to access these rights.[66] When governments pass legislation and allocate required resources, people can access adequate and appropriate services related to human rights, and thus these actions on the part of Governments enhance people's entitlements so that people can better enjoy their rights. To secure this entitlement, the implementation of Article 12 is required. The above discussion makes it clear that the extent of State responsibility is the major concern in the implementation of Article 12. Majorly, there are two principles in this regard: (a) progressive realization and (b) minimum standards. Following this progressive realization principle, a State must take steps to operationalize the right to health only 'to the maximum of its available resources, with a view to achieving

---

[64] *Ibid.* at 16.

[65] ICESCR 1966, art. 2.

[66] AMARTYA SEN, POVERTY AND FAMINES: AN ESSAY ON ENTITLEMENT AND DEPRIVATION 2 (Clarendon Press 1981).

progressively the full realization of the rights'.[67] Thus, this principle relates to the fulfilment of the duty to provide economic, social and cultural rights to the economic ability of the State. A State is only legally bound to fulfil these rights to the extent its economic resources allow. As a result, the universality of human rights loses its rigidity in the context of health. Like other economic, social and cultural rights, in the context of the right to health, the lexical primacy that is commonly thought to attend human rights does not seem to apply.[68] By criticizing the resource-dependent nature of the right to health, David P. Fidler asserted that 'the principle of progressive realization undermines the establishment of a universal health baseline of basic public health services and information because the principle renders health standards relative to the availability of economic resources'.[69]

The opposite view talks about the attainment of minimum standards with regards to the right to health. In his analysis of the right to health in the context of the ICESCR, Matthew C. R. Craven observed that the Committee on Economic, Social, and Cultural Rights favours minimum core obligations that cannot be excused by pleading lack of economic resources alone. Thus, Craven contended that 'These minimum standards should be achieved by all States, irrespective of their economic situation, at the earliest possible moment'.[70] However, the 'minimum standards' approach raises several questions: What should be the minimum standards for the provision of basic public health services? Should these minimum standards be determined as per the WHO's Health for All strategy? Should the minimum standard be restricted to more specific problems? A straightforward answer to these questions is hard to find. The WHO tried to provide answers to these questions by following a path that is more biased to the progressive realization of standards.

[67] ICESCR 1966, art. 2.

[68] Timothy Stoltzfus Jost, Readings in Comparative Health Law and Bioethics 4 (Carolina Academic Press 2001).

[69] D.P. Fidler, *International Law and Global Public Health*, 48(1) Kansas L. Rev. 1, 46 (1999).

[70] Matthew C.R. Craven, International Covenant on Economic, Social and Cultural Rights: A Perspective on Its Development 138–141 (Clarendon Press 1995).

In the World Health Report 1999, WHO presented the concept of 'new universalism' to guide its member States in formulating their health policies.[71] WHO argued that 'classical universalism' which emphasises universal access to comprehensive health services, was no longer a feasible model for health system development. The 'new universalism' concept stresses that universal access to health services remains a fundamental principle, but it recognizes that governments cannot secure universal access to all health services to their citizens. The Report highlighted that States' limited funds will not be able to pay for all of those services that the population and the health workforce would like to see provided at no charge. Thus, it admitted that the economic constraints are holding health system development back in many countries. Further, WHO did not lay down a minimum core of health services that the 'new universalism' requires. From the perspective of developing countries, such an approach is likely to encourage them to cling even more strongly to the principle of progressive realization and to demand more assistance from the developed world.[72] As a result, the hope of achieving significantly improved health for a greater proportion of the world's people has become an ever more distant prospect.[73] Under the domestic framework, practically, States cannot guarantee the highest attainable standard of health to every citizen without consideration of resource constraints. There is a chance that an attempt to meet the maximal healthcare needs for every individual would be overburdened by a state's capacity to provide other social goods, such as education, livelihood and defence. In this dilemma, equity principles and ethics should be critical considerations to ensure proper priority setting under the Governmental framework. The State should consider whether the interests of some groups or sections are unfairly promoted over those of another. Thus, proper attention to securing equity in access to health care, quality of health care and

[71] WHO, WORLD HEALTH REPORT 1999: MAKING A DIFFERENCE 43 (WHO 1999).

[72] Fidler, *supra* note 20, at 46.

[73] Solomon Benatar et al., *Global Health and the Global Economic Crisis*, 101(4) AJPH 646 (2011); George J. Annas, *Health and Human Rights in the Continuing Global Economic Crisis*, 103(6) AJPH 967 (2013).

financial protection for health care can promote a fair distribution of benefits across different populations and disease groups.[74]

IV. RIGHT TO HEALTH UNDER 1978 ALMA ATA DECLARATION

Under the auspices of the WHO and in collaboration with the United Nations Children's Fund (UNICEF), in 1978 International Health Conference was held between 6 and 12 September 1978 in Alma Ata, and the Declaration of Alma-Ata on Primary Health Care was adopted as a key approach for the attainment of the goal of 'Health for all by the year 2000' with far-reaching implications for the developing countries.[75] This Declaration for the first time attempted to shift the human right to health from vertical hospital-based technologies to horizontal public health systems and combined it with the determinants of health outside the purview of health ministries. The Declaration mainly highlighted the following: (a) the importance of health as a fundamental human right which should be achieved through collective action by societies and is a responsibility of governments, (b) the 'gross' inequities in health status, especially those between poor and rich countries, (c) the understanding that good health for all will advance social and economic development and world peace, (d) the importance of people's participation in health care as both a right and duty, (e) the recognition that primary health care should be universally accessible in a manner the community and country can afford and should bring health care as close as possible to the places where people live and work and should include 'preventive, curative, rehabilitative, and promotive', services, (f) the required coordinated effort from all sectors that have an impact on health, (g) the realization of right to health requires political will to mobilize resources for public health care, (h) the acceptance of the inter-dependence between countries

---

[74] Rebecca Dittrich et al., *The International Right to Health: What Does It Mean in Legal Practice and How Can It Affect Priority Setting for Universal Health Coverage?* 2(1) HS&R 23, 25 (2016).

[75] The Alma-Ata Declaration was adopted on 12 September 1978 by the health experts and policy makers from 134 member States of United Nations.

and that the attainment of health by people in anyone country directly concerns and benefits every other country, and (i) the recognition that armaments and military conflicts take away resources from achieving health for all and that peace and disarmament will release resources for social and economic development.[76]

The Conference declared that the health status of hundreds of millions of people in the world was unacceptable and called for a new approach to health through PHC and through economic and social development to shrink the gap between the 'haves' and 'have nots', to achieve more equitable distribution of health resources, and to attain a level of health for all the citizens of the world that would permit them to led a socially and economically productive life.[77] This approach through PHC was based on practical, scientifically sound and socially acceptable methods and at a cost that the individual and State can afford. Thus, the well-measured PHC will be the key to ensuring the delivery of health for all.[78] Thus, it seeks to realize a level of health that would allow all individuals to lead socially and economically productive lives and develop equity as a human rights imperative and a basis to assure public health.

The underlying principles of the conference were to address health problems in the community, providing preventive, curative and rehabilitative services reflecting the economic situation and the social values of the country and its communities through PHC. The Declaration specifically stated that[79]:

> The Conference strongly reaffirms that health, which is a state of complete physical, mental and social wellbeing, and not merely the absence of disease or infirmity, is a fundamental human right and that the attainment of the

---

[76] Fran Baum, *Health for All Now! Reviving the Spirit of Alma Ata in the Twenty-First Century: An Introduction to the Alma Ata Declaration*, 2(1) Soc. Med. 34(2007).

[77] 1 WHO, Evaluation of the Strategy for Health for All by the Year 2000 - Seventh Report on the World Health Situation 1 (WHO 1987).

[78] Stephen Gillam, *Is the Declaration of Alma Ata still Relevant to Primary Health Care?* 336(7643) BMJ 536, 536 (2008).

[79] International Conference on Primary Health Care, Alma-Ata, USSR, 6–12 September 1978, Declaration 1.

highest possible level of health is a most important world-wide social goal whose realization requires the action of many other social and economic sectors in addition to the health sector.

On the other way, the declaration imposed responsibility upon the governments for the health of their people which can be fulfilled only by the provision of adequate health and social measures.[80] The people have to participate individually and collectively in the planning and implementation of their health care. The Alma Ata declaration also specified that the governments should formulate national policies, strategies and plans of action to launch and sustain primary health care as an important part of the comprehensive national health system in coordination with other sectors.[81] It eschews a vision of health based on technical solutions and sees health as a technical, social and political issue, and declared that the right to health has an undeniable impact upon social and economic development.

V. RIGHT TO HEALTH UNDER AGENDA 21

The United Nations Conference on Environment and Development (UNCED) took place in Rio de Janeiro in 3–14 June 1992, popularly known as Earth Summit and Agenda 21[82] was a special product of that event. It is a vast work programme for the 21st century for protecting the environment and human health based on global partnership. The Rio Declaration on Environment and Development specified human beings as a centre of sustainable development and entitled to enjoy a healthy and productive life.[83] Agenda 21 suggests that factors creating policies of development, resource management, and poverty be integrated. This objective needs to be achieved by improving access to education, health care, safe water and sanitation.[84] Para 5 of the Agenda states:

---

[80] *Ibid.* Declaration 5.

[81] *Ibid.* Declaration 8.

[82] Agenda 21 was accepted by more than 178 States in 1992.

[83] The Rio Declaration on Environment and Development1992, Principle 1.

[84] Agenda 21, Paragraph 3.

Health services should 'include women-centred, women-managed, safe and effective reproductive health care and affordable, accessible services, as appropriate, for the responsible planning of family size…' Health services are to emphasize reduction of infant death rates which converge with low birth rates to stabilize world population at a sustainable number at the end of the century.

Agenda 21 has called to meet the basic health needs of all populations and to provide necessary specialized environmental health services. It required coordination between citizens and the health sector to provide solutions to health problems. It provides that health service coverage should be achieved by considering the population groups in greatest need, particularly those living in rural areas. The urban health hazards and risks from environmental pollution urge the inclusion of preventive measures along with curative measures to combat the same within the framework of Agenda 21.[85]

VI. RIGHT TO HEALTH UNDER THE 2000 MILLENNIUM DEVELOPMENT GOALS

The United Nations Millennium Declaration was signed at United Nations Headquarters in New York to combat poverty, disease, hunger, environmental degradation, illiteracy, and discrimination against women in September 2000. This declaration contained eight goals popularly known as UN Millennium Development Goals. A total of 189 UN member States agreed to try to achieve these goals by the year 2015.[86] Thus, it was an inclusive set of well-defined goals that primarily sought to put developmental issues at the forefront of national agendas by encouraging governments to commit resources to address socio-economic backlogs in their respective countries.[87] Among the eight Millennium Development Goals, three were directly related to health, namely to (a) reduce child mortality,[88] (b) improve maternal

---

[85] *Ibid.* Paragraph 6.

[86] *People's Union for Civil Liberties v. Union of India*, (2007) 1 S.C.C. 719.

[87] Eric O. Udjo & Pinky Laltha persad Pillay, *Assessing the Achievements of the Millennium Development Goals in Southern Africa*, 29(1) AFR. POPUL. STUD. 1460, 1461 (2015).

[88] MDGs 2000, Goal 4.

health,[89] and (c) combat HIV/AIDS, malaria and other diseases.[90] To this list fourth one, i.e. eradication of poverty and hunger[91] may also be added.[92] The Declaration, further, aims to decrease the proportion of people who suffer from hunger[93] and to reduce the under-five mortality rate by two-thirds within a period between 1990 and 2015.[94] It targeted to reduce by three quarters the maternal mortality ratio[95] and to achieve universal access to reproductive health between the abovementioned periods.[96] The indicators are the maternal mortality ratio and the proportion of births attended by skilled health personnel. Securing Universal access to reproductive health care, including family planning, is the starting point for achieving this goal, and is particularly significant for the world's young people.[97]

Further, the MDGs showed their concern under Goal 6 by directing to reverse the spread of HIV/AIDS,[98] to achieve universal access to treatment for HIV/AIDS for all those who need it by 2010,[99] and also to reverse the incidence of malaria and other major diseases.[100] Interdependency among the goals is also another aspect of the successful implementation of MDGs. Thus, in combating HIV/AIDS the issues of women's empowerment and inequality have to be addressed. Similarly, to maximize the efforts in combating malaria, capacity

---

[89] *Ibid.* Goal 5.

[90] *Ibid.* Goal 6.

[91] *Ibid.* Goal 1.

[92] The remaining MDGs are to: achieve universal primary education, promote gender equality and empower women, ensure environmental sustainability and develop a global partnership for development.

[93] MDGs 2000, Goal 1, Target 1.C.

[94] *Ibid.* Goal 4, Target 4.A.

[95] *Ibid.* Goal 5, Target 5.A.

[96] *Ibid.* Goal 5, Target 5.B.

[97] D. Shaw, *Women Right to Health and the Millennium Development Goals: Promoting Partnerships to Improve Access*, 94(3) INT. J. GYNAECOL. OBSTET. 207, 212 (2006).

[98] MDGs 2000, Goal 6, Target 6.A.

[99] *Ibid.* Goal 6, Target 6.B.

[100] *Ibid.* Goal 6, Target 6.C.

building among women and children is required. Moreover, through Target 7. C under Goal 7, the declaration intends to decrease the proportion of people without sustainable access to safe drinking water and basic sanitation; through Target 8. E of Goal 8 the declaration plans to cooperate with pharmaceutical companies to provide access to affordable essential drugs in developing countries. This declaration forces the member States to act within a time-bound health delivery framework. However, in a practical sense, the MDG was a clarion call and it mobilized many governments into concerted action, a review of the achievements to date and projections for 2015 suggests some success and much failure.[101]

VII. RIGHT TO HEALTH UNDER THE 2016 SUSTAINABLE DEVELOPMENT GOALS

The Sustainable Development Goals (SDGs) are a collection of 17 diverse global goals set by the General Assembly of the United Nations and adopted by all the member nations in 2015 for the period of 2016–2030. It set an agenda to guide and influence universal sustainable development for the next 15 years. At the Conference on Sustainable Development in Rio de Janeiro on 20–22 June 2012, the UN member States agreed to establish a process to develop new international development goals to succeed the Millennium Development Goals.[102] All these total 17 inspirational Goals and 169 quantitative and qualitative targets evolved out of this 2030 Agenda for Sustainable Development that represents the output of at least three years of intergovernmental negotiations and several workstreams across the dimensions of sustainable development. These goals are expressions of a non-codified and, at the same time, competing order of values and principles. Though the Millennium Development Goals are often seen

---

[101] Bhabani Prasad Mishra, *Health Care for All - Is It a Distant Dream?* 48(1) Civil & Military L. J. 59, 61 (2012).

[102] Diane F. Frey & Gillian Mac Naughton, *A Human Rights Lens on Full Employment and Decent Work in the 2030 Sustainable Development Agenda*, (April–June) SAGE Open 1, 6 (2016).

as the predecessors of the Sustainable Development Goals (SDGs),[103] it is clear that the SDGs also have strong intellectual roots in Agenda 21 which is evident from the nature of objectives of the 2030 goals.[104] While described some of the goals as 'unremittingly utopian', the major aim was to attain a better future and leave no one behind from this process of securing a better future.

Among these goals, two are directly connected with the determinants of health. Goal 3 specifically targets to 'ensure healthy lives and promote well-being for all at all ages'. It targets to reduce maternal mortality to less than 70 deaths per 100,000 live births and under-five mortality to 25 deaths per 1,000 live births. It also aims to achieve universal health coverage, including access to essential medicines and proposes to end epidemics such as AIDS, tuberculosis, malaria and water-borne diseases by 2030. Thus, while Goal 3 and its targets do not specifically address the social determinants of health and well-being, the importance of social factors, such as working conditions,[105] income,[106] education,[107] and housing,[108] is recognized within other Sustainable Development Goals.[109] The express inclusion of the right to health in SDGs added a legal safety net to catch and protect the most marginalized who would otherwise fall between the cracks of any global health policy.[110] Furthermore, Goal six aims to 'ensure

---

[103] The Sustainable Development Summit was held from 25 to 27 September 2015 in New York where 193 member States of the United Nations officially adopted the new agenda, entitled 'Transforming Our World: The 2030 Agenda for Sustainable Development'.

[104] Asa Persson et al., *Follow-up and Review of the Sustainable Development Goals: Alignment vs. Internalization*, 25(1) RECIEL 59, 64 (2016).

[105] Transforming Our World: The 2030 Agenda for Sustainable Development, Goal 8.

[106] *Ibid*. Goal 2.

[107] *Ibid*. Goal 4.

[108] *Ibid*. Goal 11.

[109] Philippa Howden-Chapman et al., *SDG 3 Ensure Healthy Lives and Promote Well-being for All at All Ages*, in A GUIDE TO SDG INTERACTIONS: FROM SCIENCE TO IMPLEMENTATION 81–124, 84 (Mans Nilsson et al., eds, International Council for Science, 2017).

[110] Claire E. Brolan et al., *Did the Right to Health Get Across the Line? Examining the United Nations Resolution on the Sustainable Development Goals*, 2(3) GLOB. HEALTH 1, 3 (2017).

availability and sustainable management of water and sanitation for all'. It includes targets to achieve (a) universal and equitable access to safe and affordable drinking water for all by 2030, (b) access to adequate and equitable sanitation and hygiene for all and end open defecation, paying special attention to the needs of women and girls and those in vulnerable situations by 2030, and (c) improve water quality by reducing pollution, eliminating dumping and minimizing release of hazardous chemicals and materials, halving the proportion of untreated wastewater and substantially increasing recycling and safe reuse globally by 2030. In addition, the Goals relating to 'no poverty, zero hunger and achieve food security and improved nutrition, gender equality, reduce income inequality, combat climate change'[111] also have implications on the issues related to the right to health.

VIII. RIGHT TO HEALTH UNDER THE 2018 DECLARATION OF ASTANA

The recent approach to health care is governed by the Global Conference on Primary Health Care, which is popularly known as the Declaration of Astana, as it is held in Astana, Kazakhstan on 25–26 October 2018. Two thousand delegates from more than 120 countries renewed the commitment to comprehensive PHC for all by endorsing a new declaration on Primary Health Care.[112] Thus, this new declaration has also given a chance to commemorate the Alma-Ata Declaration on Primary Health Care, 1978 and reflect on how far the same has been implemented and the work that still lies ahead. The Declaration of Astana aims to refocus efforts on PHC to ensure that everyone everywhere is able to enjoy the highest possible attainable

---

[111] Sustainable Development Goals, 2015, Goals 1, 2, 5, 10 and 13. The Sustainable Development Goals build on the principles agreed upon in Resolution A/RES/66/288, entitled 'The Future We Want'. The other goals are related to equitable quality education, access to affordable, reliable, sustainable and modern energy, sustained, inclusive and sustainable economic growth, inclusive and sustainable industrialization, sustainable cities and communities, sustainable consumption and production, life below water, life on land, peaceful and inclusive societies for sustainable development, and implementation and revitalize the global partnership.

[112] Gijs Walraven, *The 2018 Astana Declaration on Primary Health Care, Is It Useful?* 9(1) J. GLOB. HEALTH 1, 2 (2019).

standard of health. The Conference suggests prioritizing, promoting and protecting people's health and well-being, both at population and individual levels, through strong health systems by the Governments and societies. This Conference strongly affirms its commitment to the fundamental right of every human being to the enjoyment of the highest attainable standard of health without distinction of any kind.[113] Thus, equal opportunity to all individuals was the primary intention of the participants of this Conference. While the Alma-Ata declaration focused on building primary healthcare systems, especially in under-developed countries, the new declaration adopted a wider scope by re-emphasizing the importance of primary health care in addressing current health challenges, renewing political commitment to primary health care, and achieving universal health coverage.[114]

The Conference makes an effort to recognize PHC as the most inclusive, effective and efficient approach to enhance people's physical and mental health, as well as social well-being, and that PHC is a cornerstone of a sustainable health system for Universal Health Coverage and health-related Sustainable Development Goals.[115] To assure these to general citizens, the Conference affirms the primary role and responsibility of Governments at all levels in promoting and protecting the right of everyone to the enjoyment of the highest attainable standard of health.[116] Hence, the Conference expands the ambit of the PHC and stated that[117]:

> PHC will provide a comprehensive range of services and care, including but not limited to vaccination; screenings; prevention, control and management of noncommunicable and communicable diseases; care and services that promote, maintain and improve maternal, new born, child and adolescent health; and mental health and sexual and reproductive health. PHC will

[113] Global Conference on Primary Health Care 2018, Declaration I.

[114] Katharina Tabea Jungo et al., *Astana Declaration: A New Pathway for Primary Health Care*, 65(5) IJPH 511 (2020).

[115] Global Conference on Primary Health Care 2018, Declaration II.

[116] *Ibid.* Declaration IV.

[117] *Ibid.* Declaration V.

also be accessible, equitable, safe, of high quality, comprehensive, efficient, acceptable, available and affordable, and will deliver continuous, integrated services that are people-centred and gender-sensitive.

For the successful working of the PHC, the Conference encourages the involvement of individuals, families, communities and civil society through their participation in the development and implementation of policies and plans that have an impact on health.[118] Further, it provides that for implementing this Declaration, countries and stake-holders (e.g., health professionals, academia, patients, civil society, local and international partners, agencies and funds, the private sector, faith-based organizations and others) will work together in a spirit of partnership and effective cooperation, by sharing knowledge and good practices.[119] Hence, the Conference highlights the PHC approach as the fundamental way to achieving Universal Health Coverage for all and the health-related SDGs.

[118] *Ibid.* Declaration VI.
[119] *Ibid.* Declaration VII.

Right to Health in Indian Constitutional Law

The preceding chapter demonstrates that there are large numbers of international human rights instruments which provide provisions for recognition of the right to health in general. The journey from the 'survival of the fittest' as a moto of human society to a stage where 'survival of the weakest' is the main human value, can be deducted from all these human rights instruments. As a result, the absolute dominance of few individuals, who treated people as 'subjects' without any rights, could not continue for long.[1] The protection of the right to health in India can be discussed broadly in two aspects: (a) the protection under Constitutional law, and (b) the protection under specific legislative and policy frameworks. The Constitution is the highest law of the land and therefore the scope and ambit of the protection of the right to health in India has to be determined from the background of the Constitutional principles. This chapter is primarily devoted to this.

I. CONSTITUTIONAL PROTECTION OF RIGHT TO HEALTH

A. The General Framework

Health is the most precious prerequisite for happiness.[2] While international human rights law assures the right to health as an integral part of the human rights regime, at the country level, the Constitutions have a

---

[1] Rajesh Kumar, *Right to Health: Challenges and Opportunities*, 40(4) IJCM 218 (2015).

[2] Dnyneshwar Chouri, *Constitutional Perspective of Right to Health in India*, 2(1) IUP L. REV. 46 (2012).

natural and much greater legitimacy.[3] Right to health whenever guaranteed by a written Constitution may be called a fundamental law in the sense that a written Constitution is a fundamental law of the land, though it is not the exhaustive source of law that is enforceable by a Court.[4] The Constitution of India envisions establishing an egalitarian social order rendering to every citizen social, economic and political justice in a social and economic democracy.[5] The goals specified in the preamble are the guiding principles for the realization of constitutional mandates. Under the constitutional framework in a welfare state, it is the obligation of the state to ensure the creation and the sustaining of conditions congenial to good health. Maintenance and improvement of public health have to rank high as these are indispensable to the very physical existence of the community and the betterment of that society depends on the building of the society of which the Constitution makers envisaged.[6] However, the Constitution of India does not expressly declare the right to health as a fundamental right[7]; nevertheless, in Article 21, under the fundamental right to 'life', the right to health has been declared by the judiciary as an unenumerated fundamental right in several cases. In *Vincent Panikurlangara v. Union of India*,[8] the Apex Court held that the maintenance and improvement of public health is one of the fundamental rights falling under Article 21 of the Constitution. Further, in *Parmanand Katara v. Union of India*,[9] the Apex Court held that Article 21 of the Constitution casts the obligation on the state to preserve the life of its people and every injured citizen brought for treatment should instantaneously be given medical aid to preserve their life. Similarly, in *Paschim Banga Khet Mazdoor*

---

[3] Abhijit Das, *Right to Health in India: Contemporary Issues and Concerns*, 12 JNHRC 37, 42 (2013).

[4] J.K. DAS, HUMAN RIGHTS LAW AND PRACTICE 208 (PHI Learning 2016).

[5] *Samatha v. State of Andhra Pradesh*, A.I.R. 1997 S.C. 3297; *Ranjana Agnihotri v. Union of India*, (2014) 1 UPLBEC 289.

[6] Tamil Nadu Medical Officers Association *v.* Union of India, 2020 (3) S.C.T. 336 (SC).

[7] J.K. Das, *Right to Health, Consumer Justice and Deficiency in Medical Services in India*, 49(1–4) J CONSTL & PAR STUD. 8 (2015).

[8] 1986 (2) SCALE 801.

[9] A.I.R. 1989 S.C. 2039.

Samity v. State of West Bengal,[10] the Supreme Court held that the right to health of a citizen is a fundamental right guaranteed under Article 21 of the Constitution and thus all the government hospitals, nursing homes and polyclinics are liable to provide treatment to the best of their capacity to all the patients. Thus, the fundamental right to life which is the most precious human right and which forms the ark of all other rights including the right to health must therefore be interpreted in a broad and expansive spirit to invest it with significance and vitality which may endure for years to come and enhance the dignity of the individual and the worth of the human person.[11]

The Constitution of India by adopting various provisions such as directive principles of state policies,[12] fundamental duties,[13] panchayats and municipalities,[14] certain entries in Seventh Schedule as well as the Preamble to the Constitution ensures various principles relating to Constitutional philosophy which are certainly useful for the protection of the right to health and their implementation in India besides the Article 21. Under the Preamble, the Constitution provides the light for the protection of the right to health through the concept 'Justice-Social, Economic and Political'. According to Article 51A(g), every citizen of India shall have the duty to protect and improve the natural environment including forests, lakes, rivers and wildlife, and to have compassion for living creatures[15] while the right to get healthy environment is a right under Article 21 of the Constitution which is guaranteed against the State. In addition to this, health has been allowed as a limiting factor against the freedom of religion as secured under Article 25 of the Constitution.[16]

---

[10] A.I.R. 1996 S.C. 2426.

[11] *Association of Medical Super Speciality Aspirants and Residents v. Union of India*, (2019) 8 S.C.C. 607.

[12] INDIA CONST. arts. 36–51.

[13] *Ibid.* art.51A.

[14] *Ibid.* arts. 243, 243A to 243ZG.

[15] *Lalit Miglani v. State of Uttarakhand*, 2017 (2) U.C. 1564; *Chinti Devi v. Presiding Officer, Industrial Tribunal-cum-Labour Court*, 2013 (3) S.C.T. 597(P and H).

[16] The question, whether a given religious practice is an integral part of the religion or not, should be answered with the test whether it is regarded as such by the

The fundamental right to profess, practise and propagate religion is subject to public order, morality and health. Where the health of the citizens has involved the right of such practice to profess, practice and propagate religion gets controlled and is subservient to the powers of the State to regulate such practice.[17] Again in *Arjun Gopal v. Union of India*,[18] the question was whether the burning of crackers during Diwali should be allowed to be continued in the present form without any regulatory measures, as a part of religious practice, even if it is proving to be a serious health hazard. The Court held that Article 25 is subject to Article 21 and if a particular religious practice is threatening the health and lives of people, such practice is not entitled to protection under Article 25. Thus, State has the capacity to restrict any religious practices for safeguarding the health, safety and welfare of its people.[19]

Further, in *Bhartiya Govansh Rakshan Sanverdhan Parishad v. Union of India*,[20] the High Court of Himachal Pradesh observed that a combined reading of Articles 48 A and 51A(g) of the Constitution demonstrates that the citizen must be compassionate to the animal kingdom and also protect them. The Supreme Court also observed in *State of Gujarat v. Mirzapur Moti Kureshi Kassab Jamat*,[21] that by enacting Clause (g) in Article 51A in the Constitution as a fundamental duty the Parliament ensured the spirit and message of Articles 48 and 48A which is to be honoured by every citizen. Article 51A(g) provides for a fundamental duty of every citizen 'to have compassion for living creatures', which in its wider fold embraces the category of cattle spoken of specifically in Article 48.

community following the religion or not. Now, the answer to the abovementioned question can be found by judging whether the practice in question is religious in character and if it is, whether it can be regarded as an integral or essential part of the religion. *See, The Commissioner, Hindu Religious Endowments, Madras v. Lakshmindra Thirtha Swamiar of Sri ShirurMutt.*, A.I.R. 1954 S.C. 282.

[17] *Rajesh Kumar Srivastava v. A.P. Verma*, A.I.R. 2005 All 175.

[18] A.I.R. 2018 S.C. 5731.

[19] *Ramchandra Pande v. State of West Bengal*, A.I.R. 1976 Cal 164.

[20] MANU/HP/0697/2016.

[21] A.I.R. 2006 S.C. 212.

Part IX (Articles 243, 243A to 243O) and Part IXA (Articles 243P to 243ZG) of the Constitution of India provide provisions for Panchayats[22] and Municipalities[23] respectively. According to Article 243G, the Legislature of a State may, by law, endow the Panchayats with such powers and authority as may be necessary to enable them to function as institutions of self-government and such law may contain provisions for the devolution of powers and responsibilities upon Panchayats at the appropriate level, subject to such conditions as may be specified therein, concerning - (a) the preparation of plans for economic development and social justice and (b) the implementation of schemes for economic development and social justice as may be entrusted to them including those in relation to the matters listed in the Eleventh Schedule. The Eleventh Schedule enlisted several Entries which are very much useful for the protection of the right to health and its implementation. These entries relate to (a) drinking water, (b) health and sanitation, including hospitals, primary health centres and dispensaries, (c) family welfare, (d) women and child development, and (e) social welfare, including the welfare of the handicapped and mentally retarded.[24] Thus, in *Javed v. State of Haryana*,[25] the Supreme Court observed that Article 243G imposes one of the responsibilities upon Panchayats to prepare plans and implement schemes for economic development and social justice. Some of the schemes that can be entrusted to Panchayats, as spelt out by Article 243G read with Eleventh Schedule are schemes for economic development and social justice in relation to health and sanitation, family welfare, women and child development and social welfare. Nothing more needs to be said to demonstrate that the Constitution contemplates Panchayat as a potent instrument of family welfare and social welfare schemes coming true for the betterment of people's health especially women's health and family welfare. Similarly, the State legislature may entrust under Article 243W read with Entry 6 of Schedule XII, the functions of public health, sanitation conservancy and solid waste management

---

[22] Inserted by the Constitution (Seventy-third Amendment) Act, 1992.

[23] Inserted by the Constitution (Seventy-fourth Amendment) Act, 1992.

[24] Entries 11, 23, 24, 25 and 26 of the Eleventh Schedule of the Constitution of India.

[25] A.I.R. 2003 S.C. 3057.

to Municipalities. It may thus be seen that the Constitution envisages the setting up of hospitals by many different public authorities, including the Central Government, State Government, Municipalities and Panchayati Raj Institutions.[26]

The legislative power to make law for regulating different facets of the right to health is given in the Articles 245 to 260 along with the Union List, State List and Concurrent List of the Seventh Schedule of the Constitution which is more important in understanding the scope and ambit of the right to health in India.[27] Under the List I (Union List) of the Seventh Schedule to the Constitution the Union Legislature has the power to legislate on matters of port quarantine, including hospitals connected therewith; seamen's and marine hospitals,[28] insurance,[29] patents, inventions and designs; copyright; trade-marks and merchandise marks,[30] and regulation of labour and safety in mines and oilfields.[31] Like Union legislature, under Entry-6 of the List-II (State List) the State legislature is empowered to legislate on matters of public health, sanitation, hospitals and dispensaries. The objective of this Entry has been explained by the Supreme Court in *State of Bihar v. Shree Baidyanath Ayurved Bhawan Private Ltd.*,[32] where the Court observed that in the matter of liquor traffic the power of control by the State is an incident of the society's right to self-protection. It rests upon the right of the State to care for the health, moral and welfare of the people.

In *Sanjeev Kumar v. State of H. P.*,[33] the Himachal Pradesh High Court has given the widest interpretation to Entry 6 of the State List. The Court held that there is no clear and direct inconsistency

---

[26] *Meeta Sahai v. State of Bihar*, 2020 (1) S.C.T. 469 (SC).

[27] Poonam Sonwani, *Distribution of Legislative Powers under the Indian Constitution*, 7(1) RJHSS 39 (2016).

[28] INDIA CONST., List I, Entry 28.

[29] *Ibid.* Entry 47.

[30] *Ibid.* Entry 49.

[31] *Ibid.* Entry 55.

[32] A.I.R. 2005 S.C. 932.

[33] MANU/HP/0709/2013.

between the Central Act and the State Act. Though the Union has taken the control of the food industry under Entry 52 of List I, as a whole, it cannot be said that the State Legislature was not competent to exercise other powers enabling to legislate the statute in List II, more particularly, Entry 6 of the State list. This power cannot be denied to the State. Entry 8 of List II of Seventh Schedule of the Constitution empowers the State to enact the law on intoxicating liquors, that is to say, laws to control the production, manufacture, transport, possession, purchase and sale of intoxicating liquors. In *State of A. P. v. Mcdowelland Co.*,[34] the Supreme Court, by referring to all those relevant Entries from the three Lists in Seventh Schedule of the Constitution, held that the ambit and scope of a constitutional Entry cannot be determined by reference to a Parliamentary enactment. Entry 8 in List II speaks of only intoxicating liquors; therefore, it does not apply to any liquor which does not fall within the expression 'intoxicating liquors'. Henceforth, the power to make a law concerning manufacture, production, consumption and sale of intoxicating liquor is with the State alone. The State Legislature is perfectly competent to make a law prohibiting the manufacture and production in addition to sale, possession and transport of intoxicating liquors, by reference to Entries 1, 6 and 8 in List II of the Seventh Schedule of the Constitution read with Article 47 thereof.

Both the Centre and the States have the power to legislate on matters of adulteration of foodstuffs, drugs and poisons, family planning, social security and social insurance, the welfare of labour, medical professions and prevention of the extension from one state to another of infections or contagious diseases or pests affecting men, animals and plants under Concurrent List, that is, List III.[35] In *Gandhi Irwin Salt Manufacturers Association v. Government of Tamil Nadu*,[36] the Madras High Court has held that the Prevention of Food Adulteration Act is the subject relating to which there is a specific entry (Entry 18) in

[34] A.I.R. 1996 S.C. 1627.

[35] Constitution of India, List III, Entry 18, 19, 20A, 23, 24, 26 and 29 of the Seventh Schedule. *See*, S.S. Girisankar, *Constitution and Regulation of Economy*, 22 ACADEMY L. REV. 23, 48 (1998).

[36] A.I.R. 1996 Mad 109.

the Concurrent List. In *Dabur India Ltd. v. Delhi Administration*,[37] the High Court of Delhi held that medicinal products may also fall under Entry 19 of List III dealing with the subject of drugs and poisons which would give both the Parliament as well as the State legislatures the power to enact laws. Entry 20A in the Concurrent List vested the legislative power upon both the Centre and the States regarding population control and family planning.

B. Constitutional Directives to Right to Health

i. The General Framework

The framers of the Constitution of India recognized the mandate on the part of the State to improve health. In fact, they had not treated health as a fundamental right but they treated it as directive principles of state policy. With the judicial interpretations, at present, the directive principles of state policy are the Constitutional obligation of State to be performed on its own, without waiting for a citizen to demand it.[38] Accordingly, the obligation upon the State to ensure the creation and maintaining of conditions congenial to good health is cast by the constitutional directives contained in Articles 39, 41, 42, 43 and 47 (Article 47 is discussed separately). However, according to Article 37, although the directive principles are not enforceable by any Court, these principles are fundamental in the governance of the country and be applied in making laws.[39] Nevertheless, the directive principles are available for determining the legal efficacy of the actions of the State.[40] In this way, directives are fundamental in the governance of the country and they can be stated as the rock bottom level of the socio-economic development that the State is obliged to secure and maintain.

So far as the protection of the right to health of workers, men, women and children is concerned, Articles 39 (e) to (f) of the

[37] 48 (1992) D.L.T. 660.

[38] *Juhi Kumari v. State of Bihar*, 2011 (59) B.L.J.R. 2662.

[39] *Arun Kumar Bhadoria v. State*, 2018 (3) R.C.R. (Criminal) 146.

[40] *Anshu Rani v. State of U.P.*, 2019 (4) A.D.J. 809.

Constitution imposes a responsibility upon the State to follow certain policies relating to the health and strength of workers, men and women and the tender age of children. According to Article 39(e) of the Constitution, the State shall, in particular, direct its policy towards securing that the health and strength of workers, men and women, and the tender age of children are not abused and that citizens are not forced by economic necessity to enter avocations unsuited to their age or strength.

In *Bangalore Turf Club Ltd. v. Regional Director*,[41] the Supreme Court observed that:

> The State is enjoined under Article 39(e) to protect the health of the workers, under Article 41 to secure sickness and disablement benefits and Article 43 accords decent standard of life. Right to medical and disability benefits are fundamental human rights. Under Article 25(2) of Universal Declaration of Human Rights and Article 7(b) of International Convention on Economic, Social and Cultural Rights, right to health, a fundamental human right stands enshrined in socioeconomic justice of our Constitution and the Universal Declaration of Human Rights. Concomitantly right to medical benefit to a workman is his or her fundamental right.

Similarly, Article 39(f) provides that the children should be given opportunities and facilities to develop in a healthy manner and in conditions of freedom and dignity and that childhood and youth are protected against exploitation and against moral and material abandonment. In *Bandua Mukthi Morcha v. Union of India*,[42] the Supreme Court held that Article 21 provides for the right to live with human dignity which derives its life breath from the directive principles of state policy and particularly clauses (e) and (f) of Article 39 and Articles 41 and 42 and therefore, it must include protection of the health and strength of workers, men and women, and of the tender age of children against abuse, opportunities and facilities for children to develop in a healthy manner and in conditions of freedom and dignity, educational facilities, just and humane conditions of work and maternity relief. The Court held that these are the basic minimum

---

[41] A.I.R. 2015 S.C. 221.

[42] A.I.R. 1984 S.C. 802.

requirements that must exist to enable a person to live with human dignity[43] and no State neither the Central Government nor any State Government has the right to take any action which will deprive a person of the enjoyment of these nominal essentials.

Article 41 of the Constitution concentrated on providing public assistance in certain cases. Thus, Article 41 of the Constitution requires that the State *inter-alia* within the limit of its economic capacity and development, to make effective provision for securing the right to public assistance in cases of old age, sickness and disablement, and other cases of undeserved want. In contrast under Rule 9 of the Central Civil Services (Pension) Rules, 1972, the President has reserved to himself the right to withhold pension in whole or in part, whether permanently or for a specified period. Nevertheless, in *D. S. Nakara v. Union of India*,[44] the Constitution Bench of the Supreme Court held that pension is not only compensation for loyal service rendered in the past, but also has a broader significance. It is a social welfare measure that renders socio-economic justice by providing economic security in the end stage of life when physical and mental capacity is ebbing as a by-product of the ageing process and as a result, one is required to fall back on savings. One such saving in kind is when one had given his best in the heyday of life to his employer, in days of inability, economic security by way of periodical payment is assured. Therefore, it is a sort of stipend made in consideration of past service or a surrender of rights or emoluments to one retired from service. Thus, the pension is earned by rendering long and efficient service and therefore can be said to be a deferred portion of the compensation for service rendered. The most practical reason for providing the pension is the inability to provide for oneself due to old age.

Further, if the right to livelihood as enshrined in Article 41 is not treated as a part of the constitutional right to life, the easiest way of depriving a person of his right to life would be to deprive him of his

---

[43] Human dignity is an essential part of the fundamental rights. *Ashwani Kumar v. Union of India*, (2019) 2 S.C.C. 636; *Jeeja Ghosh v. Union of India*, A.I.R. 2016 S.C. 2393; *Shabnam v. Union of India*, A.I.R. 2015 S.C. 3648.

[44] A.I.R. 1983 S.C. 130.

means of livelihood to the point of abrogation.[45] Thus, by examining the scope and ambit of the public assistance under Article 41 the Supreme Court in *B. R. Kapoor v. Union of India*[46] held that the employee's right to pension is a statutory right. The measure of deprivation, therefore, must be correlative to or commensurate with the gravity of the grave misconduct or irregularity as it offends the right to assistance at the evening of his life as assured under Article 41 of the Constitution. Therefore, the order to withhold the pension as a measure of penalty is obviously illegal and is devoid of jurisdiction. However, the main hurdle in Article 41 is the words 'within the limits of its economic capacity' by which the Governments often get a course not to fulfil this obligation.[47]

According to Article 42 of the Constitution, the State shall make provision for securing just and humane conditions of work and for maternity relief. The object of maternity leave is to protect the dignity of motherhood by providing for the full and healthy maintenance of the woman and her child. Maternity leave is intended to achieve the objective of ensuring social justice for women. Motherhood and childhood both require special attention. Not only are the health issues of the mother and the child considered while providing for maternity leave but the leave is provided for creating a bond of affection between the two.[48] The Supreme Court in *Municipal Corporation of Delhi v. Female Workers*[49] held that since Article 42 specifically speaks of 'just and humane conditions of work' and 'maternity relief', the validity of an executive or administrative action in denying maternity benefit has to be examined on the versions of Article 42 which, though not enforceable in Courts, is nevertheless available for determining the legal efficacy of the action complained of. Thus, the Court granted maternity leave to the female workers on muster roll though their

---

[45] *Dinavahi Lakshmi Kameswari v. State of Andhra Pradesh*, 2020 (5) A.L.T. 77.

[46] A.I.R. 1990 S.C. 1923.

[47] Mridula Sarmah, *A Study of Right to Health under the Constitution of India*, 5(3) IJHSS 85, 88(2019).

[48] *Devshree Bandhe v. Chhattisgarh State Power Holding Company Limited*, 2017 (5) C.G.L.J. 340.

[49] A.I.R. 2000 S.C. 1274.

service was not regular and the Court further emphasized that just social order can be achieved only when inequalities are eliminated and everyone gets what is legally due.

Besides these provisions, the State shall endeavour to protect and improve the environment and safeguard the forests and wildlife of the country under Article 48A which is very useful for the enjoyment of the right to health. In *Consumer Education and Research Centre v. Union of India,*[50] the Supreme Court held that:

> [R]ight to health, medical aid to protect the health and vigour to a worker while in service or post retirement is a fundamental right under Article 21, read with Articles 39(e), 41, 43, 47, 48A and all related Articles and fundamental human rights to make the life of the workman meaningful and purposeful with dignity of a person. It is a matter of fact that a close reading of the directive principles shows that the government has the duty to provide comprehensive, creative, preventive, promotional and rehabilitative health services and proper nutrition to all the people of India.

Hence, any decision taken by the State functionaries in furtherance of any directive principles contained in Part IV of the Constitution and other Constitutional provisions cannot be termed as unreasonable. Such a decision can be justified on important competing public interests.[51]

ii. Raising Standard of Living and Improvement of Public Health

The Constitution of India under Article 47 directs the State to take measures to raise the level of nutrition and the standard of living and to improve public health. According to Article 47, the State shall

> regard the raising of the level of nutrition and the standard of living of its people and the improvement of public health as among its primary duties and, in particular, the State shall endeavour to bring about prohibition of the consumption except for medicinal purposes of intoxicating drinks and of drugs which are injurious to health.

[50] A.I.R. 1995 S.C. 922.

[51] *D.S. Rana v. Ahmedabad Municipal Corporation,* A.I.R. 2000 Guj 45.

The concepts 'standard of living' and 'improvement of public health' under Article 47 refer to both a goal for the health of a population and to professional practices aimed at its attainment. This goal can be achieved by attaining a healthy standard of living. The 'improvement of public health' is a state of attaining standard of living with a complete physical, mental and social well-being and not merely the absence of disease or infirmity. Thus, the improvement of public health is the fulfilment of society's interest in assuring the conditions in which people can be healthy. Under these circumstances, therefore it is obligatory upon the State Government to make an endeavour under Article 47 to look after the provisions for health and nutrition.[52] Further, after reading Article 47 along with Article 21, the Supreme Court in *Centre for Public Interest Litigation v. Union of India*,[53] emphasized that any food article which is hazardous or injurious to public health is a potential danger to the fundamental right to life guaranteed under Article 21 of the Constitution of India. A paramount duty is cast on the State and its authorities to achieve an appropriate level of protection to human life and health which is a fundamental right guaranteed to the citizens under Article 21 read with Article 47 of the Constitution of India.

Moreover, the grant of a licence as a measure of control of intoxicating liquor is an age-old phenomenon. In the changing circumstances, a question may arise that whether there is any contradiction in 'improvement of public health' with 'trade in liquor' and 'grant of liquor licence'. According to Article 47, it should be the policy of the State to (a) raise the standard of public health by raising the level of nutrition, and (b) bring about prohibition of consumption. Keeping in view the provision in Article 47 the Supreme Court in *Kuldeep Singh v. Government of NCT of Delhi*,[54] observed that although dealing in liquor is not a fundamental right, but indisputably the equality clause contained in Article 14 of the Constitution of India would apply. Therefore, the policy decision of opening the doors of liquor shops by the private entrepreneurs is taken to earn more revenue. However, consideration of the application for it is required to be fair and reasonable. The

---

[52] *State of West Bengal v. Tonmoy Mondal*, (2019) 16 S.C.C. 348

[53] A.I.R. 2014 S.C. 49.

[54] A.I.R. 2006 S.C. 2652.

effect of a policy decision taken by the State is to be considered having regard to the provisions contained in Article 47 of the Constitution. Thus, in *Ashok Lenka v. Rishi Dikshit*,[55] the Supreme Court held that all information supplied by the applicants for licences must undergo and satisfy the 'strict scrutiny test'. The State should not treat its right of parting with its privilege only as a means of earning more and more revenue. The importance of regulation of liquor *visa-a-vis* public health should be noted.

The importance of Article 47 of the Constitution may have to be noticed tracing the history back from the date of constitutional debate. The initial proposal of Article 47 was based on a narrow approach which is evident from the draft of April 16, 1947, of the Sub-Committee on Fundamental Rights of the Constitution. According to Clause 44 of the Report of the Sub-Committee on Fundamental Rights (dated April 16, 1947), under the Chapter on non-judicial rights, 'the State shall regard the raising of the level of nutrition and the standard of living of its people and the improvement of public health as among its primary duties'. And this proposal was critically discussed in the Constituent Assembly on 23–24 November 1948. As a result, an amendment was moved by Mahavir Tyagi and modified by Shibban Lal Saksena and Dr. Ambedker sought to add the following in the initial draft:

> and, in particular, the State shall endeavour to bring about prohibition of the consumption except for medicinal purposes of intoxicating drinks and of drugs which are injurious to health.

The original draft along with the amendment was adopted by the Constituent Assembly on 24 November 1948 as Article 38.[56] Later, at the revision stage, it was renumbered as Article 47 of the Constitution. The object of Article 47[57] has been discussed by the Supreme Court in *Ashok Lenka v. Rishi Dikshit*[58] In this case, the Court observed that the prohibition of intoxicating liquor had long been a part of the

---

[55] A.I.R. 2006 S.C. 2382.

[56] Constituent Assembly Debate, Vol. VII. at 567–568.

[57] H.M. SEERVAI, CONSTITUTIONAL LAW OF INDIA 2012 (Universal 2015).

[58] A.I.R. 2006 S.C. 2382.

policy of the Indian National Congress and its inclusion in Article 47 received support from the Mohammedan community whose social habits were reinforced by the Koranic injunction against intoxicating liquor. Alcohol (the intoxicating ingredient of liquor) is a 'narcotic', a word replaced by the word 'depressant' to describe the same effects contrary to the popular belief that it is a stimulant. It is not a mere accident that intoxicating liquor and dangerous drugs have been clubbed together in Entry 8 (List II) of the Seventh Schedule. Article 47 has a unique feature in the sense that the first part refers to public health, whereas the second part specifically refers to the prohibition of liquor. Article 47 was inserted in the draft Constitution after the first part was suggested by Shri B. N. Rau (including Seth Govind Das and Shri Bishwanath Das) specifically wanted that prohibition should find specific mention at a suitable place in the Constitution. One of the members, Kazi Sayed Karimuddin expressed his desire that such a provision should be included in a separate Article having regard to the preaching's of Mahatma Gandhi and also having regard to the fact that the same has been approved by all communities. In Article 47, however, only liquor was specifically mentioned at the instance of Shri Bishwanath Das who opined that if the prohibition of liquor is to be included in a separate Article, other harmful articles like opium, tobacco and like products should also find mention in Article 47.[59] The Supreme Court further observed:

> The relationships among medicine, public health, ethics and human rights are now evolving rapidly, in response to a series of events, experiences and struggles. In general, people equate medical care with health, but the vast majority of research into the health of populations identifies the so called 'societal factors' as the major determinants of health status. Public health, although starting as a social movement, has at least in recent years, responded relatively little to this profound knowledge about the dominant impact of society on health, such as behaviour like excess alcohol. Given that the major determinants are societal in nature, it seems evident that only a framework that expresses fundamental values in societal terms, and a vocabulary of values that links directly with societal structure and function, can be useful to the work of public health.[60]

[59] Constituent Assembly Debate, Vol. VII. at 496–498.
[60] *Ashok Lenka v. Rishi Dikshit*, A.I.R. 2006 S.C. 2382.

Although Article 47 is not enforceable, it being a directive principle, there is considerable moral force and authority in this provision to persuade the State Governments and the Government of India (GOI) to attempt at ensuring that the people, particularly those in drought-affected areas are provided adequate food grains and a cooking medium for the preparation of their meals.

C. Application of Constitutional Philosophy to Right to Health

The Constitutional philosophy in India relating to the right to health is derived from the scheme of the preamble, fundamental rights and directive principles of state policy. While the concept of social justice is laid down in the preamble as a social goal, the fundamental rights and the directive principles of the Constitution elaborates the concepts which are the foundations of social justice in India.[61] The Constitution of India is the highest law of the land and all laws, national or local, customary or statutory, past and future draw their validity and legitimacy from it. In its form and structure, the Constitution follows the Western liberal model of Constitutionalism, but it has several features founded on Indian traditions and the special needs and circumstances of the society. The Preamble to the Constitution not only talks about social justice but also aims to achieve equality of status and opportunity for all citizens. The objectives enshrined in the Preamble permeate throughout the entire Constitution.[62]

The Preamble of the Constitution serves two purposes: (a) it indicates the source from which the Constitution derives its authority, and (b) it also states the objects, which the Constitution seeks to establish and promote.[63] The Preamble and indeed the Constitution were drafted in the light and direction of the *Objective Resolutions* which was

---

[61] *Indra Das v. State of Assam*, (2011) 3 S.C.C. 380; *Dev Dutt v. Union of India*, (2008) 8 S.C.C. 725.

[62] Priti Tiwary, *The Ideology of Socialism in Indian Constitution*, 4(1) IJAR 222 (2018).

[63] Liav Orgad, *The Preamble in Constitutional Interpretation*, 8(4) Int. J. Const. Law 714, 728 (2010).

adopted on 22 January 1947 by the Constituent Assembly.[64] It was said by Jawahar Lal Nehru while moving the *Objective Resolution*[65] on 13 December 1946, that 'all power and authority of sovereign independent India, its constituent part and organs of the Government are derived from the people'. The Preamble to the Constitution assured that political justice must include real economic freedom of starving millions of people. Along with it, the Preamble provides the concept of social justice[66] based on expansive values of human rights. The founding fathers of the Constitution, therefore, in the *Objective Resolution*, speaking on behalf of, 'We, the people of India', pledged on their behalf to accord justice, social, economic and political to all the citizens, equality of status, and opportunity and dignity of the person with liberties. Further, by exercising the power provided under Article 368 of the Constitution, the objectives as specified in the Preamble cannot be amended as these are the 'basic structure'[67] of the Constitution. The Preamble and various Articles contained in Parts III and IV of the Constitution, *inter alia*, promote social justice so that the life of every individual becomes meaningful and he or she can live with human dignity.

The Preamble provides to all citizens equality of status and opportunity as well as justice - social, economic and political. In *P. A. Inamdar*

---

[64] Constituent Assembly was set up to frame the Constitution of India which began its deliberations on 9 December 1946, reassembled as the Sovereign Constituent Assembly for India after midnight of 14 August 1947.

[65] (1947) C.A.D. 304.

[66] Preamble to the Constitution of India provides: 'JUSTICE, social, economic and political'.

[67] The Supreme Court in a number of cases held that equality, rule of law, judicial review, separation of powers, supremacy of the Constitution, federalism, secularism, sovereign, democratic, republican structure, freedom and dignity of the individual, unity and integrity of the nation, equal justice, social and economic justice, balance between fundamental rights and directive principles, independence of the judiciary, efficient judicial system, powers of the Supreme Court, effective access to justice are 'basic structure' of the Constitution cannot be amended even by the amending power of the legislature under Article 368 of the Constitution of India. See, *Ram Jethmalani v. Union of India*, 2011 (6) SCALE 691; *Minerva Mills Ltd. & ORS v. Union of India*, A.I.R. 1980 S.C. 1789.

v. the State of Maharashtra,[68] the Supreme Court observed that it is well accepted by the thinkers, philosophers and academicians that JUSTICE, LIBERTY, EQUALITY and FRATERNITY, include social, economic and political justice. Granville Austin by considering the social justice mechanism, in his book,[69] states that probably no other Constitution in the world has provided so much impetus towards changing and rebuilding society for the common good.[70] The concept of elementary human needs involves a list of physiological and social aspects. It includes the minimum social needs of the right to health, food, housing, education and livelihood and provides a foundation upon which human development can occur and basic human freedoms can flourish. These minimal social rights need to be conceptualized in terms of entitlement both as individuals and as members of society. As a result, the Constitution aims at the establishment of a social welfare state, wherein the rights and welfare of all its citizens are not merely protected but insured. However, it is not an easy task to attain that goal. It requires that constant efforts be taken in that direction. In *Lala Ram v. Union of India*,[71] the Supreme Court defines the concept of welfare State and states that:

> [A]s a concept of government, in which the State plays a key role in the protection and promotion of the economic and social well-being of all of its citizens, which may include equitable distribution of wealth and equal opportunities and public responsibilities for all those, who are unable to avail for themselves, minimal provisions for a decent life. It refers to 'Greatest good of greatest number and the benefit of all and the happiness of all'. A welfare State is under an obligation to prepare plans and devise beneficial schemes for the good of the common people. Thus, the fundamental feature of a welfare state is social insurance.

It is pertinent to mention that securing does not mean only allowing the enjoyment of a right, and thus, under the Constitutional

---

[68] (2005) 6 S.C.C. 537.

[69] AUSTIN GRANVILLE, WORKING A DEMOCRATIC CONSTITUTION: THE INDIAN EXPERIENCE (OUP 1999).

[70] Saroj Bohra, *Social Justice and Indian Constitution*, 2(1) IJLLJS 1, 2 (2015); RAJKUMAR SINGH, CONTEMPORARY INDIA WITH CONTROVERSIAL NEIGHBOURS 47 (Gyan Publishing 2011).

[71] (2015) 5 S.C.C. 813.

framework, the State has the power to restrict the enjoyment of rights for the public interest. Hence, the Constitution prefers a middle path and provides such rights with certain restrictions which the government is expected to ensure for its citizen. The State may, therefore, encroach on the domain of these rights for the common good or the common interest.[72] The question of whether a fundamental right is subjected to restrictions for the common good or public interest will depend upon the conditions and circumstances prevailing at that particular time. The preamble of the Constitution also provides for social justice. The concept of 'social justice' engrafted in the Constitution consists of diverse principles that are essential for the orderly growth and development of the personality of every citizen. Thus, 'Social justice' is an integral part of justice in the generic sense. In other words, Justice is the genus, of which social justice is one of its species. The preamble and Article 38 of the Constitution envisage the concept of social justice which is one of the objects of protection of the right to health for everyone. The concept of 'social justice' consists of diverse principles that are essential for the orderly growth and development of the personality of every citizen.[73] It is notable that the concept of social justice is not narrow, one-sided or pedantic, and is not confined to a particular area. It is founded on the basic ideal of social-economic equality and it aims to assist the removal of socio-economic disparities and inequalities.[74] Hence, it cannot be limited only to subserve the interest of the affluent, the rich and the empowered.[75] In other words, the aim of social justice is to attain a substantial degree of social, economic and political equality, which is the legitimate expectation of every section of society.[76] Social justice is an integral part of the 'basic structure' of the Constitution because it gives meaning and significance to the democratic ways of life and of making life dynamic.[77] Regarding the relation between health and socio-economic object of

---

[72] *Rajesh Ranjan Yadav v. CBI*, A.I.R. 2007 S.C. 451.

[73] *Consumer Education and Research Center v. Union of India*, A.I.R. 1995 S.C. 922.

[74] *Municipal Corporation v. Female Workers*, A.I.R. 2000 S.C. 1274.

[75] *Ankit Abhishek v. Ravi Ranjan Kumar*, 2020 (2) P.L.J.R. 821.

[76] *Consumer Education and Research Center v. Union of India*, A.I.R. 1995 S.C. 922.

[77] *Ramo Services v. Subhash Kapoor*, A.I.R. 2001 S.C. 207.

social justice in *C. E. S. C. Ltd.* v. *Subhash Chanda Bose*,[78] the Supreme Court observed:

> The maintenance of health is the most imperative constitutional goal whose realization requires interaction of many social and economic factors. Just and favourable condition of work implies to ensure safe and healthy working conditions to the workmen. The periodical medical treatment invigorates the health of the workmen and harnessers their human resources. Prevention of occupational disabilities generates devotion and dedication to duty and enthuses the workmen to render efficient service which is a valuable asset for greater productivity to the employer and national production to the State.

II. JUDICIAL DIMENSIONS OF RIGHT TO HEALTH

The Indian judiciary through the interpretation technique has declared the right to health as a fundamental right under Article 21 of the Constitution of India in a large number of cases. As a result, a large number of judicial dimensions have emerged relating to the right to health. These dimensions are as follows: (a) right to health under Article 21, (b) right to access to medical aid, (c) right to receive medical treatment in emergencies, (d) right to access to medical records, (e) right to medical reimbursement, (f) right to access to medicine, (g) right to clean, hygienic and safe environment, (h) right to get treatment by qualified medical practitioners, etc. These dimensions need detailed deliberation.

A. Right to Health under Article 21

Though there is no specific provision in the Constitution of India to directly deal with the right to health yet the Supreme Court and various High Courts by a dynamic interpretation of Article 21 of the Constitution declared that the right to health is implicit in the right to life and personal liberty guaranteed under the Constitution. As per them, the right to life comprehends, *inter alia*, the right to environment, right to health care, and the right to adequate health delivery

---

[78] A.I.R. 1992 S.C. 573.

system.[79] Thus, the right to health is an unenumerated right under Article 21 of the Constitution. In *C.E.S.C. Ltd. v. Subhash Chanda Bose*,[80] the Supreme Court examined various functions of the State to protect the safety and health of the workmen and emphasized the need to provide medical care to the workmen to prevent disease and to improve the general standard of health consistent with human dignity and right to personality. Thus, it was held that the term 'health' implies more than an absence of sickness. Medical care and health facilities are not only protecting against sickness but also ensuring stable manpower for economic development. Medical facilities are, therefore, part of social security and life-gilt-edged security, it would yield immediate return to the employer in the increased production and would reduce absenteeism on the ground of sickness, etc.

In *Consumer Education and Research Center v. Union of India*,[81] a three-Judge Bench of the Supreme Court held that the jurisprudence of personhood or philosophy of the right to life envisaged in Article 21 of the Constitution enlarges its sweep to encompass human personality in its full blossom with invigorated health which is a wealth to the workmen to earn his livelihood, to sustain the dignity of the person and to live a life with dignity and equality.[82] The expression 'life' as mentioned in Article 21 does not connote mere animal existence or continued drudgery through life. It has a much wider meaning which includes the right to livelihood, better standard of living, hygienic conditions in the workplace and leisure facilities and opportunities to eliminate sickness and physical disability of the workmen. The health of the workmen enables him to enjoy the fruits of his labour, to keep him physically fit and mentally alert. Therefore, providing medical facilities is a fundamental right that is required for the protection of worker's health. In that case, health insurance, while in service or after retirement was held to be a fundamental right, and even private

---

[79] *People United for Better Living v. East Kolkata Wetlands Management Authority*, (2009) I.L.R. 2 Cal 37.

[80] A.I.R. 1992 S.C. 573.

[81] A.I.R. 1995 S.C. 922.

[82] *Kapila Hingorani v. State of Bihar*, (2003) 6 S.C.C. 1.

industries are enjoined to provide health insurance to the workman. The Court further observed:

> The right to health to a worker is an integral facet of meaningful right to life to have not only a meaningful existence but also robust health and vigour without which worker would lead a life of misery... Therefore, it must be held that the right to health and medical care is a fundamental right under Article 21 read with Articles 39(c), 41 and 43 of the Constitution and make the life of the workman meaningful and purposeful with dignity of person. Right to life includes protection of the health and strength of the worker which is a minimum requirement to enable a person to live with human dignity.

The State, Union or State government or industry, public or private are enjoined to take all such actions which will promote health, strength and vigour of the workman during the period of employment and even after retirement as essentials to live the life with health and happiness. Thus, by highlighting the responsibilities of the State in securing the right to health, in *Rajesh Kumar Srivastava v. A.P. Verma*,[83] the Allahabad High Court held that the right to health can be guaranteed only if the State provides for adequate measures for treatment and takes care of its citizen by protecting them from persons practising and professing unauthorized medical practices. Further, the health and strength of the worker is an integral facet of the right to life. Denial thereof denudes the workman from the finer facets of 'life' which violates Article 21.[84]

However, the word 'life' in Article 21 means the right to live with human dignity but it does not merely connote continued drudgery. It takes within its fold 'some of the finer graces of human civilization, which makes life worth living' and that the expanded concept of life would mean the 'tradition, culture and heritage' of the concerned person.[85] The concept of the advance medical directive is also called living will and it is of recent origin, which gained recognition in the latter part of the 20th century. Many people's living depending on machines

---

[83] A.I.R. 2005 All 175.

[84] *Paschim Banga Khet Mazdoor Samity v. State of West Bengal*, A.I.R. 1996 S.C. 2426.

[85] *K. S. Puttaswamy v. Union of India*, A.I.R. 2017 S.C. 4161.

causes great financial distress to the family with the cost of long-term medical treatment. The advance medical directive was developed as a means to restrict these kinds of medical interventions. The foundation for seeking direction regarding advance medical directives is an extension of the right to refuse medical treatment and the right to die with dignity. When a competent patient has the right to decide on medical treatment, with regard to medical procedure entailing the right to die with dignity, the said right cannot be denied to those patients, who have become incompetent to make an informed decision at the relevant time. Thus, in *Common Cause v. Union of India*,[86] the Supreme Court observed:

> The rights of bodily integrity and self-determination are the rights which belong to every human being. When an adult person having mental capacity to take a decision can exercise his right not to take treatment or withdraw from treatment, the above right could not be negated for a person who is not able to take an informed decision due to terminal illness... In case of a person who is suffering from a disease and is taking medical treatment, there are three stake holders; the person himself, his family members and doctor treating the patient. No person could take decision regarding life of another unless he is entitled to take such decision authorized under any law... The best interests of the patient had to be found out not by doctor treating the patient alone but a team of doctors specifically nominated by the State Authority.

Lastly, the inclusion of health right to the ambit of right to life is so obvious that the Supreme Court in *Indian Council of Legal Aid and Advice v. Union of India*[87] observed that there is no gainsaying that health is an important facet of the right to life guaranteed under Article 21 of the Constitution of India and it is an obligation of the State to ensure good health to the citizens.

B. Right to Access to Medical Aid

Protection of public health is now viewed very much within the rights perspective and access to medical aid is of paramount importance to

---

[86] A.I.R. 2018 S.C. 1665.

[87] (2000) 10 S.C.C. 542.

secure the right to health. The Constitution of India casts a duty upon the State to take appropriate steps to create an environment that makes it possible for people to access health services. Over the years, it is an accepted fact that life does not only mean animal existence but the life of a dignified human being with all its concomitant attributes. This would include effective health care facilities.[88] Thus, the High Court of Madhya Pradesh in *Manmohan Kaul v. Hindustan Copper Limited*,[89] held that the respondent is State within the meaning of Article 21 of the Constitution and there is an obligation upon State to preserve the life of its employees by providing immediate medical aid. Right to health and medical care is a fundamental right under Articles 21, 39(e), 41 and 43 of the Constitution and makes the life of an employee meaningful and purposeful with the dignity of the person. In *Sheri Sarif Mullah v. State of Assam*,[90] the High Court of Gauhati observed that the duty to provide medical treatment is performed by the State in view of its fundamental obligations as a welfare State and in consonance with the fundamental rights of the victims under Article 21 of the Constitution. Such obligations of the State flow from a sense of compassion. However, in cases where such compassion is not forthcoming a duty to provide medical assistance to a victim can be understood to be an obligation flowing from the provisions contained in Article 21 of the Constitution of India.

By highlighting the importance of the existence of an adequate number of health professionals to secure the right to medical treatment the Madras High Court in *Thangapandi v. Director of Primary Health Services, DMS Teynampet*,[91] held that right to health being a fundamental right as guaranteed Article 21 of the Constitution, non-availability of doctor in 24 hours maternity under Government hospital was a serious aspect required to be addressed by State Government seriously. The mere existence of a hospital was not

---

[88] Mihir Desai & Dipti Chand, *Fundamental Right to Health and Public Health Care*, in HEALTH CARE CASE LAW IN INDIA: A READER 17–35, 17 (Mihir Desai & Kamayani Bali Mahabal eds, CEHAT and ICHRL 2007).

[89] 2006 (2) M.P.L.J. 245.

[90] 2008 (1) G.L.T. 630.

[91] (2011) 256 M.L.J. 1329.

sufficient. Any defence that could be raised by the medical department or the medical officer of the primary health centre, would not be considered as a satisfactory explanation. The right to health as enshrined in Article 21 of the Constitution would be a promise of unreality to village people unless the abovementioned aspect is assured by the State Government.

C. Right to Receive Medical Treatment in Emergencies

In India, there is no specific legislation to deal with the duties of health care providers and personnel to provide emergency medical treatment. The emergency medical condition means a medical condition manifesting acute symptoms of sufficient severity where the absence of emergency medical treatment could reasonably be expected to result in (a) death of the person, (b) serious impairment of bodily functions, (c) serious jeopardy in the health of the person or in the case of a pregnant woman, in her health and the health of the unborn child, and (d) serious dysfunction of any bodily organ or part.[92] In India, the right to medical treatment in emergencies like all other issues related to health facilities falls in the shadow of Article 21. In other words, where there is a refusal to treat an emergency case, the patient may approach the Court to claim compensation for violation of his or her right to life under Article 21 of the Constitution.[93] In *Parmanand Katara v. Union of India*,[94] the Supreme Court held that Article 21 of the Constitution casts the obligation on the State to preserve life. There cannot be any second thought regarding the opinion that the preservation of human life is of paramount importance. A doctor at the Government hospital acting on behalf

---

[92] LAW COMMISSION OF INDIA, 201ST REPORT OF LAW COMMISSION OF INDIA ON EMERGENCY MEDICAL CARE TO VICTIMS OF ACCIDENTS AND DURING EMERGENCY MEDICAL CONDITION AND WOMEN UNDER LABOUR 93 (GOI 2006).

[93] Mihir Desai & Dipti Chand, *Right to Emergency Health Care*, in HEALTH CARE CASE LAW IN INDIA: A READER 37–44 (Mihir Desai & Kamayani Bali Mahabal eds, CEHAT and ICHRL 2007).

[94] A.I.R. 1989 S.C. 2039.

of the State is, therefore, duty-bound to extend medical assistance for preserving life. The Court further observed:

> Every doctor whether at a Government hospital or otherwise has the professional obligation to extend his services with due expertise for protecting life. No law or State action can intervene to avoid/delay the discharge of the paramount obligation cast upon members of the medical profession.

Thus, this obligation is total, absolute and paramount. Further, in *Paschim Banga Khet Mazdoor Samity v. State of West Bengal*,[95] the Supreme Court observed that in a welfare State the primary duty of the Government is to secure the welfare of the people and therefore providing adequate and quality medical facilities for the people is an integral part of the obligations undertaken by the Government. The Government hospitals and their medical officers are duty-bound to extend medical assistance for the preservation of human life. Failure on the part of a government-run hospital to provide timely medical treatment to a person in need of such treatment can result in a violation of his or her right to life guaranteed under Article 21. In this case, Hakim Seikh, who was a member of the petitioner samiti, faced the violation of the right to life guaranteed under Article 21 when he was denied treatment at various Government hospitals which were approached when his condition was very serious and he was in need of immediate medical attention. Moreover, in *Martin F. D'Souza v. Mohd. Ishfaq*,[96] the Supreme Court held that it is the duty of the doctor in an emergency to begin treatment of the patient and he should not wait till the completion of legal formalities or arrival of the police. The preservation of the life of a person is far more important than following the legal formalities.

D. Right to Access to Medical Records

Medical records are an integral part of medical practice and a patient's right to access his or her own medical records is one of the fundamental rights recognized under national as well as an international legal

---

[95] A.I.R. 1996 S.C. 2426.

[96] A.I.R. 2009 S.C. 2049.

framework. In general, the medical record is a confidential document and its access is limited.[97] Every health care provider is ethically and legally bound to maintain patient treatment records.[98] However, though patients' treatment records are guided primarily by patients' welfare-oriented health care principles, the record is also a legal document.[99] It serves to protect the legal interests of all participants in the health care delivery system. Thus, these ethical and legal concerns, especially issues of confidentiality have resulted in the introduction of stringent protections relating to medical records.

The Supreme Court in *Sameer Kumar v. State of U. P.*[100] by explaining the importance of medical records observed that with the growing population and increasing negligence and misconduct committed by the medical professionals, the citizens suffer and in absence of any remedial measure to check such menace, irreparable loss and injury may be caused to the patients and their attendants in due course of time. To protect the patients from such loss, it is necessary to provide medical records to patients or their attendants as the case may be. It is important to note that this aspect of the right to health is not expressly recognized under the Constitution of India, but by widening the sphere of Article 21, the Courts have included this access to medical records within the purview of the right to life. In *X v. Hospital Z*,[101] the Supreme Court observed that:

> [I]n the doctor-patient relationship, the most important aspect is the doctor's duty of maintaining secrecy. A doctor cannot disclose to a person any information regarding his patient which he has gathered in the course of treatment nor can the doctor disclose to anyone else the mode of treatment or the advice given by him to the patient.

---

[97] Nimisha Srinivas & Arpita Biswas, *Protecting Patient Information in India: Data Privacy Law and Its Challenges*, 5 NUJS L. REV. 411, 415 (2012). WILLIAM H. ROACH, MEDICAL RECORDS AND THE LAW 95 (Jones and Bartlett 1994).

[98] RONALD W. SCOTT, LEGAL ASPECTS OF DOCUMENTING PATIENT CARE 84 (Aspen Publishers 1994).

[99] Hayley Rosenman, *Patients' Rights to Access Their Medical Records: An Argument for Uniform Recognition of a Right of Access in the United States and Australia*, 21(4) FORDHAM INT. LAW J. 1500, 1506 (1997).

[100] 2014 (8) A.D.J. 742.

[101] A.I.R. 1999 S.C. 495.

But this duty is not absolute. It is subject to certain exceptions. This confidentiality may be restricted for the prevention of crime, protection of health or morals or protection of rights and freedom of others.

E. Right to Medical Reimbursement

Medical reimbursement programmes have long been used by governments to protect the finances of individuals and households affected by illness and injury and to realize Universal Health Coverage for all citizens. In modern medico-legal jurisprudence, medical expenses related to the care and treatment of the injury alleged by the claimant often constitute a significant portion of the damages that might be recovered through trial.[102] In India, the judiciary played a pivotal role in securing the right to medical reimbursement to the general people by recognizing the same under Article 21. The High Court of Punjab and Haryana in *Kartar Singh Virk v. State of Punjab*[103] opined that the right to health is an integral part of the right to life. Government is under an obligation to provide adequate facilities and to reimburse expenses incurred by serving or retired civil servants for treatment instructions issued by Government. Further, in *State of Punjab v. Mohinder Singh Chawla*,[104] the Supreme Court held that in case of sufferings of government employee if any ailment requires treatment at a specialized approved hospital and on reference, the government servant had undergone such treatment therein, then it is the duty of the State to bear the expenditure incurred by that government servant. As a result, expenditure, thus, incurred requires to be reimbursed by the State to the employee. However subsequently, the Supreme Court in *State of Punjab v. Ram Lubhaya Bagga*[105] held that the policy of reimbursement of medical expenses incurred in a private hospital is only admissible when for such ailment treatment not available in Government hospital and for this no objection certificate is obtained from the Civil

---

[102] Russell G. Thornton, *Recovery of Medical Expenses in Texas*, 20(3) Proc (Bayl Univ Med Cent) 315 (2007).

[103] (1997) 116 (2) P.L.R. 573.

[104] A.I.R. 1997 S.C. 1225.

[105] A.I.R. 1998 S.C. 1703.

Surgeon or Director of Health Services. The reason is that no State of any country has unlimited resources to spend on any of its projects and it only approves its project to the extent it is feasible. The Court further observed that:

> No right could be absolute in a welfare State. Man is a social animal. He cannot live without the cooperation of a large number of persons. Every article one uses is the contribution of many. Hence every individual right has to give way to the right of the public at large. Not every fundamental right under Part III of the Constitution is absolute and it is to be within permissible reasonable restriction. This principle equally applies when there is any constraint on the health budget on account of financial stringencies. It is however hoped that Government will give due consideration and priority to the health budget in future and render what is best possible.

However, there is another view also exists regarding the liability of the State in securing the right to medical reimbursement. In *Laxman Taneja v. the State of Rajasthan*,[106] the High Court of Rajasthan again considered that whether an individual can claim medical cost reimbursement when he made his or his relatives' treatments in the private healthcare organization and observed that in a welfare state, the welfare of people should not be frustrated just because of the bureaucratic approach of concerning authorities. While granting benefits under beneficial schemes, essential, immediate and timely medical assistance were primary considerations, the financial constraints were always secondary considerations. The Court further stated that apart from the fact that to preserve health and to obtain medical aid in the furtherance of self-preservation is part of the right of life under Article 21. The petitioner is also entitled to reimbursement of medical expenses, irrespective of the place where treatment had been received. So, the issue related to medical reimbursement for treating in private healthcare institutions remains unresolved.

F. Right to Access to Medicine

Medicine is another aspect of health care that has the capacity to control the curative aspect of health. With the development of medical science, this aspect is now having a greater impact on individual health

---

[106] R.L.W. 2005 (2) Raj 1271.

as well as public health. In pursuit of better health care outcomes, one of the many challenges Governments face is improving access to medicines and the price of medicine, in turn, can create challenges for improving access to medicines.[107] Access to medicine is a pressing concern in India today. This concern of lack of access to medicine in the Indian health scenario has forced the judiciary to include this as a fundamental right within the purview of Article 21 to secure access to the poor people and to cast a responsibility upon the State to secure the same. In *Union of India v. Mool Chand Khairati Ram Trust*,[108] the Supreme Court observed that in the wake of globalization, we are in a regime of intellectual property rights. Even these intellectual property rights have to give way to human rights. It is an obligation of the Government to provide life-saving drugs to have-nots at afford-able prices so as to save their lives, which is part of Article 21 of the Constitution of India. In *Deepa Pant v. the State of Uttarakhand*,[109] the High Court of Uttarakhand categorically held that right to get medical treatment is a fundamental right as enshrined under Article 21 of the Constitution and to provide medical assistance the family is forced to spend money sometimes by raising loans. It is the responsibility of the State Government to provide lifesaving drugs free of cost. No person can be permitted to die for want of life-saving drugs or medicine.

G. Right to Clean, Hygienic and Safe Environment

The right to enjoy a clean, hygienic and safe environment is another right recognized under Article 21 of the Constitution as a prerequisite for the enjoyment of the right to health. In *M. C. Mehta v. Union of India*,[110] the Supreme Court examined the availability of Article 21 against a private corporation engaged in an activity that has the poten-tial to affect the life and health of the people. The Court by relying on Article 21 issued certain directions regarding hazardous chemicals

---

[107] Nitsan Chorev & Kenneth C. Shadlen, *Intellectual Property, Access to Medicines, and Health: New Research Horizons*, 50(2) SCID 143 (2015).

[108] 2018 (8) SCALE 648.

[109] MANU/UC/0206/2018.

[110] A.I.R. 1987 S.C. 1086.

and observed that an enterprise that is engaged in a hazardous or inherently dangerous industry poses a potential threat to the health and safety of the persons working in the factory and residing in the surrounding areas owes an absolute and non-delegable duty to ensure that no harm results to anyone on account of hazardous or inherently dangerous nature of the activity which it has undertaken. In a similar line, in *Bangalore Medical Trust v. B. S. Muddappa*,[111] the Supreme Court highlighted the importance of protection of the environment, open spaces for recreation and fresh air and held these as matters of great public concern. The Court also held that the reservation and preservation of open spaces cannot be sacrificed by leasing or selling such sites. Any such act would be contrary to the legislative intent and inconsistent with the statutory requirements. Furthermore, it would be in direct conflict with the constitutional mandate to ensure that any State action is inspired by the basic values of individual freedom and dignity and addressed to the attainment of a quality of life that makes the guaranteed rights a reality for all the citizens. Thus, by expanding the ambit of the right to life, the Supreme Court in *M.C. Mehta v. Union of India*,[112] observed that the right to life not only meant leading a life with dignity but included within its ambit the right to lead a healthy, robust life in a clean atmosphere free from pollution. The Court further held that if there is a conflict between health and wealth, obviously, health would have to be given precedence.

The enterprise has also an obligation to ensure that the hazardous or inherently dangerous activity in which it is engaged must be conducted with the highest standards of safety and if any harm results on account of such activity, the enterprise must be absolutely liable to compensate for such harm and there should not be any argument on behalf of the enterprise that it had taken all reasonable care and that the harm occurred without any negligence on its part. In *Mathew*

---

[111] A.I.R. 1991 S.C. 1902. *Vikram Deo Singh Tomar v. State of Bihar*, A.I.R. 1988 S.C. 1782; *State of Himachal Pradesh v. Umed Ram Sharma*, A.I.R. 1986 S.C. 847; *Olga Tellis v. Bombay Municipal Corporation*, A.I.R. 1986 S.C. 180; *Francis Coralie Mullin v. The Administrator, Union Territory of Delhi*, A.I.R. 1981 S.C. 746.

[112] A.I.R. 2018 S.C. 5194.

Lukose v. Kerala State Pollution Control Board,[113] the Kerala High Court also held that Article 21 comprehends the right to a healthy environment and the duty of the State to protect these rights against air, water and environmental pollution caused by the working of the company endangering the health of the local people. Right to life is more than immunity from the extinction of life. It guarantees life in its many splendored facets, emotional, spiritual and aesthetic. A human machine that ticks or a creature that breathes are not all, we reckoned of human personality. Further, the Supreme Court in *N. D. Jayal v. Union of India,*[114] observed that the right to health is a fundamental right under Article 21. Protection of health is inextricably linked with a clean environment. Thus, a clean and healthy environment itself is a fundamental right.

H. Right to Get Treatment by Qualified Medical Practitioners

In *Rajasthan Pradesh Vaidya Samiti, Sardarshahar v. Union of India,*[115] the Supreme Court held that the citizens of India have a right under Article 21 of the Constitution to get protection and safeguard with regard to health and life from mal-medical treatment. Similarly, the Supreme Court, in *Laxman Balkrishna Joshi v. Trimbak Bapu Godbole,*[116] held that a person who holds himself out ready to give medical advice and treatment impliedly undertakes that he is possessed skill and knowledge for the purpose. He owes a duty of care to the patient in deciding whether to undertake the case and what treatment to give. A breach of such duty gives a right of action to the patient for the negligence of the doctor. Thus, every citizen has the right to get treatment from qualified medical practitioners. This right has been protected under the Indian Medical Council Act 1956. Thus, no person other than a doctor having qualifications recognized by the Medical Council of India and

---

[113] I.L.R. 1991 (1) Kerala 328.

[114] (2004) 9 S.C.C. 362; *M. C. Metha v. Union of India,* (2001) 3 S.C.C. 756.

[115] A.I.R. 2010 S.C. 2221.

[116] A.I.R. 1969 S.C. 128.

registered with the Medical Council of India/State Medical Council (s) is allowed to practise modern system of medicine or surgery. A person who obtained the qualification in any other system of medicine is not allowed to practice the modern system of medicine. By applying this principle, in *Dr. Mehboob Alam v. State of U. P.*,[117] the Allahabad High Court also observed that a person qualified and registered in any branch of medicine cannot practice any other branch. Thus, Section 15 of the Indian Medical Council Act, 1956 provides that if a person practises medicine without possessing either the requisite qualification or enrolment under the Act on any State Medical Register, he becomes liable to be punished with imprisonment or fine or both.[118]

The High Court of Madras in *Dr. Mukhtiar Chand v. State of Punjab*,[119] held that right to practise any profession or to carry on any occupation trade or business was no doubt a fundamental right guaranteed under Article 19(1)(g) of the Constitution. However, that right to practise any profession or to carry on any occupation trade or business is subject to the laws relating to professional or technical qualifications necessary for practising such profession or carrying on such occupation or trade or business. Thus, regulatory measures on the exercise of this right both with regard to the standard of professional qualifications and professional conduct had been applied keeping in view not only the right of medical practitioners but also the right to life and proper health care of persons who need medical care and treatment. Therefore, there was no compromise on the professional standards of medical practitioners. Similarly, by interpreting Article 19(1)(g) and its restrictions under Article 19(6), the Allahabad High Court in *Charan Singh v. State of U.P.*,[120] held that the right to practice medicine is subject to reasonable restrictions under Article 19(6) of the Constitution of India. The right to health included under Article 21 of the Constitution of India is to be balanced with the right to practice medicine under Article 19(1)(g) of the Constitution of India and is

---

[117] A.I.R. 2001 All 374.

[118] *Poonam Verma v. Ashwin Patel*, A.I.R. 1996 S.C. 2111.

[119] (1998) 7 S.C.C. 579.

[120] A.I.R. 2004 All 373.

subject to reasonable restrictions under Article 19(6). Only those persons who hold valid and recognized degree and are registered under the existing legislation can be allowed to practice medicine in the State. Recently, in *Kerala Ayurveda Paramparya Vaidya Forum v. State of Kerala,*[121] the appellants filed the petition against Indian Medical Council Act 1956 which debarred them from practising medicines unless registered under Act, but the appellants had failed to show that they possessed requisite recognized qualification for registration entitling them to practice medicines or their names had been entered in appropriate registers after commencement of Act. By flowing its decision of *Dr. Mukhtiar Chand case,*[122] the Supreme Court again dismissed the appeal and upheld the right to get treatment from qualified medical practitioners.

[121] A.I.R. 2018 S.C. 1995.

[122] (1998) 7 S.C.C. 579.

General Legislative and Policy Framework of Right to Health in India

The status of health of citizens of a nation is a priority and it reflects the quality of life enjoyed by its people.[1] In the previous chapter, an attempt has been made to discuss the constitutional framework of the right to health in India. To realize the constitutional mandate for the protection of the right to health and its related issues certain special health-centric legislations have been enacted over time.[2] These health-generic legislations are responsible to provide facilities for the fullest enjoyment of the fundamental right to health. To examine the contemporary relevance of the health-related legislative framework in India, it is essential to study the working of these legislations. Along with these legislations, policy frameworks are also there for the promotion of health in India. These policies are the mirror reflecting the mind and the will of the nation.[3] This chapter is primarily devoted to this aspect.

I. GENERAL LEGISLATIVE FRAMEWORK OF RIGHT TO HEALTH IN INDIA

In addition to the International Conventions and the Constitutional provisions, in India, the Parliament has enacted a good number of

---

[1] IRDA, Report of the Committee on Health Insurance for Senior Citizens 11 (IRDA 2007).

[2] Jugal Kishore, *Legislation and Health Promotion in India*, 3(2) RGMHR 75, 80 (2012).

[3] Gautam Chikermane, 70 Policies That Shaped India: 1947 to 2017, Independence to US$2.5 Trillion xi (Observer Research Foundation 2018).

legislations that protect the health interests of the people in general.[4] These legislations relating to the right to health can be divided under the following heads: (a) legislations applied to prevent abuse of drugs and their distribution and storage, (b) legislations applied for maintaining the quality of food and securing nutrition, (c) legislation applied in case of organ transplantation and (d) legislations applied to maintain high standards in medical services.

A. Legislations Applied to Prevent Abuse of Drugs and Their Distribution and Storage

With the development of science, drugs and medicines became one of the major curing agents of health issues. Along with the development, there are various incidents of misusing such drugs and medicines by compromising with the quality, delivery system and storage procedure. To regulate the quality, distribution and storage of drugs various legislations have been enacted in India from time to time. All these legislations have a direct impact on the right to health of individuals.

i. Drugs and Cosmetics Act, 1940

The 1940 Drugs and Cosmetics Act[5] was enacted as the pioneer legislation to regulate the import, manufacture, distribution and sale of drugs and cosmetics which has a direct relation with medical and health aspects of the individual. It also specifically prevents substandard drugs and directs to maintain high standards of medical treatment.[6] Section 3(b)(i) of the Act defines 'drug' and includes within its ambit all medicines for external or internal use of human beings or animals and all substances intended to be used for or in the prevention, diagnosis, treatment or mitigation of any disease in human beings or animals, including preparations applied on the human body for the purpose of repelling insects like mosquitoes. Thus, the 1940 Act

---

[4] P.K. Rana, 'Right to Health Care for All' - Is It a Distant Dream in India? 7(1) NAYA DEEP 55, 60 (2011).

[5] Act No. XXIII of 1940. It was enacted on 10 April 1940.

[6] Chimanlal Jagjivandas Sheth v. State of Maharashtra, A.I.R. 1963 S.C. 665.

provides a broad definition of drugs and includes substances such as cotton wool, bandages, absorbent gauze, gauze bandages or roller bandages necessary for treating surgical or other cases.[7] It is interesting to note that the inclusive definition of 'drug' also includes 'blood' as it is undoubtedly a substance that can be used for or in the diagnosis, treatment, prevention of any disease in human being.[8] The Act also includes Ayurvedic, Siddha and Unani systems of medicine within its sphere. Section 10 of the Act prohibits the importation of drugs that are misbranded, adulterated and spurious, and not of standard quality.

Further, Chapter IV containing Sections 16 to 33-A of the Act, deals with the manufacture, sale and distribution of drugs and cosmetics. Sections 18 and 27 are substantive provisions whereas other provisions are in the nature of adjutant procedural prescriptions. As per Section 18, manufacturing, selling and stocking of any drug is prohibited unless a person obtains a licence issued for that specific purpose. The newly manufactured drugs and cosmetics have to conform with the quality and standards as prescribed under Sections 16 and 17.[9] Section 18A of the Act requires that every person who has acquired a drug or cosmetic if required shall disclose to the inspector the name, address and other particulars of the persons from whom the drug or cosmetic was acquired.[10] Further, any drug to which the 1940 Act applies, cannot be sold by a grocer or a general store, the specific medical shop required for the selling of such drug.[11] In conformity with these provisions in *Hakkimuddin Taherbhai Shakor v. State of Gujarat*,[12] the Gujarat High Court observed that no person can manufacture for sale or distribute or sell or stock or exhibit or offer for sale or distribute any drug, except in accordance with the conditions of the licence issued for such purpose under Chapter IV of the 1940 Act. A licence is a must

---

[7] *Jagjivandas Sheth v. State of Maharashtra*, A.I.R. 1963 S.C. 665. *See*, S. Bhat et al., Healthcare in India: An Introduction to Law and Legal System 213 (Bloomsbury 2016).

[8] *Subodh S. Shah v. Director, Food and Drugs, Ahmedabad*, A.I.R. 1997 Guj 83.

[9] *Reckitt and Benckiser (India) Ltd. v. State of Andhra Pradesh*, 2009 (2) A.L.T. 562.

[10] *State of Karnataka v. Pratap Chand*, A.I.R. 1981 S.C. 872.

[11] M.C. Gupta, *What are the Legal Aspects of Over-the-Counter Sale of Allopathic Medicines?* 23(12) IJCP 864, 865 (2013).

[12] 2017 Cri. L.J. 3143.

for such a purpose. Under Section 26A, the Central Government is empowered to regulate, restrict or prohibit the manufacture, etc., of drugs and cosmetics in the public interest. For applying this authority, the Central Government must be 'satisfied' that any drug or cosmetic is likely to involve (a) any risk to human beings or families; or (b) that any drug does not have the therapeutic value claimed or purported to be claimed for it; or (c) contains ingredients in such quantity for which there is no therapeutic justification.[13]

ii. Drugs Control Act, 1950

The 1950 Drugs Control Act[14] was enacted to control the piece of the drugs and to ensure the availability of drugs in all parts of India. It replaced the Drugs Control Ordinance, 1949.[15] Section 4 of the Act states that the Chief Commissioner may fix in respect of any drug (a) the maximum price which may be charged by a dealer or producer, (b) the maximum quantity which may be possessed by a dealer or producer at any one time, and (c) the maximum quantity which may be sold in any single transaction to any person. However, the prices or rates and the quantities fixed in respect of any drug under this Section may be different in different localities or for different classes of dealers or producers.[16] Further, the Act prohibits selling or agreeing to sell or storage of exceeding drugs than the maximum amount as specified by the Chief Commissioner.[17] Section 7 of the 1950 Act casts a responsibility upon the person having in his possession a quantity of any drug, exceeding the limit as permitted by this Act, to report that fact to the Chief Commissioner and to take such action as to the distribution, disposal or storage of that excess quantity as the Chief Commissioner may direct. Moreover, no person can refuse to sell any drug to any person within the specified limit.[18] This provision is the

---

[13] *Union of India v. Pfizer Limited*, A.I.R. 2018 S.C. 265.

[14] Act No. XXVI of 1950.

[15] *Aphali Pharmaceuticals Ltd. v. State of Maharashtra*, A.I.R. 1989 S.C. 2227.

[16] Drugs Control Act 1950, Section 4(2).

[17] *Ibid*. Section 5.

[18] *Ibid*. Section 8.

basic backbone structure for ensuring access to medicine to all without any discrimination.

iii. Drugs and Magic Remedies (Objectionable Advertisements) Act, 1954

The 1954 Drugs and Magic Remedies (Objectionable Advertisements) Act[19] was enacted to control the advertisement of drugs and to prohibit the advertisement in cases of remedies alleged to possess magic qualities. Thus, the necessary condition for the application of this Act is that the advertisement must induce others to use the advertised 'drug'.[20] Section 3 of the Act says that no person shall take any part in the publication of any advertisement referring to any drug which leads to the use of that drug for (a) the maintenance or improvement of the capacity of human beings for sexual pleasure, (b) the procurement of miscarriage in women or prevention of conception in women, (c) the correction of menstrual disorder in women, and (d) the prevention, diagnosis, treatment, cure, or mitigation of any disease, disorder or condition specified in the Schedule. Moreover, the ambit of this Section includes all categories of drugs, whether they are licensed or not and whether they are prohibited or not.[21] The Supreme Court in *Hamdard Davakhana v. Union of India*[22] explained the aim and object of the Act. The Court held that the object of the Act was merely to put a curb on advertisements that offend against decency or morality but the object truly and properly understood is to prevent self-medication or treatment by prohibiting instruments which may be used to advocate the same or which tend to spread the evil. The Court further held that no doubt in Section 3 of the Act diseases is expressly mentioned which have relation to sex and disorders peculiar to women but taken as a whole it cannot be said that the object of the Act was to deal only with matters which relate to indecency or immorality. The name and

---

[19] Act No. XXI of 1954. It was enacted on 30 April 1954.

[20] *K. S. Saini v. Union of India*, A.I.R. 1967 P and H 322.

[21] *GMT Teleshopping Private Limited v. Union of India*, 2013 (5) Mh.L.J. 661.

[22] A.I.R. 1960 S.C. 554.

the preamble are indicative of the purpose being the control of all advertisements relating to drugs and the use of the word 'animals' negatives the claim that the object of the Act is to curb the emphasis on sex and indecency.

Moreover, the Act provides prohibition on misleading advertisements relating to drugs[23] and advertisement of magic remedies.[24] It shows that no person shall take any part in the publication of any advertisement relating to a drug if the advertisement contains any matter which directly or indirectly gives a false impression regarding the true character of the drug or makes a false claim for the drug or otherwise false or misleading in any material particular.[25] In case of violation of these provisions, the Drug Controller has the power to put an embargo on the telecasting of the advertisement after scrutinizing the same. However, there is no provision in the Act to place the interim bar on the telecast of the advertisement pending such scrutiny.[26] Thus, the Act is concerned about the bad impact of advertisement with false promises relating to drugs and empowers the presidency magistrate, magistrate of the first class or anyone of higher rank to try any offence relating to those misleading advertisements.[27]

iv. Patent Act, 1970

In general, the patent is concerned to protect the right of the manufacturer of any marketable process or product. However, this law has an overriding effect on the pharmaceutical manufacturing process and pharmaceutical products. India has amended the 1970 Patents Act[28] in the year 1999 and 2002 to comply with the obligations of

---

[23] Drugs and Magic Remedies (Objectionable Advertisements) Act 1954, Section 4.

[24] *Ibid.* Section 5.

[25] *Sreedhareeyam Ayurveda Medicines Private Limited v. State of Kerala*, 2014 Cri.L.J. 2167.

[26] *Tele World Marketing v. Entorr-10 Television Pvt. Ltd.*, A.I.R. 2016 M.P. 212.

[27] *Ibid*. Section 10.

[28] Act No. XXXIX of 1954. It was enacted on 19 September 1970.

Trade-related Aspects of Intellectual Property Rights (TRIPs). The only pending obligation with regard to TRIPS was the introduction of product patents to medicines and agro-chemicals. After the enforcement of the 2002 Amendment Act, Section 5 of the Act was written as 'in the case of inventions being claimed relating to food, medicine, drugs or chemical substances, only patents relating to the methods or processes of manufacture of such substances could be obtained'.[29] This deliberate strategy was the result of the Iyengar Committee Report. The Committee in its report stated that product patent is a machinery of multinational companies to achieve monopolistic control over the market, especially food, chemical and pharmaceutical markets and recommended that certain inventions be only granted process patent protection, not the product one. However, this was in contradiction with Article 27.1 of the TRIPs Agreement which states that patents shall be available for any invention, whether products or processes, in all fields of technology, which clearly encompasses pharmaceutical products.[30] To remove such contradiction, India has amended the 1970 Patent Act further in 2005 and omitted that Section and provides product patent benefit on the pharmaceutical product for a term of 20 years.[31]

The 1970 Act explains 'pharmaceutical products' as any patented product or product manufactured through a patented process of the pharmaceutical sector that is needed to address public health problems and shall include ingredients necessary for their manufacture and diagnostic kits required for their use. The 1970 Act further states that any process for the medicinal, curative, surgical, prophylactic diagnostic, therapeutic or other treatment of human beings or any process for a similar treatment of animals to render them free of disease or to increase their economic value or that of their products is out of the scope of the definition of 'inventions' so that patent protection

---

[29] Sougata Talukdar, *Access to Medicine and Its Journey from TRIPS to Doha: A Discussion from Human Rights Perspective*, 9(1) IHRLR 33 (2018).

[30] Abhinav Bhalla, *Pharmaceutical Patents: India and Beyond*, 12–13 NATIONAL CAPITAL L.J. 178, 183 (2007–2008).

[31] Monoj Pillai, *The Patents (Amendment) Act, 2005 and TRIPS Compliance - A Critique*, 10(3) JIPR 235 (2005).

cannot claim on those processes.[32] Moreover, through Section 47(4) the 1970 Act specifies that the grant of a pharmaceutical patent under this Act shall be subject to the condition that the medicine or drug may be imported by the Government for the purpose of its own use or for distribution in any dispensary, hospital or other medical institution maintained by the Government or any other dispensary, hospital or other medical institution which the Central Government may specify in this behalf by notification in the Official Gazette. Thus, the 1970 Act also allows using this as a ground of defence in any suit for infringement of a patent for importation, use or distribution of any medicine or drug.[33] However, in *F. Hoffmann-LA Roche Ltd. v. Cipla Ltd.*,[34] by highlighting the need for the balance of interest it was argued that public interest in low-cost generic drugs has to be balanced by the public interest in the protection of patent rights. The Central Government also has the authority to grant permission to make, use, exercise or import the medicine or drug.[35] These provisions use to help the Government to secure the supply of medicines or drugs in special cases even though the same has been patented and not available in the requisite price or quantity.

Further to secure the access of pharmaceutical products the 1970 Act provides for the compulsory licence of the patent to a third party by the Controller, on an application made at any time after the expiry of three years from the date of sealing of the patent, on the grounds that (a) the reasonable requirements of the public with respect to the patented invention have not been satisfied, (b) the patented invention is not available to the public at a reasonably affordable price, and (c) the patented invention is not worked in India.[36] However, the applicability of this provision for emergency purposes is doubtful, as a compulsory licence can be obtained through a lengthy process.

---

[32] Patent Act 1970, Section 3(i).

[33] *Id.* Section 107(2).

[34] 159 (2009) D.L.T. 243.

[35] Patent Act 1970, Section 100(4).

[36] Patent Act 1970, Section 84. *See*, Surabhi Shekhawat, *Compulsory Licensing of Pharmaceutical Patents*, 5 MLJ 26, 35 (2014).

Thus, in *Indoco Remedies Ltd. v. Bristol Myers Squibb Holdings Ireland Unlimited Company*,[37] before the Delhi High Court, it was argued that the exercise of applying for the grant of the compulsory license is cumbersome and time-consuming, and is intended to cater to ordinary times, and not to a pandemic situation. The Court at the time of passing the verdict considered this contention but denied the benefit of compulsory licencing to the petitioner. The 1970 Act also has a special provision for granting compulsory licences for the manufacture and export of patented pharmaceutical products to any country having insufficient or no manufacturing capacity for the concerned product to address public health problems of that country. The only required precondition is that a compulsory licence has been granted by such country or such country has allowed the importation of the patented pharmaceutical products from India.[38] In *Bayer Corporation v. Union of India*,[39] the petitioner submitted that the Patent Act expressly stipulates, by Sections 84 and 92A, situations where the Central Government can issue compulsory licenses. Such being the reality, the Central Government should not defeat patent owners' rights by granting permission to manufacture, or market drugs or formulations for which applicants do not have any such rights. Moreover, Section 107A ensures the availability of a competitor's product immediately after the expiry of a patent in the Indian market without having to wait for regulatory approval on post-patent expiry.[40] Thus, at present, the patent law recognizes product and process patent in case of a pharmaceutical product which is the reason behind a sharp rise to the cost of medicine and causes hindrance to access to medicine. It was also strongly argued that, while fulfilling its commitment under the TRIPS agreement, the Government must not bring a patent regime where all the gains achieved by the Indian pharmaceutical industry are dissipated.[41]

---

[37] 2020 (83) P.T.C. 551 (Del).

[38] Patent Act 1970, Section 92A.

[39] 162 (2009) D.L.T. 371.

[40] *Bayer Corporation v. Union of India*, 2019 (78) P.T.C. 521 (Del).

[41] *Novartis AG v. Union of India*, A.I.R. 2013 S.C. 1311.

v. Narcotic Drugs and Psychotropic Substances Act, 1985

The 1985 Narcotic Drugs and Psychotropic Substances (NDPS) Act[42] came into force on November 14, 1985, by replacing the Opium Acts and the Dangerous Drugs Act 1934. The 1985 Act was enacted in order to provide adequate penalties for drug trafficking, strengthen enforcement powers, implement the provisions of international conventions to which India was a party and enforce controls over psychotropic substances. Thus, it intends to curb and penalize the usage of drugs that are used for intoxication or for getting a stimulant effect.[43] Section 8 of the 1985 Act prohibits the cultivation, production, possession, sale, purchase, trade, import, export, use and consumption of narcotic drugs and psychotropic substances except for medical and scientific purposes.[44] Along with the punitive provisions, the NDPS Act also contains provisions to regulate drugs. Under the scheme of the Act, 'essential narcotic drug' means a narcotic drug notified by the Central Government for medical and scientific use.[45] In a similar line, under Section 4, the Central Government has the responsibility to take all measures for ensuring the medical and scientific use of narcotic drugs and psychotropic substances. However, the term 'medical and scientific purpose' is neither defined nor described in the Act. As per the Act, some activities are reserved exclusively for the government, and some others can be carried out by private entities under license. The regulatory system also includes the supply of opium to registered users, who are dependent on opium, for consumption on medical advice which is a measure of contemporary harm reduction strategies.[46] Similarly, the Central Government has the duty to incur expenditure for supplying drugs to addicts where such supply is a medical necessity through the creation of the National Fund for

---

[42] Act No. LXI of 1985. It was enacted on 16 September 1985.

[43] *State of Punjab v. Rakesh Kumar*, A.I.R. 2019 S.C. 84.

[44] *Kangujam Ananda Meitei v. CBI, SCB, Kolkata*, 2020 (208) A.I.C. 498.

[45] Narcotic Drugs and Psychotropic Substances Act 1985, Section 2(viiia).

[46] *Ibid.* Section 10(1)(a)(vi).

Control of Drug Abuse.[47] However, in reality, though it is permitted by law, the practice is not popular at all. The Supreme Court in *Union of India v. Sanjeev V. Deshpande*,[48] observed that dealing in narcotic drugs and psychotropic substances is permissible only when such dealing is for medical purposes or scientific purposes. Further, the mere fact that the dealing in narcotic drugs and psychotropic substances is for a medical or scientific purpose does not by itself lift the embargo created under Section 8. Such dealing must be in the manner and extent provided by the provisions of the Act, Rules or Orders made thereunder. Sections 9 and 10 enable the Central and State Governments respectively to make rules permitting and regulating various aspects of dealing in narcotic drugs and psychotropic substances.

vi. Cigarettes and Other Tobacco Products Act, 2003

The 2003 Cigarettes and other Tobacco Products (COTPA) Act (Prohibition of Advertisement and Regulation of Trade and Commerce, Production, Supply and Distribution) Act[49] (COTPA Act) was enacted by repealing the Cigarettes (Regulation of Production, Supply and Distribution) Act, 1975 and came into effect on May 1, 2004. The Act prohibits the advertisement of cigarettes and other tobacco products and regulates trade and commerce, production, supply and distribution of the same. Further, the Act aims (a) to implement the measures to ensure that effective protection is provided to non-smokers from involuntary exposure to tobacco smoke, (b) to protect children and young people from being addicted to the use of tobacco, (c) to ensures effective measures to protect citizens with the requirement of special attention such as pregnant women and children from involuntary exposure to tobacco smoke, (d) to discourage the use of tobacco, and (e) to impose progressive restrictions and take concerted action to eventually eliminate all direct and indirect advertising, promotion and

[47] *Ibid*. Section 7A.

[48] A.I.R. 2014 S.C. 3625.

[49] Act No. XXXIV of 2003. It was enacted on 18 May 2003.

sponsorship concerning tobacco.[50] The Act is expedient to prohibit the consumption of cigarettes and other tobacco products which are injurious to health with a view to implementing Article 47 of the Constitution.[51] Section 5(1) of the Act thus states that

> no person engaged in or purported to be engaged in the production, supply or distribution of cigarettes or any other tobacco products shall advertise and no person having control over a medium shall cause to be advertised cigarettes or any other tobacco products through that medium and no person shall take part in any advertisement which directly or indirectly suggests or promotes the use or consumption of cigarettes or any other tobacco products.

Further, the 2003 Act prohibits smoking in a public place[52] and also the sale of cigarettes to a person below the age of eighteen years.[53] Thus, the main objective of the 2003 Act is to see that there is no smoking in public premises and the persons who are addicted to smoking should go to a particular place where they can smoke. This has been done as smoking is injurious to health and not to exposed non-smokers to the bad effects of smoking.

B. Legislations Applied for Maintaining Quality of Food and Securing Nutrition

Adequate food and nutrition are the two basic components of the preventive healthcare mechanism. In the Indian legal system from the mid of 20th century, adequate quality food and nutrition has been regulated with the enactment of the Prevention of Food Adulteration Act, 1954. However, this Act was repealed and substituted by the Food Safety and Standard Act of 2006. Further, in the year 2013, the National Food Security Act was enacted to secure food and nutrition for people. All these legislations required detailed deliberation.

---

[50] COTPA Act 2003, Preamble.

[51] *Narinder S. Chadha v. Municipal Corporation of Greater Mumbai*, A.I.R. 2015 S.C. 756.

[52] COTPA Act 2003, Section 4.

[53] *Id.* Section 6.

i. Food Safety and Standard Act, 2006

The right step towards addressing the problem of food adulteration was taken in the year 1954 by enacting central legislation on the subject keeping in view the limits of the existing penal code. The Prevention of Food Adulteration Act, 1954[54] provides for strict liability and the conditions of adulterated food to be treated as 'noxious'.[55] Thus, in *Dinesh Chandra Jamadars Gandhi v. State of Gujarat*,[56] the Supreme Court observed that the object and the purpose of the 1954 Act are to eliminate the danger to human life from the sale of unwholesome articles of food. The legislation is on the topic 'adulteration of food stuff and other goods' (Entry 18 list III Seventh Schedule). It is important to note that this 1954 Act has been repealed by the Food Safety and Standards Act 2006,[57] which provides new mechanisms to address this issue.[58]

The 2006 Act aims to establish the Food Safety and Standards Authority of India for laying down science-based standards for articles of food and to regulate their manufacture, storage, distribution, sale and import to ensure the availability of safe and wholesome food for human consumption.[59] Further, the Act defines 'hazard' by considering health as a determining factor and states that hazard means a biological, chemical or physical agent in, or condition of, food with the potential to cause an adverse health effect.[60] Further, the 2006 Act defines 'risk' as the probability of an adverse effect on the health of consumers of such food and the severity of that effect, consequential to a food hazard[61] and 'risk management' as the process of evaluating policy alternatives for the protection of

[54] Act No. XXXVII of 1954. It was enacted on 29 September 1954.

[55] Anubha Dhulia, *Laws on Food Adulteration: A Critical Study with Special Reference to the Food Safety and Standards Act, 2006*, 1(1) ILI L. Rev. 163, 169 (2010).

[56] A.I.R. 1989 S.C. 1011.

[57] Act No. XXXIV of 2006. It was enacted on 23 August 2006.

[58] Bharat Paul et al., *Food Safety: The Indian Perspective*, 6(2) NJCM 286, 287 (2015).

[59] *Toni v. State of U. P.*, 2017 (3) A.D.J. 285.

[60] Food Safety and Standard Act 2006, Section 3(u).

[61] *Ibid.* Section 3(zm).

the health of consumers.[62] The Act declares 'unsafe food' as an article of food whose nature, substance or quality is so affected as to render it injurious to health.[63] The 2006 Act has redefined the roles and responsibilities of the food regulatory workforce and calls for highly skilled human resources as it involves complex management procedures.[64] Thus, the Act directs to the creation of two authoritative bodies for the working of the Act, namely the Food Safety and Standards Authority of India and the Central Advisory Committee. It is interesting to note that at the time of implementation of the Act, the Central Government, the State Governments, the Food Authority and other agencies shall be guided by the principle of endeavouring to achieve an appropriate level of protection of human life and health.[65] From the detailed descriptions of the other guiding principles, it is clear that the protection of health is the frontline concern in the case of the implantation of the 2006 Act. The food business operator has the responsibility not to manufacture, store, sell or distribute any article of food if such activities are prohibited in the interest of public health.[66] Before applying this provision, it must be looked into to ascertain whether the material available on the record discloses the commission of offences under any of these provisions.[67] By explaining the duties of the manufacturers, the Bombay High Court in *M/s. Dhariwal Industries Limited v. State of Maharashtra*,[68] observed that the Parliament does not require the manufacturers like the petitioners to wait for any declaration to be made by the Food Authority or the Central Government or the State Government to declare any food as injurious to health or unsafe. It is the statutory duty of the manufacturers to ensure that they do not manufacture any article of food which is unsafe. Moreover, the

---

[62] *Ibid.* Section 3(zq).

[63] *Ibid.* Section 3(zz).

[64] Anitha Thippaiah et al., *Challenges in Developing Competency-based Training Curriculum for Food Safety Regulators in India*, 39(3) IJCM 147, 147 (2014).

[65] Food Safety and Standard Act 2006, Section 18(1)(a).

[66] *Ibid.* Section 26(2).

[67] *Shiv Kumar Agrawal v. State of Bihar*, 2019 (4) P.L.J.R. 282.

[68] 2013 (2) BomCR 383.

2006 Act also defines offences under the Act by keeping injury to health as its central determinants. Thus, Section 48(1) provides:

> A person may render any article of food injurious to health by means of one or more of the following operations, namely (a) adding any article or substance to the food; (b) using any article or substance as an ingredient in the preparation of the food; (c) abstracting any constituents from the food; or (d) subjecting the food to any other process or treatment, with the knowledge that it may be sold or offered for sale or distributed for human consumption.

Further, the Act is also concerned with an adverse effect on health by the consumption of food at the time of determining whether any food is unsafe or injurious to health.[69]

ii. National Food Security Act, 2013

This 2013 National Food Security Act[70] provides food and nutritional security in the human life cycle by ensuring access to an adequate quantity of quality food at affordable prices to people to live a life with dignity.[71] It aims to cover almost two-thirds of the Indian population.[72] The right to obtain food grains and essential commodities at controlled prices and the entitlements to the benefits of various distribution schemes are vested in the cardholders by the National Food Security Act, 2013.[73] Section 4 of the Act deals with the maternity benefits for pregnant and lactating women. It cast a duty upon the Central Government to arrange (a) meal, free of charge, during pregnancy and six months after the childbirth, through the local Anganwadi, so as to meet the nutritional standards; and (b) maternity benefit of not less than rupees six thousand. Section 5 provides nutritional support to children, in the case of children in the age group of six months

[69] Food Safety and Standard Act 2006, Section 48(2).

[70] Act No. XX of 2013. It was enacted on 10 September 2013.

[71] S. Sivakumar, *Central Legislation*, 49 ASIL 1117, 1122 (2013).

[72] Manvendra Singh & Surabhi, *Critical Analysis of National Food Security Act with Context of Global Economy*, 20(8) IOSR-JHSS 63, 63 (2015).

[73] *Nazuk v. State of U. P.*, 2019 (12) A.D.J. 832.

to six years, age-appropriate meals, free of charge, through the local Anganwadi so as to meet the nutritional standards. Significantly by virtue of Section 6, the State Government is under an obligation to identify and provide meals through Anganwadi Centres to children, who suffer from malnutrition so as to meet the prescribed nutritional standards specified in Schedule II to the Act.[74] Section 8 provides for food security allowance to persons who have for any reason are denied their entitlement of food grains. The 2013 Act in this manner appropriately compensates the cardholders for denial of food grains.[75] This describes the government's concern for various sections of society, ranging from women to children.

The inability to provide food security to them shall be compensated in the form of food security allowances to be paid by the State Government. Section 31 provides that the Central Government, the State Governments and Local Authorities shall strive to realise the objectives specified in Schedule III of the Act for the purpose of advancing food and nutritional security. Along with the other purposes, Schedule III secures access to health care and access to nutritional, health and education support to adolescent girls.[76] Though various provisions under the 2013 Act want to provide the impetus for extricating food insecurity in the country and for ensuring a better standard of living for the poor people, in practical terms, the Act has many loopholes such as heavy burden on the fiscal policy, no role for State Governments in decision making, etc. which are providing obstacles in the path of effective implementation of the Act.[77] The beneficiaries who belong to the vulnerable class are not equipped with suitable mechanisms to raise issues of non-implementation and not providing food articles complying with nutritional standards as provided in the Statute.[78]

---

[74] *Veterans Forum for Transparency in Public Life v. Union of India*, I.L.R. 2017 IV HP 1.

[75] *Arvind v. State of U. P.*, 2019 (12) A.D.J. 711.

[76] National Food Security Act 2013, Entry 3 of Schedule III.

[77] Sougata Talukdar & Rakesh Mondal, *Rethinking of National Food Security Act, 2013 under Human Right Prospective*, 3(4) IJAR 642, 645 (2017).

[78] *Dipika Jagatram Sahani v. Union of India*, A.I.R. 2021 S.C. 523.

C. Legislation Applied in Case of Human Organ Transplantation

Among health-centric legislations in India, another issue is the legislation related to human organ transplantation. The applicability of the Transplantation of Human Organ Act, 1994 in this regard is vital. The scheme of this Act required detailed discussion.

i. Transplantation of Human Organ Act 1994: Background of the Act

The advancements in the field of science, technology and medicine have made it possible to remove organs from living as well as deceased persons and to transplant such organs into the body of others to save the lives of suffering human beings.[79] Therefore, the transplantation of human organs both by natural and man-made substitutes is a landmark achievement in the aspects of curative techniques in the field of healthcare.[80] Although organ transplantation or donation is a personal issue, the process has medical, legal, ethical, organizational and social implications. In India, the legislation relating to organ transplantation got its final shape in 1994 with the name 'Transplantation of Human Organ Act'.[81] This Act provides regulations for the removal, storage and transplantation of human organs for therapeutic purposes and to prevent commercial dealings in human organs.[82] Before the enactment of this Act, a doctor who removed an organ without the informed consent of his patient could be charged for criminal liability under the Indian Penal Code for offences against the human body like assault and battery and could also face civil liability for professional negligence under the law of torts.[83] The Act defines 'human organ' as

---

[79] *Balbir Singh v. Authorisation Committee*, A.I.R. 2004 Delhi 413.

[80] C. Manickam, *Organ Transplantation and the Law*, 19 CULR 176 (1995). For discussion on man-made human organs *see*, Mitchel E. De Bakery, *The Future of Organ Transplantation*, in BIOLOGY IN HUMAN AFFAIRS 107 (Hardy Boardman & Stuart A. Ross eds, Estados Unidos 1974).

[81] Act No. XLII of 1994. It was enacted on 8 July 1994.

[82] Transplantation of Human Organ Act 1994, Preamble.

[83] Seema Rathi, *Organ Transplantation Law in India: It's Legal and Ethical Issues*, 47(1) CMLJ 52, 53 (2011).

any part of a human body consisting of a structured arrangement of tissues which, if wholly removed, cannot be replicated by the body[84] and 'transplantation' means the grafting of any human organ from any deceased person or living person to some other living person for therapeutic purposes.[85] The Transplantation of Human Organ Act being a special Act and the matter relating to dealing with offences thereunder having been regulated by reason of the provisions thereof, this Act will prevail over the provisions of the Code of Criminal Procedure, 1973.[86]

ii. Conditions for Removal of Human Organ

The human organ may be removed as per the will of the donor when he is alive or after his death. The Act provides that the donor may authorize the removal of any human organ or tissue or both of his body, before his death, for therapeutic purposes to transplant the same in the body of near relatives of the donor.[87] Whereas, for the donation of the human organ after death, the donor has to unequivocally authorize in writing the removal of any human organ of his body for therapeutic purposes in the presence of two or more witnesses. At least one of those witnesses should be near relative of the donor.[88] In that case, the person who is in possession of the body after the death of that wilful donor shall grant all reasonable facilities for the removal of that organ or tissue or both from the dead body of the donor through a registered medical practitioner unless he has any reason to believe that the donor had subsequently revoked the aforesaid authority. It is interesting to note that the Act not only allows the personal donation of the human organ but the donation for therapeutic purposes may be made by the near relatives also who are in lawful possession of the dead body.

But this can be done only if the other relatives have no objection to that and the person from whose body donation will be made did not give

---

[84] Transplantation of Human Organ Act 1994, Section 2(h).

[85] *Ibid.* Section 2(p).

[86] *Jeewan Kumar Raut v. Central Bureau of Investigation*, A.I.R. 2009 S.C. 2763.

[87] Transplantation of Human Organ Act 1994, Section 3(1).

[88] *Ibid.* Section 3(2).

objection before his death.[89] The authority to remove the organ for therapeutic purposes can only be given to a registered medical practitioner or a technician possessing such qualifications and experience.[90] The exception to the near relatives rules is laid down in Section 9(3) which states that any donor can authorize the removal of any of his organs or tissues or both before his death for transplantation into the body of a recipient who is not a near relative by the reason of affection or attachment towards the recipient or for any special reasons, but this can only be done with the prior approval of the Authorization Committee. The Authorization Committee can pass any order after giving an opportunity of being heard to the donor, recipient and any other related person.[91] Thus, Section 9 of the Act is impairing the right to health as an integral part of the right to life of the class of patients who do not have near relative, willing relative or no altruistic donor to some extent.[92]

In *S. Samson v. Authorization Committee for Implementation of Human Organ Transplantation*,[93] the respondent rejected the application of the petitioner to get a kidney from a non-relative person on the ground that the donor is very young and he is not a relative to the petitioner and both of them know each other only for the last two years and suspected financial bonding was involved. The Supreme Court overruled the decision of the respondent due to lack of evidence of financial transaction between the petitioner and donor and held that impugned minutes of the respondent is vitiated by non-compliance of Section 9(6) of the Transplantation of Human Organs Act, 1994 and observed that the action of the respondent in rejecting the petitioner's case is the result of sheer non-application of mind and arbitrary exercise of power. Further, the Act emphasizes getting free and informed consent in a written form.[94] Moreover, in the case of brain death,[95] the registered

---

[89] *Ibid.* Section 3(3).

[90] *Id.* Section 3(4).

[91] *Mehul Kishorsinh Jadeja v. Amarjit Singh*, (2007) 2 G.L.R. 1780.

[92] Anju Vali Tikoo, *Transplantation of Human Organs: The Indian Scenario*, 1 ILI L. Rᴇᴠ. 147, 160 (2017).

[93] A.I.R. 2008 Mad 227.

[94] Transplantation of Human Organ Act 1994, Section 12.

[95] *Ibid.* Section 2(d).

medical practitioner has a responsibility to make sure by personal examination that such an event has truly happened.[96] All these prior conditions are provided to secure the donor's right to the body and to assure the right to have the best possible healthcare of the donee.

iii. Prevention of Commercial Transaction

Except for the aforementioned preventive measures for the removal of human organs and tissues the 1994 Act has addressed the major issue of commercial transaction. The Act specified that only for therapeutic purposes organ can be transplanted.[97] The shocking exploitation of the abject poverty of many donors for even small sums of money provides the foundation for enacting this Act.[98] Thus, Section 19 declares commercial trading of human organs as offence and punishable with imprisonment for a term not less than five years but which may extend to ten years and may also be liable to a fine which shall not be less than twenty lakhs rupees but may extend to one crore rupees. Even for any other illegal use like offers to supply any human tissue for payment, seeks to find a person willing to supply for payment can be punished with imprisonment for a term not less than one year but which may extend to three years and is also liable to fine which shall not be less than five lakh rupees but which may extend to twenty-five lakh rupees.[99] Therefore, the Authorization Committee has to be satisfied that the authorization for removal of organ or tissue is not for commercial consideration.

iv. Punishment for Commercial Transaction

The Act makes it mandatory for the institutions conducting transplantation to register with an authority appointed by the State Government.[100] Persons associated with hospitals conducting transplantation without

---

[96] *Ibid.* Sections 3(5)-3(7).

[97] *Ibid.* Section 11.

[98] *Kuldeep Singh v. State of Tamil Nadu*, A.I.R. 2005 S.C. 2106.

[99] Transplantation of Human Organ Act 1994, Section 19A.

[100] *Ibid.* Sections 10(1) and 14.

proper registration are punishable with imprisonment for a term that may extend to ten years and with a fine that may extend to twenty lakh rupees.[101] This would be followed by the removal of the name from the register of the State Medical Council for a period of three years for the first offence and permanently for the subsequent offence.[102] Thus, it is probably for the first time in Indian legislation that an external body has been given legal power to scrutinize and monitor the activities of medical institutions and doctors.[103] After all these efforts, yet the legislation fails to achieve its purpose in the long run and it is important to note that to date the commercial dealings with human organs are visible in India. The lacunas in the law and the lack of implementation of the law are the main reasons for that.[104] Ignorance of law among donors, considerable monetary gains and feeling among offenders that they can easily get away from the law may be the reasons behind the growing menace of offences concerning human organs.[105]

D. Legislations Applied to Maintain High Standards in Medical Services

Medical services are subjective, complex and multidimensional and with the recent development in the medical arena high standard of medical service is the desired goal for every nation. The factors affecting the quality of medical services can be grouped into two main categories: (a) patient-related factors, and (b) physician-related factors. In India, to address these factors and to secure a high standard of medical service various laws have been enacted over time to provide guidelines for the doctors or physicians and to regulate their activities.

---

[101] *Ibid.* Section 18(1).

[102] *Ibid.* Section 18(2).

[103] K.P. Singh & Chitrangada Singh, *Human Organ Transplant: Legal and Ethical Contours*, 45(4) IPJ 16, 21(2008).

[104] Smrithi Surendranatharya & V. Aswini Anjana, *Organ Donation and Transplant Tourism - A Legal Perspective*, 2(2) IJLDAI 159, 162 (2016).

[105] Prateek Rastogi et al., *Human Organ Trade: Is Enough Being Done?* 29(4) JIAFM 52 (2007).

i. Indian Nursing Council Act, 1947

The 1947 Indian Nursing Council Act[106] was enacted to establish a uniform standard of training for nurses, midwives and health visitors through the Indian Nursing Council. Accordingly, each State or a group of States has its own organization for the registration of nurses called the State Nursing Council. After the successful completion of training, a nurse must register her name with the State's Nursing Council to be eligible for employment. Section 3(1) of the 1947 Act provides for the constitution of the Indian Nursing Council, an autonomous body under the Government of India, Ministry of Health and Family Welfare, which governs the nursing services and education in India. Further, the Act directs the Council to maintain the Indian Nurses Register in the prescribed manner for nurses, midwives, auxiliary nurse-midwives and health visitors, which shall contain the names of all persons who are for the time being enrolled in any State Register.[107] To comply with this provision the 1947 Act cast a duty upon each State Council to supply twenty printed copies of the State Register as soon as may be after the 1st day of April of each year and inform the Indian Nursing Council without delay of all additions to, and other amendments in, the State Register made from time to time.[108] Further, Section 11 states that notwithstanding anything contained in any law, any recognized qualification under Parts I and II of the Schedule can be sufficient for enrolment in any State Register. Thus, the 1947 Act helps to provide proper education and training to the nurses and regulates the performance of the nurses.

ii. Dentists Act, 1948

The 1948 Dentists Act[109] is directly concerned with the statutory regulation of the dental profession.[110] Section 3 of the 1948 Act empowers

---

[106] Act No. XLVIII of 1947. It was enacted on 31 December 1947.

[107] Indian Nursing Council Act 1947, Section 15A(1).

[108] *Id.* Section 15B.

[109] Act No. XVI of 1948. It was enacted on 29 March 1948.

[110] R. Kesavan et al., *Knowledge of Dental Ethics and Jurisprudence among Dental Practitioners in Chennai, India: A Cross Sectional Questionnaire Study*, 8(2) J. OROFAC. 128, 129 (2016).

the Central Government to constitute a Council which will be known as the Dental Council of India to prescribe the standards of professional conduct and etiquette or the code of ethics for dentists.[111] The violations of such regulations shall constitute infamous conduct in any professional respect or professional misconduct.[112] Section 21 relating to the Dental Council of India states that there have to be State Councils in every State except where a Joint State Council is constituted in accordance with an agreement made under Section 22. The Councils have to maintain a register with the details information regarding the dentists to be known as the Indian Dentists Register[113] and if any person whose name is not there in the register falsely represents that it is so entered, then that person shall be punished with a fine which may extend to five hundred rupees on first conviction and any subsequent conviction with imprisonment which may extend to six months or with fine not exceeding one thousand rupees or with both.[114] Moreover, Section 49(1) provides that no person, other than a registered dentist, registered dental hygienist, or registered dental mechanic shall practise dentistry or the art of scaling, polishing or cleaning teeth or repairing dentures and dental appliances. Thus, the Dentists Act controls the training, practising regulations for the Dentists and provides specific punishments for violation of the same.

iii. Indian Medical Council Act, 1956

The 1956 Indian Medical Council Act[115] was enacted by repealing the Indian Medical Council Act 1933 with the primary aim of reconstitution of the Medical Council of India (MCI) and maintenance of a Medical Register for India. Section 3 of the 1956 Act empowers the Central Government to constitute the Medical Council. The MCI is empowered to grant recognition of medical qualifications awarded by

---

[111] Dentists Act 1948, Section 17A(1).

[112] *Ibid.* Section 17A(2).

[113] *Ibid.* Section 18.

[114] *Ibid.* Section 47.

[115] Act No. CII of 1956. It was enacted on 30 December 1956.

universities or medical institutions in India,[116] and of such qualifications granted by medical institutions in other countries.[117] The MCI has the duty to lay down the minimum standards of medical education for granting degrees including postgraduate degrees,[118] to prescribe standards of professional conduct and etiquette and to provide a code of ethics for medical practitioners.[119] In *Preeti Srivastava v. State of Madhya Pradesh*,[120] the Supreme Court held that the power of the Medical Council of India to prescribe the minimum standards of medical education is not only advisory but binding in nature. Further, the Act directs the MCI to maintain an all-India register that will contain the names of all the medical practitioners possessing recognized medical qualifications.[121] It is the primary medical qualification that entitles a person to be registered on the Indian Medical Register and to practice as a medical practitioner. Thus, Section 27 of the Act provides the prerequisites for practising. It states:

> Subject to the conditions and restrictions laid down in this Act regarding medical practice by persons possessing certain recognised medical qualifications, every person whose name is for time being borne on the Indian Medical Register shall be entitled according to his qualifications to practise as a medical practitioner in any part of India and to recover in due course of law in respect of such practice any expenses, charges in respect of medicaments or other appliances, or any fees to which he may be entitled.

By analysing these preconditions in *J. Sai Prasanna v. Medical Council of India*,[122] the Andhra Pradesh High Court held that recognition of a medical qualification under the 1956 Act gives the right for enrolment in Indian Medical Register and/or State Medical Register. Unless and until the medical practitioner is permanently registered in State

---

[116] MCI Act 1956, Section 11 and Schedule I.

[117] *Ibid.* Section 12 and Schedule II.

[118] *Ibid.* Section 20(1).

[119] *Ibid.* Section 20A.

[120] (1999) 7 S.C.C. 120.

[121] *Ibid.* Section 21.

[122] 2008 (4) A.L.D. 484.

or Indian Medical Register, such a person cannot practise medicine as a medical practitioner in any part of India. Therefore, recognition of medical qualification and registration in State or Indian Medical Register is the alone fruitful logical end for a person who obtains medical qualifications. In other words, persons enrolled on the Indian Medical Register is allowed to practise as a medical professional in any part of India.[123] Furthermore, under Section 20A with the previous sanction of the Central Government, the MCI is empowered to make regulations relating to the standards of professional conduct and etiquette and code of ethics to be observed by medical practitioners.[124] Such power obviously does not confer upon the MCI to usurp the power of appellate authority of the Central Government to remove the name of a person from the State Medical Register on grounds of professional misconduct. By explaining both these provisions in *Tokugha Yepthomi v. Apollo Hospital Enterprises Ltd.*,[125] the Supreme Court observed that 'Hippocratic Oath' is not enforceable in a Court of law as it has no statutory force. Medical information about a person is protected by the Code of Professional Conduct made by the MCI and thus it is true that in the doctor-patient relationship, the most important aspect is the doctor's duty of maintaining secrecy. A doctor cannot disclose any information regarding his/her patient which he/she has gathered in the course of treatment including the mode of treatment of the patient. Further, Section 24 sets out that where the name of any person is removed from the State Medical Register on the ground of professional misconduct or any other ground except that he is not possessed of requisite medical qualifications, that he can appeal in the prescribed manner to the Central Government and the Central Government after consulting the MCI, communicate its decision. Such a decision is binding on the State Medical Council. Thus, this provision assured the consultative or supervisory role of MCI.[126] However, the MCI fails to attain all the desired goals due to

---

[123] *Shashi Bhushan v. State of Haryana*, 2019 (1) R.C.R. (Criminal) 694.

[124] MCI Act 1956, Section 33(m).

[125] 1999 (1) R.C.R. (Civil) 324.

[126] *Shalik Bhaurao Ade v. Medical Council of India*, 2016 (1) ALLMR 182.

inefficiency, arbitrariness and lack of transparency.[127] It is important to note that the disciplinary jurisdiction exercised by the MCI does not extend to adjudication of complaints brought against the doctors for the purpose of awarding compensation or damages.[128]

iv. Indian Medicine Central Council Act, 1970

The 1970 Indian Medicine Central Council Act[129] was enacted for the constitution and maintenance of a Central Register of Indian Medicine. Section 2(1)(e) stipulates that 'Indian Medicine' means the system of Indian medicine commonly known as Ashtang Ayurveda, Siddha or Unani Tibb. The allopathic system of medicine is not at all included in the aforesaid definition.[130] The Act empowers the Central Government to constitute the Central Council of Indian Medicine.[131] The Central Council has the power to constitute from amongst its members, (a) a committee for Ayurveda, (b) a committee for Siddha, and (c) a committee for Unani.[132] The Central Council has a duty to maintain a register of practitioners with a separate part for each of the systems of Indian medicine, known as the Central Register of Indian Medicine (CCIM) which shall contain the names of all persons who are for the time being enrolled on any State Register of Indian Medicine and who possess any of the recognized medical qualifications.[133] The Act has also given the responsibility upon the Central Council to prescribe standards of professional conduct and etiquette and a code of ethics for practitioners of Indian medicine.[134] The violations of such standards shall constitute professional misconduct. Similar to Section 27 of the MCI Act, 1956, Section 28 of this Act states that every person whose

---

[127] Sunil K. Pandya, *Medical Council of India: The Rot Within*, 4(3) IJME 125, 125 (2009).

[128] *A. S. Chandra* v. *Union of India*, 1992 (1) A.L.T. 713.

[129] Act No. XLVIII of 1970. It was enacted on 21 December 1970.

[130] *Praveen Kumar* v. *State of U.P.*, 2014 (1) A.D.J. 66.

[131] Indian Medicine Central Council Act 1970, Section 3.

[132] *Ibid.* Section 9.

[133] *Ibid.* Section 23(1).

[134] *Ibid.* Section 26.

name is for the time being borne on the Central Register of Indian Medicine is entitled according to his qualification to practice Indian Medicine in any part of India, thus secure right to every individual to get treatment from a qualified medical practitioner which is an integral part of the right to health.[135] By interpreting this provision, in *Vinod Kumar Chauhan v. Ved Prakash Tyagi*,[136] the Uttarakhand High Court observed that the registration of a doctor has to be done with only one State Board. Logically it would also mean that a person cannot be registered with two or more different Boards at a time. The scheme of the Act leaves no doubt that registration has to be done only with one State Board, though such registration can be transferred from one State Board to another, by due process. This is for the reason that on the strength of his registration with a particular State Board, his name is automatically registered with the CCIM. Therefore, if a person is registered with more than one Board at a time, this would cause an obvious anomaly, particularly in the calculation of seats of members of a particular State in CCIM.

v. Homoeopathy Central Council Act, 1973

The Homoeopathy Central Council Act[137] of 1973 was enacted primarily to regulate the conduct of homeopathic practitioners in India. The Act defines the term 'Homoeopathy' as the Homoeopathic system of medicine and includes the use of Bio-chemic remedies within its ambit.[138] The 1973 Act empowers the Central Government to constitute the Central Homoeopathy Council[139] to prescribe uniform minimum standards for admission, curriculum and syllabus and duration of course of training for homeopathy professionals. To secure this, it has been specified that no homeopathic medical

---

[135] *Hakim Arjeena Jabeen v. Central Council for Research in Unani Medicine*, 2007 (6) A.L.D. 667.

[136] A.I.R. 2016 Utr 117.

[137] Act No. LIX of 1973. It was enacted on 19 December 1973.

[138] Homoeopathy Central Council Act 1973, Section 2(d).

[139] *Ibid.* Section 3.

college shall be established without the previous permission of the Central Government.[140] This Act also provides for maintaining a Central Register by the Central Council[141] and also for regulating the professional conduct of homeopathic professionals by the formulation of a code of ethics.[142] Thus, the 1973 Act plays an important role in regulating the education, training and profession related to Homoeopathy practice.

vi. Clinical Establishments (Registration and Regulation) Act, 2010

The issue of regularization of private healthcare institutes is increasingly becoming important for securing the right to health.[143] To address this issue, the 2010 Clinical Establishments (Registration and Regulation) Act[144] was enacted which aims to provide registration and regulation of clinical establishments in the country. From the statement of the object, it is clear that the registration and regulation of clinical establishments are required to ensure minimum standards of facilities and services so that mandate of Article 47 of the Constitution for improvement in public health may be achieved. The 2010 Act is applicable to both diagnostic and therapeutic clinical establishments from public and private sectors of all recognized systems of medicine. The only available exception is clinical establishments run by the Armed forces.[145] As per this Act, at the National level a multi-member body namely 'National Council for Clinical Establishments' has to be established by the Central Government[146] which is responsible for categorization of clinical establishments, prescribing category-wise

---

[140] *Ibid.* Section 12.

[141] *Ibid.* Section 21.

[142] *Ibid.* Section 24(1).

[143] Anant Phadke, *Regulation of Doctors and Private Hospitals in India*, 51(6) EPW 15, 15 (2016).

[144] Act No. XXIII of 2010. It was enacted on 18 August 2010.

[145] The Clinical Establishments (Registration and Regulation) Act 2010, Section 2(c).

[146] *Ibid.* Section 3.

minimum standards, compilation, and publication of a National Register of Clinical Establishments and collect the information and statistics from clinical establishments.[147] In various States to implement this 2010 Act, there are 'State Council for Clinical Establishments'[148] and 'District Registering Authority'[149] in each district. Section 11 of the Act prevents any person from running a clinical establishment without registration under this Act. Further, Section 12 of the Act lays down that for the registration and continuation a clinical establishment has to fulfil certain conditions such as (a) the minimum standards of facilities and services, (b) the minimum requirement of personnel, (c) provisions for maintenance of records and reporting, etc. The minimum standards for clinical establishment are implemented on the basis of the level of care provided by such establishments. Further the Act guides for compiling a register of clinical establishments by the Registering Authority and supplies a digital copy of the same to the State Council.[150] The State Council has to provide the details to the Central Council and has to keep the record updated all time.[151]

Section 40 of the Act also provides penalties for contraventions of any provision with a fine which may extend to rupees ten thousand, and for any second offence which may extend to fifty thousand rupees and for any subsequent offence which may extend to rupees five lakh. Furthermore, Section 41 of the Act states that running a clinical establishment without registration shall, on the first contravention, be liable to a monetary penalty up to rupees fifty thousand, for the second contravention be liable to a monetary penalty up to rupees two lakh and for any subsequent contravention with a monetary penalty which may extend to rupees five lakh. However, the 2010 Act is not the perfect one. There are various loopholes in the Act such as the manpower requirements cannot be met in practical situations, certain provisions like the requirement to provide emergency care are vague.

[147] *Ibid.* Section 5.
[148] *Ibid.* Section 8.
[149] *Ibid.* Section 10.
[150] *Ibid.* Section 37.
[151] *Ibid.* Section 38.

Further, there is no provision for handling the additional workload of regulating private clinical establishments and the minimum standards should not be limited to structural standards like physical space, equipment and staff, it should include human rights of patients within its ambit.[152] Moreover, monitoring the compliance with standards as specified by the Act required a large number of officials to cover all the establishments. Further, as health is a State matter as per the Seventh Schedule of the Constitution, various States have their own law and there have certain differences with the Central Act of 2010, which creates confusion among the private healthcare authorities.

II. PROTECTION OF RIGHT TO HEALTH THROUGH VARIOUS NATIONAL HEALTH RELATED POLICIES IN INDIA

A. National Vaccine Policy 2011

Vaccines are important preventive medicines for primary healthcare as well as are critical for a nation's health security and play a useful role in public health by reducing morbidity and mortality due to communicable diseases. The Ministry of Health and Family Welfare, Government of India published the National Vaccination Policy in April 2011. The Expanded Program for Immunization (EPI) was launched for the first time in 1978 in India under which every vaccinator was re-designated as an 'Immunizer' and was required to perform the tasks of vaccinations/inoculations for smallpox, cholera, typhoid, diphtheria, tetanus, and pertussis.[153] The ambit of EPI was increased with the inclusion of the measles vaccine in 1985 and it was renamed the Universal Immunization Program (UIP).[154] For almost two decades, UIP did not include any additional vaccine within its schedule. However, since 2006, vaccines, namely Hepatitis B, a second dose of Measles and the Japanese Encephalitis vaccine have been introduced.[155] The 2011

---

[152] Sandhya Srinivasan, *Regulation and the Medical Profession: Clinical Establishments Act, 2010*, 48(3) EPW 14, 15 (2013).

[153] *Narendra v. Municipal Corporation of Delhi*, 2014 (146) D.R.J. 179.

[154] Yennapu Madhavi, *Vaccine Policy in India*, 5(2) POLS MED. 387, 388 (2005).

[155] GOI, NATIONAL VACCINE POLICY, 2011(GOI 2011), Paragraph 1.1.

Vaccine Policy is indeed a welcome development as it successfully provides an epidemiologically sound rationale vaccination programme in the country. This 2011 Vaccine Policy intends to provide a broader policy framework to create evidence-based guidelines to justify needs for Research and Development, production, procurement, quality assessment of vaccines for UIP in India. This Policy addresses the broad issues of strengthening the institutional framework, processes along with the framework required for decision making for new vaccine introduction. It is also concern about vaccine security and program management, regulatory issues, and product development.[156]

B. National Policy for Containment of Antimicrobial Resistance 2011

i. Background of the Policy

Anti-Microbial Resistance (AMR) in pathogens causing important communicable diseases has become a matter of grave public health concern globally including India. The factors like widespread use and availability of practically all the antimicrobials across the counter meant for human, animal and industrial consumption are responsible for the emergence of policy for antimicrobial resistance. This global threat of AMR calls for collaborative action for developing effective strategies in combating these diseases. In this background the Ministry of Health and Family Welfare, Government of India started an initiative in this direction by creating a task force, comprising the experts from all the fields of medicine including the Indian Council of Medical Research (ICMR), veterinary, agriculture and horticulture sciences, and Central Scientific and the Industrial Research Organization.[157] Finally, a national policy on AMR was introduced in 2011. The policy intends to (a) understand the emergence, spread and factors influencing AMR, (b) set up the antimicrobial programme to rationalize the use of antimicrobials, and (c) encourage the innovation of newer

---

[156] National Vaccine Policy, 2011, Paragraph 1.2.

[157] Chand Wattal & Neeraj Goe, *Tackling Antibiotic Resistance in India*, 12(1) EXPERT REV. ANTI INFECT. THER. 1427, 1431 (2014).

effective antimicrobials.[158] It also addresses the intervention strategies required and the steps for formulation and implementation of a standard antibiotic policy.

ii. National Surveillance System for AMR and Regulatory Provisions

Reliable data on AMR is an essential prerequisite for developing appropriate guidelines for the use of antimicrobials. Before the AMR Policy, there was no accepted national database of antimicrobial resistance in different pathogens except for those where there is a specific national health programme. Therefore, the 2011 Policy specifies the need for Surveillance System for Antimicrobial Resistance. Three types of surveillance can be done for AMR: (a) Comprehensive Surveillance, which means AMR surveillance through giving an actual estimate of AMR burden, includes the study of the whole population at risk and needs the involvement of a large number of laboratories, (b) Sentinel Surveillance, this study is a suitable mode of surveillance when prolonged and detailed data is needed, and (c) Point Prevalence, this study is useful for validation of the representativeness of the surveillance data. Among these, Sentinel Surveillance seems to be the best approach for our country.[159] The AMR Policy demonstrates that surveillance networks at different levels of the healthcare system should be set up with unified protocols, at least up to district level with a clause of future expansion up to peripheral health facility level and to obtain community-based data on AMR. The laboratory should preferably be a part of a large hospital having different types of facilities such as outdoor and indoor, ICU, operation theatres, etc.[160]

The AMR Policy suggested establishing an Inter-Sectoral Coordination Committee with the function (a) to review the available data regarding the use of antimicrobials, (b) to generate detailed information and

---

[158] Rajesh R. Uchil et al., *Strategies to Combat Antimicrobial Resistance*, 8(7) JCDR 1, 2 (2014).

[159] National Policy for Containment of Antimicrobial Resistance 2011, Paragraph 2.2.

[160] *Ibid.* Paragraph 2.3.2.

data by undertaking studies on the use of antimicrobials as Animal Growth-Promoters, (c) to specify the antibiotics for use in livestock, (d) to develop regulations on the usage of antimicrobials in poultry and other animals as well as the requisite labelling requirements in food, and (e) to review of Prevention of Food Adulteration Rules, 1995.[161] Thus, this policy for antimicrobial resistance is very important for the protection of the health of the population of India, particularly the rural people.

C. National Mental Health Policy 2014

i. Principles and Objectives of the Policy

In India, there is a wide treatment gap in mental healthcare and allied issues. These gaps and issues cause substantial losses to individuals, families, society, and the nation.[162] To address this issue in 2011 the Central Government constituted a policy group to recommend a Mental Health Policy for the country and subsequently in October 2014 the Central Government, in particular, Ministry of Health and Family Welfare, has introduced the National Mental Health Policy for the promotion of mental health, prevention of mental illness, enabling recovery of mental illness, promoting de-stigmatization and desegregation, and ensuring socio-economic inclusion of persons affected by mental illness by providing accessible, affordable and quality health and social care through their life span, within a right-based framework.[163]

This Policy is backed by the Mental Health Action Plan 365, which defines the specific roles of the central government, the state governments, local bodies, and civil society organizations. To achieve its objectives and goals, the policy stipulates certain principles such as equity, justice, integrated care, evidence-based care, quality,

---

[161] *Ibid*. Paragraphs 4.2.1 and 4.2.2.

[162] Reetinder Kaur & R. K. Pathak, *Treatment Gap in Mental Healthcare Reflections from Policy and Research*, 52(31) EPW 34 (2017).

[163] GOI, New Pathways New Hope - National Mental Health Policy of India (GOI 2014) at Paragraph 1.

participatory and right-based approach, grievance and effective delivery, value-based training and teaching programmes, and holistic approach to mental health. The 2014 Policy fixed its goal to (a) reduce distress, disability, exclusion morbidity and premature mortality associated with mental health problems across the life span of the person, (b) enhance understanding of the mental health in the country, and (c) strengthen the leadership in the mental health sector at the national, state and district levels.[164] Apart from these goals, the Mental Health Policy also specifies ten objectives. The Policy aims (a) to provide universal access to mental health care, (b) to increase access to and utilization of comprehensive mental health services by persons with mental health problems, (c) to increase access to mental health care especially to vulnerable groups including homeless persons, persons in remote areas, educationally, socially deprived sections, (d) to reduce prevalence and impact of risk factors associated with mental health problems, (e) to reduce incidence of suicide and attempted suicide, (f) to ensure respect for rights and protection from harm of persons with mental health problems, (g) to reduce stigma associated with mental health problems, (h) to enhance availability and equitable distribution of skilled human resources for mental health, (i) to progressively enhance financial allocation and improve utilization for mental health promotion and care, and (j) to identify and address the biological, social and psychological determinants of mental health problems and to provide appropriate interventions.[165]

ii. Issues Addressed by the Policy

The 2014 Policy highlights stigma to be one of the major issues of persons with mental health problems and identifies the absence of available, effective and affordable services as a major barrier to these people. And this has been often accompanied by a lack of knowledge, fear and even hostility towards these people.[166] The Policy also casts a duty to design the implementation programmes from a rights-based

---

[164] *Ibid*. Paragraph 3.1.

[165] *Ibid*. Paragraph 3.2.

[166] *Ibid*. Paragraph 4.1.

perspective which will help to reduce stigmatizing and discriminatory behaviours.[167] Mental Health services should take into account the needs of vulnerable people. The policy has linked inextricably poverty and mental ill-health in a negative vicious cycle. Persons from lower socioeconomic groups are more vulnerable to mental health problems. Out-of-pocket health spending in accessing mental health services and lost productivity due to disability can also lead to poverty.[168] Besides poverty, the policy also addresses the issues of homelessness, persons inside custodial institutions, orphaned persons with mental illness, children with mental health problems, elderly caregivers, internally displaced persons, persons affected by disasters and emergencies, and other marginalized populations.[169] The Mental Health Policy recognizes the role of the family in bearing the direct financial cost of treatment and other associated costs besides the emotional and social costs of providing care for a family member with mental illness.[170] It also argues for a healthy, safe and enriching physical and social environment for the promotion of individual and community mental health.[171]

iii. Directions and Recommendations

The National Mental Health Policy 2014 propagates numerous suggestions to address the abovementioned cross-sectional issues. The Policy recognizes interventions like effective governance and delivery mechanism for mental health, universal access to mental health services, and community participation in mental health development to achieve the vision of the Policy. It also argues for effective governance and accountability for mental health by developing relevant policies, programmes, laws and regulations along with budgetary provisions for the implementation of evidence-based mental health plan and actions.[172] For the promotion of mental health, the Policy recommends

---

[167] *Ibid.* Paragraph 4.2.

[168] *Ibid.* Paragraph 4.3.1.

[169] *Ibid.* Paragraphs 4.3.2–4.3.9.

[170] *Ibid.* Paragraph 4.5.

[171] *Ibid.* Paragraph 4.8.

[172] *Ibid.* Paragraph 5.1.

re-designing the Anganwadi Centres to supply the early child care and training of Anganwadi workers and school teachers with the knowledge and skill that build the self-confidence of parents and caregivers in understanding the physical and emotional needs of children and persons with mental illness.[173] However, for the prevention of mental illness and reduction of suicide and attempted suicide, the Mental Health Policy aims to ensure that there is no discrimination against persons with mental problems and to create an environment where these persons are able to take part in regular activities along with participating in social and economic activities.[174] Further, it calls for an enhanced understanding of mental health and strengthening of leadership in the mental health sector at all levels to achieve universal access to mental health care. This Mental Health Policy has a positive impact on the status and position of persons with mental illness in India.

D. National Health Policy 2017

i. Background of the Policy

India introduced the first National Health Policy (NHP) in 1983 and then there was the introduction of the NHP in 2002 for the second time. Both of them have served well in guiding the approach for the health sector in the Five-Year Plans. Since the last NHP in 2002, there have been few changes in the overall health scenario of India. These include the following:

1. The health priorities are changing. Although India has achieved gradual improvement in the Infant Mortality Rate (IMR) and Maternal Mortality Rate (MMR) along with control of infectious diseases to a larger extent, there is a growing burden on account of non-communicable diseases and some infectious diseases,
2. The emergence of a robust health care industry,
3. The growing incidences of catastrophic expenditure due to health care costs, which are presently estimated to be one of the major contributors to poverty, and

[173] *Ibid.* Paragraph 5.2.
[174] *Ibid.* Paragraph 5.3.

4. Rising economic growth enables enhanced fiscal capacity.[175] During the framing of the NHP in 2016, the Supreme Court in *Devika Biswas v. Union of India*[176] observed that the draft of a NHP was put up on the website on the Ministry of Health and Family Welfare of the Government of India in December 2014 for comments, suggestions and feedback but even after more than one and a half years, the website of the said Ministry shows that the NHP has not been finalized. And ultimately directs the Union of India to take a decision on or before December 31, 2016, on whether it would like to frame a NHP or not.

Against this backdrop, new NHP was adopted in 2017 which aims at providing good quality healthcare services in an assured manner to all by addressing current and emerging challenges arising from the ever-changing epidemiological, technological and socio-economic scenarios.[177] The primary aim of the 2017 Policy is to strengthen, clarify and inform the role of the Government in shaping health systems in all its dimensions including investments in health, prevention of diseases, promotion of good health through cross-sectoral actions, organization of healthcare services, developing human resources, access to technologies, encouraging medical pluralism, developing better financial protection strategies, building the knowledge base and strengthening regulation and health assurance.

Thus, by explaining the role of the NHP in achieving primary health goals the Gujarat High Court in *United India Insurance Company Ltd. v. Mohanlal Aggarwal*,[178] observed that:

> Improvement of public health is one of the primary duties of the State under Article 47 of the Constitution of India. Protecting health of the citizens against infectious diseases, promoting better standards of healthcare and ensuring that there are adequate safeguards against financial risks connected

---

[175] NHP 2017, Paragraph 1.

[176] A.I.R. 2016 S.C. 4405.

[177] Rajiv Kumar Gupta & Rashmi Kumari, *National Health Policy 2017: An Overview*, 19(3) JK Sc. 135, 135 (2017).

[178] A.I.R. 2004 Guj 191.

with severe ailments would constitute key objectives of the public health policy in a welfare State. The socially and economically marginal groups in the society can hardly afford the financial burden involved in treatment of diseases. This calls for an equitable distribution of the financial burden of ill-health. Such disproportionate economic burden on the poor sections demands State intervention to ensure that private health insurance is regulated in a manner that would promote the goals of the National Health Policy in the context of the directive principles of securing high standards of living of the people, to improve public health and to secure that the operation of the economic system does not result in the concentration of wealth and means of production to the common detriment, as mandated by Articles 39 and 47 of the Constitution.

ii. Objectives and Goals

The NHP 2017 envisages its goal to attain the highest possible level of health and wellbeing for all at all ages through a preventive and promotive health care orientation in all developmental policies and to assure universal access to good quality health care services without facing financial hardships.[179] The 2017 NHP specifies professionalism, equity, affordability, universality, accountability, integrity and ethics, patient-centred care, pluralism, decentralization and dynamism, inclusive partnerships and adaptiveness as the key principles behind the aims and objectives of the Policy.[180] These quantitative goals and objectives are the benchmark against which the achievements of the health policy can be judged in time to come.[181] To achieve Universal Health Coverage by 2025, the NHP assures comprehensive primary care to all with regard to reproductive, maternal, child, and adolescent health, communicable, non-communicable and occupational diseases.

The 2017 NHP also ensures improved access and affordability of quality secondary and tertiary health care services through a combination of public hospitals and well-measured strategic purchasing of services in health care deficit areas, from private care providers and also

---

[179] NHP 2017, Paragraph 2.1.

[180] *Ibid.* Paragraph 2.2.

[181] Vikas Bajpai, *National Health Policy, 2017 Revealing Public Health Chicanery*, 53(28) EPW 31 (2018).

specifies its aim for a reduction in out of pocket expenditure for getting healthcare services.[182] Further, the policy influences the operation and growth of the private health care sector and medical technologies to ensure alignment with public health goals.[183] Under the 2017 NHP, the indicative, quantitative goals and objectives are outlined under three broad components: (a) health status and programme impact, (b) health systems performance, and (c) health system strengthening. With the ambit of health status and programme impact, it fixes the goals to increase life expectancy at birth from 67.5 to 70 by 2025.[184] In connection to mortality by age and/or cause the 2017 Policy aims to (a) reduce under-five mortality to 23 by 2025 and maternal mortality rate to 100 by 2020, (b) reduce neo-natal mortality to 16 and stillbirth rate to 'single digit' by 2025, and (c) reduce the infant mortality rate to 28 by 2019.[185] The 2017 Policy wants to increase the utilization of public health facilities by 50 per cent from current levels by 2025.[186] With regard to finance in healthcare, the Policy is ambitious to increase health expenditure by Government as a percentage of GDP from the existing 1.15 per cent to 2.5 per cent by 2025.[187] Moreover, to reduce the number of deaths and illnesses from hazardous chemicals and air and water pollution, this Policy also intends to levy pollution cess.[188]

iii. Mainstreaming the Potential of AYUSH

This 2017 NHP ensures access to AYUSH remedies through co-relation among public facilities and introduced Yoga in schools and workplaces as part of the promotion of good health as adopted in the National AYUSH Mission. It also identifies the need to standardize and validate

---

[182] NHP, 2017, Paragraph 2.3.1.

[183] *Ibid.* Paragraph 2.3.3

[184] *Ibid.* Paragraph 2.4.1.1.

[185] *Ibid.* Paragraph 2.4.1.2.

[186] *Ibid.* Paragraph 2.4.2.1.

[187] *Ibid.* Paragraph 2.4.3.1.

[188] Shailja Sharma et al., *National Health Policy 2017: Can It Lead to Achievement of Sustainable Development Goals?* 11(1) AJMS 4, 5 (2018).

Ayurvedic medicines and establish a robust and effective quality control mechanism for AYUSH drugs. The NHP promotes research and public health skills for preventive and promotive healthcare. Linking AYUSH systems with ASHAs is an important plank of this policy. The present NHP continues mainstreaming of AYUSH with the general health system and supports the integration of AYUSH systems at all levels of knowledge systems, by validating processes of health care promotion and cure. The policy further recognizes the need and importance of integrated courses for the Indian System of Medicine, Modern Science and Ayurgenomics.[189]

iv. Collaboration with Non-government Sector

The NHP 2017 suggests exploring collaboration for primary care services with not-for-profit organizations having a track record of public services. It also permits collaboration where the team of specialized human resources and domain-specific organizational experience is required. In the case of private providers working in rural and remote areas or with under-serviced communities the NHP provides provision for encouragement through the provision of appropriate skills to meet public health goals, opportunities for skill up-gradation to serve the community better, participation in disease notification and surveillance efforts, and sharing and supporting certain high-value services. The present policy supports voluntary service in rural and under-served areas on a pro-bono basis by recognized healthcare professionals by motivating them under a 'giving back to society' initiative.[190] The NHP advocates coordination between the National Council for Skill Development, Ministry of Health and Family Welfare and State Government(s) for engaging private hospitals or private general medical practitioners in skill development to minimize the gaps in technicians, nursing and para-nursing, and para-medical staff in select areas.[191] It casts a duty upon the private sector to use the company's

---

[189] NHP, 2017, Paragraph 9.

[190] *Ibid.* Paragraph 13.

[191] *Ibid.* Paragraph 13.2.

social responsibility platform to play an active role in the awareness generation through campaigns on occupational health, adolescent health, blood disorders, safe health practices and accident prevention, anti-microbial resistance, micronutrient adequacy, screening of children and ante-natal mothers, psychological problems linked to misuse of technology, etc.[192] The Policy also aims to improve health outcomes and reduce out-of-pocket payments through the effective implementation of Arogyasri and RSBY schemes.[193]

v. Regulatory Framework

According to the 2017 Policy, modernization and effective functioning of clinical establishments, professional and technical education, food safety, medical technologies, medical products, clinical trials, research and implementation of other health-related laws are required for the better protection of health.[194] It advocates strengthening the professional councils of Medical, Ayurveda, Unani and Siddha, Homeopathy, Nursing, Dental and Pharmacy through expanding the membership of these councils between three key stakeholders - doctors, patients and society in balanced numbers. It also supports the setting up of the National Allied Professional Council to regulate all allied health professionals and ensure quality standards.[195] The Policy further recommends placing and strengthening the necessary network of offices, laboratories, e-governance structures and human resources needed for the enforcement of the Food Safety and Standards Act, 2006.[196] This Policy encourages (a) the streamlining of the system of procurement of drugs, (b) a strong and transparent drug purchase policy for bulk procurement of drugs, (c) spread of low-cost pharmacy chains such as 'Jan Aushadhi' stores, and (d) prescription of generic medicines.[197]

---

[192] *Ibid.* Paragraph 13.3.

[193] *Ibid.* Paragraph 13.6.2.

[194] *Ibid.* Paragraph 14.

[195] *Ibid.* Paragraph 14.1.

[196] *Ibid.* Paragraph 14.3.

[197] *Ibid.* Paragraph 14.4.

III. PROTECTION OF RIGHT TO HEALTH THROUGH NATIONAL HEALTH MISSIONS

The National Health Mission (NHM) was introduced in 2013 by the Central Government along with National Urban Health Mission (NUHM) as a Sub-mission under it and included the National Rural Health Mission (NRHM) as the other Sub-mission under its scheme. The NHM envisages the achievement of universal access to equitable, affordable and quality health care services that are accountable and responsive to people's needs with effective inter-sectoral convergent action to address the wider social determinants of health.

A. National Rural Health Mission (NRHM)

i. Background and the Focus States

To strengthen the health care delivery, improve access to quality health services and make them functional and available at the doorsteps of the rural population, the Government of India formulated NRHM on April 12, 2005. The NRHM aims to provide accessible, affordable and accountable quality health services to the poorest households in the remotest rural regions.[198] At the time of introduction, the duration of NHRM was from 2005 to 2012. In 2013 it became a part of the National Health Mission and further, it was extended till March 2020. It aims to secure effective delivery of quality healthcare to rural populations throughout the country with a special focus on 18 States, which have weak public health indicators and/or weak infrastructures. These states are Arunachal Pradesh, Assam, Bihar, Chhattisgarh, Himachal Pradesh, Jharkhand, Jammu and Kashmir, Manipur, Mizoram, Meghalaya, Madhya Pradesh, Nagaland, Orissa, Rajasthan, Sikkim, Tripura, Uttaranchal and Uttar Pradesh. The Government of India would provide funding for key components in these 18 high focus States.[199] The thrust of the mission is to establish a fully community-owned decentralized health delivery system with

---

[198] *Javed Iqbal Bhat v. State*, 2010 (4) J.K.J. 771.

[199] Umesh Kapil & Panna Choudhury, *National Rural Health Mission (NRHM): Will It Make a Difference?* 42 INDIAN PEDIATR. 783, 783 (2005).

inter-sectoral conversance at all levels to ensure simultaneous action on a wide range of determinants of health like sanitation, water, nutrition, education, social and general equality.

Further, under the NRHM several schemes are also provided for securing basic and fundamental health awareness and health protection systems at the village, panchayat block and district level.[200] Moreover, it also provides cash schemes for delivery and post-delivery care.[201] The NRHM has treated the village as a unit, therefore, a village health plan is prepared through a local team headed by the Health and Sanitation Committee of the Panchayat. For effective implementation of the scheme, various committees are established at National Level, State Level, District Level, Block Level, Zila Parishad Level and village level.[202] Thus, it focuses on the process of decentralization with concomitant convergence.

ii. Goals and Strategies

The NRHM provides a broad operational framework for the health sector. The aim of the Mission is to improve an access to quality health care for people, especially those residing in rural areas.[203] In detail the goals of the NRHM include: (a) reduction in infant mortality rate and maternal mortality ratio, (b) universal access to integrated comprehensive public health services, water, sanitation and hygiene, (c) prevention and control of communicable and non-communicable diseases, including locally endemic diseases, (d) population stabilization, gender and demographic balance, (e) revitalization of local health traditions

---

[200] *Rajkumar v. State of Rajasthan*, A.I.R. 2016 Raj 176.

[201] *Laxmi Mandal v. Deen Dayal Harinagar Hospital*, 172 (2010) D.L.T. 9.

[202] The Committee which are established in different levels under the NRHM at: National Level: Mission Steering Group and Empowered Programme Committee; State Level: State Health Mission and State Health and Family Welfare Society; District Level: District Monitoring Council, District National Rural Health Mission Committee, District Governing Council, and Rugna Kalyan Committee; Block Level: Block Governing Council Committee; Zila Parishad Level: Executive Committee; Village Level: Sub Centre Strengthening Committee, Village Health Nutrition Water Supply and Sanitary Committee.

[203] *Devendra Pratap Singh v. Union of India*, 2011 (7) A.D.J. 169.

and main-stream Ayurvedic, Yoga, Unani, Siddha and Homeopathy Systems of Health (AYUSH), and (f) promotion of healthy lifestyles. The strategies to achieve these goals include (a) process to train and enhance the capacity of Panchayati Raj Institutions to own, control and manage public health services, (b) health plan for each village through Village Health Committee of the Panchayat, (c) strengthening sub-centre through an untied fund to enable local planning and action, (d) provision of 24-hour service in 50 per cent PHCs by addressing the shortage of doctors, especially in high focus States, (e) preparation and implementation of an inter-sectoral District Health Plan prepared by the District Health Mission, including drinking water, sanitation, hygiene and nutrition, (f) integrating vertical health and family welfare programs at National, State, Block, and District levels. It also aims to introduce effective risk-pooling mechanisms and social health insurance and takes advantage of local health traditions through public-private partnerships.[204]

iii. Accredited Social Health Activists

The NRHM will cover all the villages in these 18 States through approximately 2.5 lakh village-based 'Accredited Social Health Activists' (ASHA) who would act as a link between the health centres and the villagers. One ASHA will be raised from every village or cluster of villages across 18 States.[205] The NRHM even embodies the role of ASHA at the village level for mobilizing the opinion about the importance of health care among villagers or self-help groups through personal contacts, discussions, consultations and dissemination of information.[206] The ASHA would be trained (a) to advise village populations about sanitation, hygiene, contraception, and immunization, (b) to provide primary medical care for diarrhoea, minor injuries and fever, (c) to escort patients to medical centres, (c) to deliver direct observed short-course therapy for tuberculosis and oral rehydration,

---

[204] A.K. Sharma, *The National Rural Health Mission: A Critique*, 63(2) SOCIOL. BULL. 287, 289 (2014).

[205] To note that exactly one ASHA use to be selected for 1,000 populations.

[206] *Inder Prakash Gupta v. State*, 2008 (1) J.K.J. 386.

(d) to give folic acid tablets and chloroquine to patients, and (e) to alert authorities to unusual outbreaks.[207] These ASHA volunteers will receive performance-based compensation for promoting universal immunization, referring and escorting services for primary health-care, constructing household toilets, and other health care delivery programs.

B. National Urban Health Mission (NUHM)

Urban population growth has been exponential over the last few decades in India. While India's rural population has doubled between 1961 and 2001, the urban population has grown four-fold.[208] As a result, the need for planning with regard to the health of urban people was also considered by the Central Government and thus, the NUHM has emerged as the sub-part of the NHM and through this, the health needs of the urban population are being systematically and nationally addressed for the first time. It envisages meeting the health care needs of the people living in urban areas with a focus on the urban poor. It aims to provide essential primary health care services to the urban poor and to reduce their out-of-pocket expenses for treatment. This will be achieved by strengthening the existing health care service delivery system and targeting the people living in slums.[209]

The aims of the NUHM will clearly be on alleviating the distress and duress of the urban poor in seeking quality health services.[210] Apart from this, the NUHM policy framework places high focus on the urban poor and vulnerable, the social determinants of health and the strengthening of institutional capacity of urban local governments. The urban primary health centre, on the lines of a rural primary health centre, is envisaged as the nodal point for the delivery of health care services under the NUHM. While the basic concept remains the same

---

[207] G. Mudur, *India Launches National Rural Health Mission*, 330 BMJ 920 (2005).

[208] S. Agarwal & K. Sangar, *Need for Dedicated Focus on Urban Health Within National Rural Health Mission*, 49(3) IJPH 141 (2005).

[209] GOI, National Urban Health Mission Framework for Implementation (GOI 2013) Paragraph 1.10.

[210] *Ibid.* Paragraph 1.8.

as of the NRHM, the services and service delivery mechanisms of urban primary health centres are modified to address the unique health and livelihood challenges faced by the urban population. It provides a three-tier system of health care, viz, (a) Community Level, (b) Urban Health Centre Level, and (c) Secondary or Tertiary level. The NUHM covers all State capitals, district headquarters and other towns with a population of 50,000 and above (as per census 2011) in a phased manner. It is important to note that cities and towns with a population below 50,000 will continue to be covered under the NRHM.[211]

The NUHM endeavours to achieve its goal through (a) institutional mechanism and management systems to meet the health-related challenges of a rapidly growing urban population, (b) need-based city-specific urban health care system to meet the diverse health care needs of the urban poor and other vulnerable sections, (c) partnership with the community and local bodies for more proactive involvement in planning, implementation, and monitoring of health activities, (d) availability of resources for providing essential primary health care to urban poor, and (e) partnerships with NGOs and other stakeholders. Thus, with the help of various schemes, the NUHM is playing an important role in protecting the health of the urban population.

IV. PROTECTION OF RIGHT TO HEALTH THROUGH VARIOUS NATIONAL HEALTH SCHEMES

Along with policy and programmes, there are various schemes of the Government of India which are also beneficial for the protection of the right to health in India. Among these schemes, the Pradhan Mantri Swasthya Suraksha Yojana (PMSSY) was launched in 2003 with the aim of correcting regional imbalances in the availability of affordable or reliable tertiary healthcare services and for attaining self-sufficiency in graduate and postgraduate medical education and training.[212] Initially, the PMSSY had two components (a) setting up of AIIMS like institutions, and (b) up-gradation of Government Medical College

---

211 GOI, Ninety Third Report Demands for Grants 2016–17 (Demand No. 42) of the Department of Health and Family Welfare 1 (GOI 2016).

212 *Seema Agency v. Union of India*, II (2018) B.C. 364 (Chhattis.).

Institutions (GMCIs) for securing health for all. In March 2006, the Phase-I of the PMSSY was approved by the Government which comprised of (a) setting up six AIIMS like institutions (later re-named as new AIIMS), and (b) up-gradation of 13 existing State Government Medical Colleges or Institutions.[213] Upgradation of GMCIs envisaged improvement in health infrastructure through the construction of Super Specialty Blocks or Trauma Centres and procurement of medical equipment for selected existing GMCIs.[214] Further in Twelfth Five Year Plan, the Government again decided to increase the number of new AIIMS and to upgrade other GMCIs in subsequent phases. As a consequence, over the years, the scheme has been expanded to cover 20 new AIIMS and 71 Government Medical College Institutions. The Cabinet Committee on Economic Affairs approved the PMSSY for ₹332 crores per institution in March 2006. The cost, however, escalated to ₹820 crores per institution in March 2010.[215]

The Janani Suraksha Yojana (JSY) is a safe motherhood intervention scheme implemented with the objective of reducing maternal and neonatal mortality by promoting institutional delivery among poor pregnant women under the National Rural Health Mission. This was launched on April 12, 2005.[216] The important features of the JSY scheme are to motivate, counsel and ensure safe delivery particularly among women belonging below the poverty line and Scheduled Castes and Scheduled Tribes and to identify them for antenatal care, delivery, postnatal care, immunization and family planning services.[217] It is a centrally-sponsored scheme. Some States, for example, Andhra Pradesh launched their own similar schemes by increasing the amount of cash assistance for institutional deliveries. Tamil Nadu has introduced a

---

[213] Anita Nath, *India's Vision for Health: Perspectives from the XII Five-Year Plan (2012–2017)*, 4(1) INT. J. PUBLIC HEALTH 46 (2014).

[214] PAC, PRADHAN MANTRI SWASTHYA SURAKSHA YOJANA, ONE HUNDRED AND THIRTY FOURTH REPORT 6 (Lok Sabha Secretariat 2018).

[215] PLANNING COMMISSION, REPORT OF THE WORKING GROUP ON TERTIARY CARE INSTITUTIONS FOR 12TH FIVE YEAR PLAN (2012–2017) 28 (GOI 2011).

[216] *Laxmi Mandal v. Deen Dayal Harinagar Hospital*, 172 (2010) D.L.T. 9.

[217] R.V. Deshpande, *Is Janani Suraksha Yojana (JSY) Contributing to the Reduction of Maternal and Infant Mortality? An Insight from Karnataka*, 57(1) J. FAM. WELF. 1, 2 (2011).

separate scheme for providing ₹1000/- per month to mothers for six months i.e., three months prior to the delivery and three months after the delivery.[218] The JSY recognizes the Accredited Social Health Activist (ASHA) as an effective link between the Government mechanism and the poor pregnant women. ASHA usually works under an Auxiliary Nurse Midwife and their works have to be supervised by a Medical Officer. A child under the JSY is entitled to emergency care including integrated management of neonatal and childhood illness, care of routine childhood illness, essential newborn care, promotion of exclusive breastfeeding for 6 months. One of the features of the JSY is that only a woman, who belongs below the poverty line (BPL) and is more than 19 years of age, can be a beneficiary in the High Performing States (HPS). Cash assistance in HPS is limited to two live births. The disbursement is made at the time of delivery. Cash assistance of ₹700 in the case of rural and of ₹600 in the case of urban is given for institutional delivery and of ₹500 is given for home delivery. In rural areas, cash assistance for transportation to the nearest health centre for delivery of the child is also provided under the scheme.

In addition to these, for quality healthcare assurance, the Rashtriya Swasthya Bima Yojana (RSBY) is an ambitious new public health insurance scheme for the poor. It was launched in August 2007. The aim of the scheme is to improve access to quality medical care involving hospitalization and surgery through an identified network of healthcare providers for below poverty line families. By allowing the hospital to bill an insurance company for the cost of treatment, the RSBY secures health services to the poor and by subsidizing the annual premium, the government makes the scheme nearly free for beneficiaries.[219] The RSBY generally provides for annual coverage up to ₹30,000 per household. The Scheme extends its coverage to five members of the family which includes the head of a household, spouse and up to three dependents. The scheme also covers hospitalization, related tests, consultations, day-care treatment and medicines along with the pre and post-hospitalization expenses for some 700 medical and surgical

[218] People's Union for Civil Liberties v. Union of India, A.I.R. 2008 S.C. 495.

[219] D. Rajasekhar et al., Implementing Health Insurance: The Rollout of Rashtriya Swasthya Bima Yojana in Karnataka, 46(20) EPW 56, 56 (2011).

conditions and procedures. Pre-existing conditions are included within the scheme and there is a provision for transport allowance subject to a limit of ₹1,000 per year.[220] The Central Government will bear 75 per cent and State Government will bear 25 per cent of the beneficiary's premium to the insurer and the State Government has the duty to select the insurer following a competitive bidding process.[221]

Further, India cannot realize its demographic dividends without its citizen being healthy and thus, the Government of India conceived 'Ayushman Bharat - National Health Protection Mission' (Healthy India) on September 23, 2018, as a shift from traditional health planning approaches towards a comprehensive healthcare vision. The Ayushman Bharat Programme aims to build a New India by 2022 and ensure enhanced productivity, well-being and avert wage loss and impoverishment. It warrants health for all, specifically the poorest and most vulnerable people by utilizing core technology as its backbone. NITI Aayog proposes the imperative need to completely redesign the flow of people, money, and information, as well as introduces a layered approach to provide comprehensive foundational health functions for all the States through Ayushman Bharat Programme, grounded strongly in an inclusive and inter-operable technology strategy.[222] The combination of 'Universal Health Coverage' and 'Ayushman Bharat Programme' has the potential to place health higher in future public and political discourses in India. Ayushman Bharat Programme aims to provide coverage of 500,000 per family annually, benefiting more than 10 crore poor families. It includes the beneficiaries beyond the traditional approach of targeting the 'below poverty line' population. Inclusion of 'vulnerable and deprived population' identified through socio-economic and caste census will nearly double the number of people to be benefited. The Ayushman Bharat Programme combines two initiatives. It includes Health and Wellness Centres

---

[220] *Ibid.* at 57.

[221] Prateek Rathi, Evaluation of Rashtriya Swasthya Bima Yojana (RSBY): A Case Study of Amravati District 9 (IIM 2012).

[222] S.A. Tabish, Transforming *Health Care in India: Ayushman Bharat-National Health Protection Mission*, 7(12) IJSR 16, 17 (2018).

and the National Health Protection Scheme aiming for increased accessibility, affordability and availability of primary, secondary and tertiary level healthcare services in India. The Health and Wellness Centres were proposed by the task force on strengthening primary healthcare in India in 2016 and first announced in the Union Budget of 2017–2018, whereas the National Health Protection Scheme was first announced in the Union Budget of 2016–2017.[223] Subsequently, the National Health Protection Scheme has been renamed as Pradhan Mantri Rashtriya Swasthya Suraksha Mission. These two initiatives will meet the range of healthcare needs across the nation. Hence, this can help to make progress towards Universal Health Coverage in India.

---

[223] GOI, REPORT OF THE TASK FORCE ON PRIMARY HEALTH CARE IN INDIA (MOHFW 2017).

Right to Health in Context of Women and Children

Health is now a societal issue for the global community and should be considered as a global good.[1] However, along with the general framework, the human rights framework relating to the right to health of women and children is important to discuss. The notion of the human right to health of women is primarily originated from international endeavours. The human rights paradigm provides an important perspective on the relationship between reproduction and health, as well as it remains an essential tool for ensuring that reproductive health is achieved and reproductive rights are protected. Hence, to understand the health right of women, detailed deliberation with respect to recognition of reproductive choice and its allied rights under the international instruments and domestic law of India is required.

Along with the women, the perspective of the children and the importance of noticing their health issues is another area of concern. Early childhood is crucial for cognitive and emotional development as well as overall physical and mental health.[2] In addition to this, special care is required for the child till they attain the age of 18 years. In parity, the UDHR proclaimed that childhood is entitled to special care

---

[1] R. SMITH et al., eds, GLOBAL PUBLIC GOODS FOR HEALTH: HEALTH ECONOMICS AND PUBLIC HEALTH PERSPECTIVES (OUP 2003); D.J. Sullivan, *The Nature and Scope of Human Rights Obligations Concerning Women's Right to Health*, 1(4) HHR 368 (1995).

[2] Sonia B. Nagarale, *Plight of Right to Education of Underprivileged Children in India: A Pertinent Outlook*, 1(1) J. RIGHTS CHILD 44–45 (2016).

and assistance.[3] In this background, this chapter is primarily devoted to understanding the issues relating to the right to health of women and children under international and Indian law.

I. CONCEPTUAL HUMAN RIGHT ORIENTATION TO REPRODUCTIVE HEALTH OF WOMEN

While women and men share more or less similar health challenges to some extent, the particular biological and social differences are such that the health of women deserves particular attention.[4] Among those, maternal health and its realization through recognition of reproductive rights is the most significant aspect of women's health. Sometimes a combination of these two concepts is known as reproductive health. In general legal terms, reproductive health broadly encompasses those health conditions and social conditions that affect reproductive functioning. Thus, reproductive health requires that people have the ability to reproduce, the ability to regulate their fertility[5] and the ability to practice and enjoy sexual relationships.[6] By recognizing reproductive health, the human rights paradigm provides an important perspective on the relationship between reproduction and health and provides effective tools for securing reproductive health. Its embodiment under the international and domestic legal framework is always significant considering its impact on the life and survival of women, their children and families. Thus, women's health should be reconstructed by considering gender, class, culture and social needs. More detailed elaboration of right-based approach to the health of women includes:

---

[3] Anu & Pawan Kumar, *Children's Right to Health in India: Legal Perspective*, 1(6) IJSR 91 (2012).

[4] Neelam Singh, *Issues of Women's Health*, 15(1) NYAYA DEEP 46 (2014).

[5] This definition of reproductive health has focused on both supporting reproductive functioning and self-regulation of fertility by women. *See for example*, Mahmoud F. Fathalla, *Promotion of Research in Human Reproduction: Global Needs and Perspectives*, 3(1) HUMAN REPROD. 7 (1988).

[6] Mahmoud F. Fathalla, *Reproductive Health: A Global Overview*, 626(3) ANN. N. Y. ACAD. SCI. 1 (1991).

(a) right to marry and form a family, (b) right to health, reproductive health and family planning, (c) right to decide the number and spacing of children, (d) right to be free from gender discrimination, (e) right to be free from sexual assault and exploitation, and (f) right to modify customs that discriminate against women along with other gender-neutral rights.

Reproductive health rights exist at the convergence of two human rights models: (a) the reproductive rights model and (b) the right to a health model. The reproductive rights model has typically revolved around the protection of the rights of women to make autonomous reproductive decisions, grounded in civil and political rights to privacy, liberty, equality, autonomy and dignity. Particularly this view includes the rights, conditions and determinants that support the ability of an individual to make autonomous decisions without coercion.[7] The dominant rights discourse under this model focuses on women's reproductive decisions by considering human rights of decisional autonomy, bodily integrity, privacy and dignity.[8] Whereas, the right to health model employs a different approach than the reproductive rights model to conceptualize reproductive health rights.

This model, by taking the broad aspects of the right to health into consideration, seeks to uphold the foundational aspects of human rights and related conditions integral to reproductive health which made efforts to provide conditions and determinants necessary to allow good reproductive health to flourish. Further, the protection of human rights relating to the availability of health services and protection from violence always have a direct influence on the ability of a woman to exercise her decisional rights related to reproductive choice.[9] Thus, as reproductive health and human rights are inextricably linked, the attainment of reproductive health rights demands the realization of other supportive human rights also.

---

[7] Lance Gable, *Reproductive Health as a Human Right*, 60(4) CASE W. RES. L. REV. 957–969 (2010).

[8] *Ibid.* at 975.

[9] Rosalind P. Petchesky, *Human Rights, Reproductive Health and Economic Justice: Why They Are Indivisible*, 8(15) RHM 12–13 (2000).

II. RIGHT TO HEALTH OF WOMAN UNDER GENERAL INTERNATIONAL INSTRUMENTS

A. Right to Health of Woman under ICESCR, 1966

i. General Comment Number 14: An Indirect Approach

To make a binding law on economic social and cultural rights in 1966 the International Covenant on Economic Social and Cultural Rights (ICESCR) was adopted.[10] While the right to health was specifically included in the ICESCR through Article 12, it does not explicitly establish a discrete human right to reproductive health. It recognizes the right of every person to the enjoyment of the highest attainable standard of physical and mental health. The implementation of the ICESCR is monitored by the Committee on Economic, Social and Cultural Rights (CESCR) composed of independent experts elected by the State parties.[11] The ICESCR through its General Comment No. 14 'The Right to the Highest Attainable Standard of Health (Article 12)', by giving a greater interpretation to Article 12.2(a)states that[12]:

'The provision for the reduction of the stillbirth rate and of infant mortality and for the healthy development of the child' (art. 12.2 (a))[13] may be understood as requiring measures to improve child and maternal health, sexual and reproductive health services, including access to family planning, pre- and post-natal care, emergency obstetric services and access to information, as well as to resources necessary to act on that information.

ii. General Comment 22: A Broader Approach

Additionally, in 2016, the CESCR extensively addressed the right to sexual and reproductive health.[14] It specifically emphasized States'

---

[10] Audrey R. Chapman, *Monitoring Women's Right to Health under the International Covenant on Economic, Social, and Cultural Rights*, 44 AUILR 1157, 1158–1159 (1995).

[11] Dina Bogecho, *Putting It to Good Use: the International Covenant on Civil and Political Rights and Women's Right to Reproductive Health*, 13(2) S. CAL. REV. L. & WOMEN'S STUD. 229–239 (2004).

[12] CESCR General Comment No. 14, Paragraph 14.

[13] According to WHO, the stillbirth rate is no longer commonly used, infant and under-5 mortality rates being measured instead.

[14] UN DOC. E/C.12/GC/22 (2 May 2016).

legal duties towards securing the right to sexual and reproductive health in general. This Comment affirms that this right is an integral part of the right of everyone to the highest attainable physical and mental health[15] and is interdependent on a series of human rights to life, personal dignity, and others- that has enjoyed longstanding recognition based on already existing international human rights instruments. The Comment further defined the four cornerstones of the right to health such as availability, accessibility, affordability, acceptability with respect to reproductive health.[16] The Committee also specifies that State parties to the ICESCR have the obligation to respect the right to sexual and reproductive health, which includes not denying access to health services such as abortion, or not maintaining laws or practices that criminalize abortion, or not requiring third-party authorization to access contraception or abortion. As an enforcement scheme, the Committee states that the right to sexual and reproductive health should be enshrined in laws and policies and should be fully justiciable at the national level and that judges, prosecutors and lawyers should be made aware of that so that these rights can be enforced.[17]

B. ICPD, 1994 and Woman Health

The United Nations drafted the International Conference on Population and Development (ICPD) from 5–15 September 1994, in Cairo, Egypt. Hundreds of nongovernmental organizations and 173 States participated in this Conference in 1994.[18] This Conference resulted in the formulation of a plan designed to control the growth of the global population over the next twenty years.[19] During preparations for the conference, it was announced that one of the major objectives of the

---

[15] General Comment No. 22, Paragraph 11.

[16] *Ibid.* Paragraphs 12–20.

[17] *Ibid.* Paragraph 64.

[18] Jennifer Jewett, *The Recommendations of the International Conference on Population and Development: The Possibility of the Empowerment of Women in Egypt*, 29(1) Cornell Int. L.J. 191–192 (1996).

[19] ICPD Program of Action 1994. UN Doc A/CONF.171/13 (1994).

conference would be the establishment of abortion as an international human right.[20] Accordingly, the ICPD has opted to establish standards in family planning services including the right to reproductive autonomy and collective gender equality. A 'Programme of Action', entitled 'The Cairo Document for the International Conference on Population and Development of 1994', was adopted in this conference and along with other part Chapter 7 of the document deals with 'Reproductive Rights and Reproductive Health' whereas Chapter 8 stated about 'Health, Morbidity and Mortality'. It defines reproductive health as a state of complete physical, mental and social well-being and not merely the absence of disease or infirmity, in all matters relating to the reproductive system and to its functions and processes, and specifies the requirements for achieving the same to its fullest extent. According to it, the preconditions are (a) right to have access to a safe, effective, affordable and acceptable method of family planning of their choice, and (b) the rights to access to appropriate healthcare services that will enable a woman to go safely to pregnancy and childbirth process couples with the best chance of having a healthy infant.[21] The right to attain the highest standard of sexual and reproductive health also includes the right to make decisions concerning reproduction free of discrimination, coercion and violence.[22] Reproductive health, therefore, implies that women are able to have a satisfying and safe sex life and that they have the capability to reproduce and the freedom to decide if, when and how often to do so.[23] Building on the foundation and momentum generated by the Vienna Declaration, which had been issued the prior year, participants in the ICPD sought to directly link reproductive health to human rights.[24] The programme provides

---

[20] Gregory M. Saylin, *The United Nations International Conference on Population and Development: Religion, Tradition, and Law in Latin America*, 28 VJTL 1245, 1253 (1995).

[21] ICPD Program of Action 1994, Principle 7.2.

[22] *Ibid.* Principle 7.3.

[23] Lucia Berro Pizzarossa, *Here to Stay: The Evolution of Sexual and Reproductive Health and Rights in International Human Rights Law*, 7(3) Laws 29–34 (2018).

[24] Laura Reichenbach, *The Global Reproductive Health and Rights Agenda: Opportunities and Challenges for the Future*, in Reproductive Health and Human Rights 21–39, 26–27 (Laura Reichenbach & Mindy Jane Roseman eds, Pennsylvania University Press 2009).

directions to the member States to make reproductive health available to all individuals of appropriate ages through accessible primary health care by expanding the ambit of primary health care as soon as possible and no later than the year 2015. It States[25]:

> Reproductive health Care in the context of Primary Health care should, *inter alia*, include: family planning counselling, information, education, communication and services, education and services for prenatal care, safe delivery and postnatal care especially breastfeeding and Infant and women's health care; prevention and appropriate treatment of infertility; abortion including prevention of abortion and management of the consequences of abortion; treatment of reproductive tract infections; sexually transmitted diseases and other reproductive health conditions; information, education and counselling as appropriate on human sexual reproductive health and responsible parenthood.

Further, the document recognizes that women play an essential role in the programme of population development, and thus, they must gain complete control over their reproduction rights.[26] Consequently, the ICPD Programme of Action emphasizes that for the programme to succeed, nations must strive to empower their female citizens and provide them with adequate family planning services and information.[27] Largely ICPD Programme of Action aims to enhance gender equality, promote reproductive health, strengthen partnerships and mobilize resources.[28] However, the Programme of Action is not a binding treaty but rather a standard that the member participants will strive to attain. Thus, this Programme document creates a tangible shift from a narrowly focused policy on population and fertility reduction to a broadened agenda that addresses the range of sexual and reproductive health issues that constitute the individual lives of men and women.[29]

---

[25] ICPD Program of Action 1994, Principle 7.6.

[26] *Ibid.* Principle 4.1.

[27] *Ibid.* Principles 7.7–7.8.

[28] M. Wheeler, *ICPD and Its Aftermath: Throwing Out the Baby?* 77 (9) BWHO 778 (1999).

[29] Mindy Jane Roseman & Laura Reichenbach, *International Confe. ence on Population and Development at 15 Years: Achieving Sexual and Reproductive Health and Rights for All?* 100(3) AJPH 403 (2010).

Additionally, the right to reproductive health care is the right to lead safe and satisfying sex lives, with the freedom to decide if, when, and how often to reproduce. The State must provide women and men with information regarding reproductive health so that they may effectively exercise these rights.[30] The Conference recommended that reproductive health care encompass the areas of family planning, prenatal care, delivery and postnatal care, health care for women and infants, prevention of infertility and sexually transmitted diseases, prevention of abortion, and management of abortion complications. Thus, the Conference noted that reproductive health care includes respect for the human body, as well as the right to informed free choice as to whether or not to have children.[31]

C. Cairo+5 Key Actions Document, 1999

In 1999, the United Nations Fund for Population Activities hosted the five-year follow-up meetings to the 1994 Cairo conference on Population and Development and the General Assembly adopted a new plan of action known as the Cairo+5 Key Actions Document[32] by reviewing its pledge in ICPD and renewed its pledge to the advancement of health and reproductive rights of women. The mandate of this United Nations review was to assess progress to date in implementing the 20-year ICPD Programme of Action and to articulate strategies for moving forward. This Key Actions Document also lays out specific strategies for dealing with the reproductive and sexual health needs of adolescents. Along with this, it outlines crucial steps needed for better addressing maternal mortality and morbidity, including unsafe abortion, and the impact of the HIV/AIDS pandemic on women and young people. The Cairo+5 Key Actions Document directs the State parties to enhance their efforts in protecting the human rights of women and to incorporate a human rights approach in addressing reproductive health issues.[33]

---

[30] ICPD Program of Action 1994, Principles 7.7–7.8.

[31] *Ibid*. Principle 7.12.

[32] Cairo+5 Key Actions Document, 1999 was adopted on 2 July 1999.

[33] *Ibid*. Paragraph 8.8.

However, similar to the ICPD Programme of Action, the Cairo+5 Key Actions Document also fails to integrate reproductive health care with the need for reform of the health sector, although it did emphasize that 'the reduction of maternal mortality and morbidity should be prominent and used as an indicator for the success of such reforms'.[34] A possible reason for this omission may have been the limited involvement of health experts in either meeting, as opposed to that of population and family planning experts and advocates.

D. UN Millennium Development Goals, 2000

Since September 2000, a major shift has taken place under international law, through the induction of the United Nations Millennium Declaration, 2000. Among the eight Millennium Development Goals, two goals, namely (a) reduction of child mortality,[35] (b) improvement of maternal health[36] are directly related to women's health along with children's health. As such, these MDG targets echo a 1994 UN goal set at the Cairo Conference on Population and Development[37]; however, these new Goals side-line the broader right based approach towards sexual and reproductive health as articulated in the 1994 ICPD, and focus on narrow select interventions even within the health sector. Thus, they relatively depoliticize the realm of maternal health in the context of International human rights. In terms of functioning, these two goals can be described as extending the lives of two specifics, especially vulnerable members of society (children and mothers), while the third goal is about being free from major diseases for the society at large.

---

[34] *Ibid.* Paragraph 62(b).

[35] MDGs 2000, Goal 4.

[36] *Ibid.* Goal 5. Obiajulu Nnamuchi, *Health and Millennium Development Goals in Africa: Deconstructing the Thorny Path to Success*, in THE RIGHT TO HEALTH: A MULTI-COUNTRY STUDY OF LAW, POLICY AND PRACTICE 3–42 (Brigit Toebes et al., eds, Springer, 2014).

[37] Amir Attaran, *An Immeasurable Crisis? A Criticism of the Millennium Development Goals and Why They Cannot Be Measured*, 2(10) PLoS MED. 955–957 (2005).

Among its targets, the Millennium Development Goals Target 5. A 'to reduce by three quarters, between 1990 and 2015, the maternal mortality ratio' is more ambitious than most of the other Goals 1 to 7, as a three-quarters reduction would constitute more rapid progress than was achieved between 1960 and 1990.[38] However, at the same time as the U.N. High Commissioner for Human Rights has criticized MDGs for lack of ambition, arguing that most maternal deaths are easily avoidable.[39] It further targets to achieve universal access to reproductive health between the abovementioned periods.[40] In reality, though the rate declined it fails to achieve the target. This target related to the reproductive health of women was the subject of subsequent political wrangling, thus suffered a lack of domestic policy implementation to some extent.[41] However, in comparison to the other international instruments, the MDGs have undoubtedly raised the profile and popular awareness of development issues was changed the terms of international development policy and helped to bring a stronger focus to the right to food and health.

With regard to reproductive health, several authors highlight the fact that targets for reproductive health were absent before 2007 and are still insufficient. Omissions of the issues of abortion, a 'fertility regulation indicator' and the 'availability and use of obstetric services' are also major lacunas on the part of MDGs and their implantation mechanism. It is further notable that only Goals 3 and 5 are to some extent gender-specific. This limited explicit inclusion in two MDGs is too narrow and clearly indicates that the gender issue and its dynamics have not yet been fully understood nor integrated into policy dialogues.[42]

---

[38] Jan Vandemoortele, *If Not the Millennium Development Goals, then What?* 32 TWQ 9, 14 (2011).

[39] Mac Darrow, *The Millennium Development Goals: Milestones or Millstones? Human Rights Priorities for the Post-2015 Development Agenda,* 15(1) YHRDLJ 55, 63 (2012).

[40] MDGs 2000, Goal 5, Target 5.B.

[41] David Hulme & James Scott, *The Political Economy of the MDGs: Retrospect and Prospect for the World's Biggest Promise,* 15(2) NEW POLIT. ECON. 293, 296 (2010).

[42] Marta Lomazzi et al., *The Millennium Development Goals: Experiences, Achievements and What's Next,* 7(1) GLOB. HEALTH ACTION 1, 5 (2014).

E. UN World Summit 2005

The United Nations World Summit 2005 was held on 16 September 2005, at United Nations headquarter in New York, to adopt the 2005 World Summit Outcome document which consisted largely of a set of goals and principles for the United Nations and its members. It brought together representatives from more than 170 countries. The coverage of this Summit is broad, including matters such as international economic and social development, peace and collective security, human rights and the rule of law, and strengthening the United Nations. Further, the 2005 Summit culminated with an agreement that the international community, acting through the United Nations, bears a responsibility to help protect populations from genocide and other atrocities when their own governments fail to do so. The Outcome document further announces a willingness to take collective action through the Security Council to protect populations if peaceful means prove inadequate.

The issues related to women's health rights were again strongly debated during this World Summit where world leaders resolved to achieve universal access to reproductive health by 2015, as envisioned at the 1994 ICPD; promote gender equality, and end discrimination against women.[43] The Summit Outcome[44] calls for integrating universal access to reproductive health in strategies for achieving the Millennium Development Goals[45] and as a means to promote gender equality and women's empowerment.[46] Thus, through these measures, the 2005 Summit looked to promote gender equality and eliminate pervasive gender discrimination.[47]

---

[43] HILKKA PIETILA, THE UNFINISHED STORY OF WOMEN AND THE UNITED NATIONS 26 (United Nations 2007).

[44] World Summit Outcome, 2005. Resolution adopted by the General Assembly through Sixtieth session on 16 September 2005. UN Doc A/res/60/1.

[45] *Ibid.* Paragraph 57(g).

[46] *Ibid.* Paragraph 58(c).

[47] VED NANDA & GEORGE PRING, INTERNATIONAL ENVIRONMENTAL LAW AND POLICY FOR THE 21ST CENTURY 644 (Martinus Nijhoff 2013).

F. Sustainable Development Goals, 2015

A worldwide discussion on the successor to the MDGs began several years before 2015, which expresses the international concern with regard to the future policy after 2015. Finally, on September 25, 2015, Heads of States and Governments from the193 UN member States gathered at the 70th Session of the UN General Assembly in New York to adopt *Transforming our world: The2030 Agenda for Sustainable Development*[48] a 'comprehensive, far-reaching and people-centred set of universal and transformative goals and targets'[49] which will 'stimulate action over the next 15 years in areas of critical importance for humanity and the planet'.[50] Among these, Goal 5 articulates the aim to 'achieve gender equality and empower all women and girls'. Within the targets fixed under Goal 5, the Sustainable Development Goals wants to 'ensure universal access to sexual and reproductive health and reproductive rights as agreed in accordance with the Programme of Action of the International Conference on Population and Development and the Beijing Platform for Action and the outcome documents of their review conferences'.[51] From the language of Target, it is clear that Sustainable Development Goals does not provide any new guidance with respect to the reproductive health of women. It only reaffirms the goals which were decided in the ICPD and Beijing Platform. However, Inga T. Winkler and Carmel Williams rightly observed that these reproductive health targets under Goal Five refrain from taking a rights-based approach, focus on a technical approach, and do not address underlying structural issues impeding women's right to equality and their ability to control their own lives.[52]

---

[48] UN Doc. A/RES/70/1 (2015).

[49] Transforming Our World: The 2030 Agenda for Sustainable Development, Paragraph 2.

[50] *Ibid.* Preamble.

[51] *Ibid.* Goal 5, Targets 6.

[52] Inga T. Winkler & Margaret L. Satterthwaite, *Leaving No One Behind? Persistent Inequalities in the SDGs*, 21(8) IJHR 1073 (2017).

III. CEDAW, 1979: THE WOMEN CONVENTION AND HEALTH OF WOMAN

A. The CEDAW and Its Approach

i. General Overview

The Convention on the Elimination of Discrimination against Women (CEDAW), 1979[53] expressly addressed reproductive rights with the broadest approach in the international legal arena. The CEDAW requires State parties to eliminate discrimination between women and men in the area of health[54] along with the areas related to education,[55] employment,[56] marriage[57] and full participation in economic and social activities.[58] Hence the CEDAW aimed to take all appropriate measures to eliminate discrimination against women in all areas of life. This includes equality in legal status, healthcare, employment, education, political participation, and family structure. The CEDAW character-izes women's inferior status and oppression not just as a problem of inequality between men and women but rather as a function of sex and gender discrimination against women. It also recognized the fact that discrimination against women hampers economic growth and prosperity and detrimentally affects society in general. Thus, it describes 'discrimination against women' as any distinction, exclusion or restriction made on the basis of sex which has the effect or purpose of impairing or nullifying the recognition, enjoyment or exercise by women, irrespective of their marital status, on a basis of equality of men and women, of human rights and fundamental freedoms in the political, economic, social, cultural, civil or any other field.[59] Thus, the Convention's non-discrimination clause provides a very broad

---

[53] Adopted by General Assembly Resolution 34/180 of 18 December 1979 and came into force 3 September 1981 in accordance with Article 27(1).

[54] CEDAW 1979, Article 12.

[55] *Ibid.* Article 10.

[56] *Ibid.* Article 11.

[57] *Ibid.* Article 16.

[58] *Ibid.* Article 17.

[59] *Ibid.* Article 1.

understanding of discrimination against women by including all three dimensions of distinction, exclusion or restriction on the basis of sex.[60] By focusing on both legal and development policy to guarantee the rights of women, this Convention emphasized that there must be the practical realization of rights which is different in approach than its prior international instruments.[61] To date, 190 countries have ratified the convention, which has been hailed as the International Bill of Rights for Women. In pursuance to the affectability of the CEDAW, many renowned scholars argued that the CEDAW's recognition of the inter-dependence and indivisibility of civil, political, social and economic rights makes it the instrument with the greatest potential to address the close relationship between woman's marginalization, social rights and inequalities.[62]

ii. Primary Health Rights under CEDAW

The preamble of 1979 CEDAW, like earlier international instruments, reiterates that discrimination against women violates the principles of equality of rights and respect for human dignity.[63] It also expresses concern regarding the situations of poverty, where women have the least access to food, health, education, training and opportunities for employment and other needs.[64] As a result, the Convention entitles women to equal enjoyment with men not only of the so-called 'first generation' of human rights which includes civil and political rights, such as the right to marry and found a family but also of the 'second generation' of human rights which includes economic, social and cultural rights, such as the right to health. It deals with the right

---

[60] Marijke De Pauw, *Women's Rights: From Bad to Worse? Assessing the Evolution of Incompatible Reservations to the CEDAW Convention*, 29(77) UTRECHT J. INT. EUR. LAW 51, 52 (2013).

[61] A. Saksena, *CEDAW: Mandate for Substantive Equality*, 14(3) IJGS 481, 483 (2007).

[62] L. Farha, *Committee on the Elimination of Discrimination Against Women: Women Claiming Economic, Social and Cultural Rights - The CEDAW Potential*, in SOCIAL RIGHTS JURISPRUDENCE. EMERGING TRENDS IN INTERNATIONAL AND COM PARAGRAPHTIVE LAW 553–568 (M. Langford ed, CUP 2008).

[63] *Meenakshi Dubey v. M.P. Poorva Kshetra Vidyut Vitran Co. Ltd.*, 2020 (1) M.P.L.J. 657.

[64] CEDAW, Preamble, Paragraph 8.

to healthcare under Article 12. However, there are other Articles in the Convention that have a bearing on women's health also. The Convention requires States Parties to ensure that family education includes a proper understanding of maternity as a social function.[65] This provision lays the basis for an approach to enhancing women's human rights that goes beyond the well-known distinction between formal and substantive equality and includes transformative equality within its ambit.[66] Furthermore, Article 10 requires States parties to ensure equal access to education, thus enabling women to access health care more readily and reducing female students' drop-out rates, which are often due to premature pregnancy. More specifically, States parties have the duty to provide specific educational information to ensure the wellbeing of families, including information and advice on family planning.[67]

The CEDAW also looks after securing the right to health and right to safety in working conditions, including the safeguarding of the function of reproduction.[68] Thus, the duty to protect the right of a woman in her reproductive choices is sacrosanct.[69] In addition, the convention directs the States Parties to ensure access for rural women to adequate health care facilities, including information, counselling and services in family planning,[70] and to take all appropriate measures to ensure adequate living conditions, particularly housing, sanitation, electricity and water supply, transport and communications,[71] all of which are critical for the prevention of disease and the promotion of good health care.

---

[65] *Ibid.* Article 5(b).

[66] Rikki Holtmaat, *The CEDAW: A Holistic Approach to Women's Equality and Freedom*, in WOMEN'S HUMAN RIGHTS: CEDAW IN INTERNATIONAL, REGIONAL AND NATIONAL LAW 27–61 (Anne Hellum & H.S. Aasen eds, CUP, 2013).

[67] CEDAW, 1979, Article 10(h).

[68] *Ibid.* Article 11(1)(f).

[69] *S v. State of Rajasthan*, 2019 (4) R.L.W. 2916 (Raj.).

[70] CEDAW, 1979, Article 14(2)(b).

[71] *Ibid.* Article 14(2)(h).

iii. Specific Right to Healthcare

Further, through Article 12, the CEDAW secures equal access to healthcare for women. It states that:

1. States Parties shall take all appropriate measures to eliminate discrimination against women in the field of health care in order to ensure, on a basis of equality of men and women, access to health care services, including those related to family planning.
2. Notwithstanding the provisions of paragraph 1 of this article, States Parties shall ensure to women appropriate services in connection with pregnancy, confinement and the post-natal period, granting free services where necessary, as well as adequate nutrition during pregnancy and lactation.[72]

In other words, Article 12 of the Convention stipulates that State parties shall take all appropriate measures to eliminate discrimination against women in the field of health care in order to ensure, on a basis of equality of men and women, accesses to health care services, including those related to family planning.[73] Therefore, Article 12 specifically calls on States to take all appropriate measures to eliminate discrimination against women in the field of health care, while others have a direct or indirect bearing on the enjoyment of the highest attainable standard of health.[74] To understand Article 12, an understanding of the normative content of the right to health and the relationship between gender equality and health is inherently required. Its impact on the abortion law always raised questions about the interpretation of Article 12's prohibition of gender discrimination in the provision of health care services. Opponents to the Convention have expressed concern that this provision may prohibit private or government restrictions on abortions, including

---

[72] R.J. Cook & V. Undurraga, Article 12, in THE UN CONVENTION ON THE ELIMINATION OF ALL FORMS OF DISCRIMINATION AGAINST WOMEN: A COMMENTARY 311–326, 311 (M.A. Freeman et al., eds, OUP, 2012).

[73] Z v. State of Bihar, A.I.R. 2017 S.C. 3908.

[74] WHO, WOMEN'S HEALTH AND HUMAN RIGHTS: MONITORING THE IMPLEMENTATION OF CEDAW 8 (WHO 2007).

the ability to not offer or provide funding for abortion services if other medical services are offered or subsidized.[75]

However, this counter-argument is not established as Article 12 does not specify limits itself within the abortion issues. It can be demonstrated in a far broader way. Under this provision, first the State is obligated to eliminate discrimination in the field of healthcare, which in terms of Article 1 articulates that the State is obligated to ensure those distinctions in health do not impede equality. Second, it assures that the State has to eliminate discrimination 'in order to ensure' the equal rights for women in health. The goal of eliminating discrimination is gender equality. Equality is both the analytical frame for evaluating the state's law and policies on health and the state's goal to achieve equal access to health care.[76] For attaining these objects, the States need to address structural barriers - such as cost, stigma, and unnecessary procedural requirements, so that there is a legal and practical framework in place, which emphasized the health needs of women. Thus, it is important to note that barriers to women's access to appropriate health care include laws that criminalize medical procedures only applicable to women and punish them for undergoing those procedures.

Moreover, to prevent discrimination against rural women, the State parties are directed to secure access to adequate health care facilities, including information, counselling and services in family planning.[77] Further a harmonious construction of Articles 12 and 16 reveals that State parties have the duty to secure for every woman a right to make free and informed decisions about health care and medical treatment, including decisions about her own fertility and sexuality.[78]As a whole,

---

[75] Julia Ernst, *U.S. Ratification of the Convention on the Elimination of All Forms of Discrimination Against Women*, 3(1) MICH. J. GEND. LAW 299, 331 (1996).

[76] Meghan Campbell, *Women's Rights and the Convention on the Elimination of all Forms of Discrimination Against Women: Unlocking the Potential of the Optional Protocol*, 34(4) NJHR 247–255 (2016).

[77] CEDAW, 1979, Article 14.

[78] Srinivas Kosgi et al., *Women Reproductive Rights in India: Prospective Future*, 10(1) JHAS 1, 2 (2011).

Article 12 of the CEDAW states the duty of States to ensure equality of men and women in access to health care services.[79] It sets goals to measure governments' observance of their international duties to put the rights of women into effect.[80] In essence, the State should be able to identify concrete steps required to be taken to fulfil the right to maternal health of the poor,[81] and it should protect reproductive health along with reproductive choices of women.[82] Hence, this strong language of Article 12 supporting women's health enabled the Committee on the Elimination of Discrimination against Women to be the first international treaty body to hold a national government responsible for preventable maternal death.

IV. WOMAN HEALTH UNDER OTHER WOMEN CENTRIC INTERNATIONAL INSTRUMENTS

A. DEVAW, 1993

The 'women's rights are human rights' movement was prominent at the Vienna World Conference on Human Rights in 1993. It succeeded to include the issues of women's rights and violence against women successfully within the final Declaration and Program of Action.[83] However, pressure by the women's movement for a new instrument to deal specifically with violence against women also led to the adoption of a Declaration on the Elimination of Violence against Women (DEVAW) in 1993.[84] This Declaration was adopted for the universal recognition of women's rights with regard to equality, security, liberty, integrity and dignity and to eliminate violence against women.[85] Hence, it aims

[79] WHO, *supra* note 74, at 8.

[80] Rebecca J. Cook, *International Human Rights and Women's Reproductive Health*, 24(2) STUD. FAM. PLAN. 73, 76 (1993).

[81] MEGHAN CAMPBELL, WOMEN, POVERTY, EQUALITY: THE ROLE OF CEDAW 129 (Hart Publication 2018).

[82] *Supra* note 73.

[83] Vienna Declaration and Programme of Action 1993, UN Doc AICONF. 157123.

[84] Elizabeth Evatt, *Women and Human Rights*, 28 MON. L. REV. 1, 3 (2002).

[85] Proclaimed by General Assembly Resolution 48/104 of 20 December 1993.

to fill up the gaps left by CEDAW.[86] This declaration was the first international instrument explicitly addressing violence against women, providing a framework for national and international action. It defines violence against women as any act of gender-based violence that results in or is likely to result in, physical, sexual or psychological harm or suffering to women, including threats of such acts, coercion or arbitrary deprivation of liberty, whether occurring in public or in private life.[87] Thus, for addressing gender violence or violence against women, this Declaration has explicitly used the due diligence principle to frame and expound State obligations.[88] It draws links between violence against women and reproductive health and rights. Further, it includes the right to just and favourable conditions of work and the right not to be subjected to torture, or other cruel, inhuman or degrading treatment or punishment within the framework of the right to the highest standard attainable of physical and mental health.[89] Although DEVAW is the only international instrument relating to domestic violence as of yet,[90] it does not recognize directly such violence as a violation of human rights. Instead, violence against women is understood as a 'barrier' to women's enjoyment of human rights.[91]

B. Beijing Conference on Women, 1995

On 4–15 September 1995, the Fourth World Conference on Women was held in Beijing.[92] This was the aftermath of the three previous Women's Conferences held in Mexico City (1975), Copenhagen (1980) and Nairobi (1985). The purpose of these UN-sponsored Women's

---

[86] *Union of India v. Fancy Babu*, 2016 (5) K.H.C. 767.

[87] DEVAW, 1993, Article 1.

[88] Julie Goldscheid & Debra J. Liebowitz, *Due Diligence and Gender Violence: Parsing Its Power and Its Perils*, 48 CORNELL INT. L.J. 301, 317 (2015).

[89] *Supra* note 87, Article 3.

[90] BONITA MEYERSFELD, DOMESTIC VIOLENCE AND INTERNATIONAL LAW 37 (Hart Publishing 2010).

[91] ALICE EDWARDS, VIOLENCE AGAINST WOMEN UNDER INTERNATIONAL HUMAN RIGHTS LAW 22 (CUP 2011).

[92] Fourth World Conference on Women, *Beijing Declaration and Platform for Action*, (17 October 1995). UN DOC A/CONF.177/20.

Conferences is to bring together diverse systems, cultures, and traditions and seek consensus on women's issues.[93] However, during the preparation period, the stated purpose of the Beijing event was to address constraints and obstacles which impede progress and perpetuate inequalities between women and men. Gertrude Mongella, Secretary-General of the Conference, stressed the need to look at women's issues holistically. Further, As the Deputy Secretary of the United Nations, Ismat Kittani, stated in his opening speech at the Beijing Conference: '[T] he challenge is how to make existing laws take effect in the daily lives of women'.[94] The final draft specifically focuses on twelve areas concerning the implementation of women's human rights and sets out an agenda for women's empowerment. It reaffirms gender equality as a fundamental prerequisite for social justice. The Platform for Action includes a series of strategic objectives to eliminate discrimination against women and achieve equality between women and men.[95] The Platform for Action is the most comprehensive expression of States' commitments to the human rights of women. It also aims to formulate and operationalize national policy on women through member States and to set up a commission to defend women's human rights in the domestic arena.[96] On the issue of women's health, the Platform for Action reiterates that the highest standard of mental, physical and social health is a necessity for all women and is critical to their ability to fully take part in all areas of life, public and private.[97] It states:

> Women have the right to the enjoyment of the highest attainable standard of physical and mental health. The enjoyment of this right is vital to their life and well-being and their ability to participate in all areas of public and

---

[93] Mona Zulficar, *From Human Rights to Program Reality: Vienna, Cairo, and Beijing in Perspective*, 44 AULR 1017, 1035 (1995).

[94] Margaret Plattner, *The Status of Women Under International Human Rights Law and the 1995 UN World Conference on Women, Beijing, China*, 84 KENTUCKY L.J. 1249, 1250 (1995–1996).

[95] OFFICE OF THE HIGH COMMISSIONER, WOMEN'S RIGHTS ARE HUMAN RIGHTS 14 (United Nations 2014).

[96] *Ashish Kumar Das v. North Eastern Hill University*, 2018 (2) G.L.T. 477.

[97] Lauren Danner & Susan Walsh, *'Radical' Feminists and 'Bickering' Women: Backlash in U.S. Media Coverage of the United Nations Fourth World Conference on Women*, 16 CSMC 63, 66 (1999).

private life… Women's health involves their emotional, social and physical well-being and is determined by the social, political and economic context of their lives, as well as by biology.[98]

Hence, the document represents not only a call for equality and empowerment by half the world's population but takes a challenge to change the course of social and economic development in a direction that places women firmly at the centre of analysis and objectives. It admits that women have different and unequal access to and use of basic health resources, including primary health services for the prevention and treatment of various diseases under the present structure of Healthcare.[99] Further, the Platform for Action highlights lack of social, psychological and economic support, deterioration of public health systems, privatization of healthcare systems without appropriate guarantees of universal access to affordable health care, and the roles of women within the family and the community, as catalysts, for not securing equal access to healthcare to women.[100] It also calls for greater attention to a comprehensive health programme rather than one that focuses on health problems related to sexuality. It then points out that women have been 'the victims of irresponsible sexual behaviour'.[101] The outcome of the fierce debate over human reproduction in Beijing is reflected in the careful wording of Paragraph 94 of the Platform for Action which discusses 'reproductive health'. The paragraph provides

Reproductive health therefore implies that people are able to have a satisfying and safe sex life and that they have the capability to reproduce and the freedom to decide if, when and how often to do so. Implicit in this last condition [is] the right of men and women to be informed and to have access to safe, effective, affordable and acceptable methods of family planning of their choice, as well as other methods of their choice for regulation of fertility which are not against the law, and the right of access to appropriate health-care services that will enable women to go safely through pregnancy and childbirth and provide couples with the best chance of having a healthy infant. In line with the above definition of

[98] Beijing Declaration 1995, Paragraph 89.

[99] *Ibid.* Paragraph 90.

[100] *Ibid.* Paragraph 91.

[101] Valentine M. Moghadam, *The Fourth World Conference on Women: Dissension and Consensus*, 3(1) Bull. Centre for Women's Dev. Stud. 93, 97 (1996).

reproductive health, reproductive health care is defined as the constellation of methods, techniques and services that contribute to reproductive health and well-being by preventing and solving reproductive health problems.

Under this paragraph, the discussion rounds with the phrases 'choice' regarding 'regulation of fertility', but that discussion is coupled with the strong proviso that 'choice' does not extend to fertility options that are 'against the law'. This specific paragraph also asserts that 'reproductive health' includes 'the constellation of methods, techniques and services' that 'prevent' or 'solve' 'reproductive health problems'.[102] It also states that 'Good health is essential to leading a productive and fulfilling life, and the right of all women to control all aspects of their health, in particular their own fertility, is basic to their empowerment'.[103]

The Platform for Action reports that women are subject to particular health risks due to inadequate responsiveness and lack of services to meet health needs related to sexuality and reproduction. Complications related to pregnancy and childbirth are among the leading causes of mortality and morbidity of women of reproductive age in many parts of the developing world. To address these issues, the Platform for Action suggests that the ability of women to control their own fertility forms an important basis for the enjoyment of other rights.[104] Shared responsibility between women and men in matters related to sexual and reproductive behaviour is also essential to improving women's health.[105] Further, this Beijing Platform expressly articulates that abortion is a matter of domestic policy. It provides that 'Any measures or changes related to abortion within the health system can only be determined at the national or local level according to the national legislative process'.[106] Paragraph 106(e) further provides more specifics, calling for sexual and reproductive health care that is accessible, available, and affordable, with particular emphasis on maternal

---

[102] Richard G. Wilkins & Jacob Reynolds, *International Law and the Right to Life*, 4(1) AVE MARIA L. REV. 123, 153 (2006).

[103] Beijing Declaration 1995, Paragraph 92.

[104] *K. Kalaiselvi v. Chennai Port Trust*, 2013 (2) C.T.C. 400.

[105] *Supra* note 103, Paragraph 97.

[106] *Ibid.* Paragraph 106(k).

and emergency obstetric care. Paragraph 106(i) further calls upon governments to 'reduce ill health and maternal morbidity and achieve worldwide the agreed-upon goal of reducing maternal mortality by at least 50 per cent of the 1990 levels by the year 2000 and a further one half by the year 2015'. The Platform for Action also recommends that States should consider reviewing laws containing punitive measures against women who have undergone illegal abortions. The Beijing Platform for Action also states that the human rights of women include their right to have control over and decide freely and responsibly on matters related to their sexuality, including sexual and reproductive health, free of coercion, discrimination and violence.[107] The Platform for Action has recommended that governments should work in collaboration with the UN system, the medical community, research institutions, and nongovernmental organizations to design and implement gender-sensitive health programs; provide affordable primary health care; and promote research on women's health. It further urged Governments to enact and enforce legislation against the perpetrators of practices and acts of violence against women, such as female infanticide and prenatal sex selection.[108]

V. SPECIFIC WOMEN CENTRIC LEGISLATIVE FRAMEWORK OF RIGHT TO HEALTH IN INDIA

Along with the international framework for securing the right to health, there are certain legislations in India that are women health-centric. The Constitution of India under Article 15(3) permits the legislatures to make special laws for the benefit of women and accordingly legislatures have enacted numerous laws for protecting various rights of women including the right to health.

A. Abortion and Ethical Issues of Women Rights

Abortion is a medico-legal issue that is overshadowed and shrugged with glaring questions of morality, infanticide, suicide, ethics, religious

---

[107] *KGP v. PKP*, 2020 (2) A.B.R. 431.

[108] *Supra* note 33.

beliefs and women's rights. Apart from these, the sex composition of living children, women's autonomy, urban residence, couple's education, and wealth status were found to be significantly associated with the experience of abortion among women.[109] Thus, to what extent, abortion should be permitted, encouraged, restricted is a socio-legal issue that has effectively divided theologians, philosophers, legislators and the general mass. The laws dealing with this delicate sphere of the woman's autonomy reflect immensely on the plight of women in the society and encompass emotive and poignant sets of views making it a mammoth task for the legislators to ensure every aspect of this medico-legal subject.[110] At the early stage of the 20th century, abortion was illegal in almost every country of the world. Indeed, it appears that China is the only country that has not placed criminal restrictions on abortion.[111] During the second half of the 20th century, however, several countries enacted laws that allowed abortion on specified grounds. In 1971, the Indian Government liberalized its abortion laws by enacting the Medical Termination of Pregnancy Act. Until then, the Indian penal code only permitted abortion if it was required to save the life of the woman.[112] Thus, these two pieces of legislation form the abortion law in India.

i. Traditional Approach to Abortion under IPC

In India, abortion primarily got its legal recognition under the Indian Penal Code, 1860[113] and this Act declares abortion as a crime. In order to save the life of women only, abortion is permissible. It is argued that this was done by keeping in view the religious, moral, social and ethical background of the Indian community[114] and to avoid causing

---

[109] Sutapa Agrawal, Determinants of Induced Abortion and Its Consequences on Women's Reproductive Health: Findings from India's National Family Health Surveys 2 (USAID 2008).

[110] *Ashaben v. State of Gujarat*, 2015 (4) Crimes 1 (Guj.).

[111] Jeanne Marecek et al., *Abortion in Legal, Social, and Healthcare Contexts*, 27(1) Fem. Psychol. 4, 5 (2017).

[112] T. Boler et al., Medical Abortion in India: A Model for the Rest of the World? 11 (Marie Stopes International 2009).

[113] Act No. XLV of 1860. It was enacted on 6 October 1860.

[114] K.D. Gaur, *Abortion and the Law in India*, 28(3) JILI 348 (1986).

injury to sentiments of the traditionally bound Indian community.[115] Thus, it can be stated that early legal recognition to abortion came from a negative point of view. This criminalizing viewpoint was in conformity with the English law of that time. Therefore, Section 312 of the Code provides:

> Whoever voluntarily causes a woman with child to miscarry, shall, if such miscarriage be not caused in good faith for the purpose of saving the life of the woman, be punished with imprisonment of either description for a term which may extend to three years, or with fine, or with both and if the woman be quick with child, shall be punished with imprisonment of either description for a term which may extend to seven years, and shall also be liable to fine.
>
> Explanation—A woman who causes herself to miscarry, is within the meaning of this section.

It is interesting to note that the abovementioned section does not contain the word 'abortion'. In contrast, the Section has used the word 'miscarriage' though it is not defined in the Code. This was perhaps done with a view to avoiding injury to sentiments of the traditional Indian community as miscarriage technically refers to spontaneous abortion and voluntarily causing miscarriage constitutes an offence under the Code.[116] Thus, in *Sushma Das v. State of Tripura*,[117] the Guwahati High Court explained the word 'miscarriage' as the premature expulsion of the child or foetus from the mother's womb at any period of pregnancy before the term of gestation is completed. Medically, three distinct terms *i.e.*, abortion, miscarriage and premature labour are used to denote the expulsion of a foetus at different stages of gestation. The term, abortion, is used only when an ovum is expelled within the first three months of pregnancy before the placenta is formed. Miscarriage is used when a foetus is expelled from the fourth to the seventh month of gestation, before it is viable, while premature labour is the delivery of a viable child possibly capable of being reared before it has become fully mature. However, in its popular sense, miscarriage is a synonym with abortion and used in

[115] *Ibid.* at 349.
[116] K.D. Gaur, *Abortion and the Law in India*, 15 CULR 123, 124 (1991).
[117] 2013(2) G.L.T. 1037.

an interchangeable manner as the foetus being regarded as 'human life from the moment of fertilization'.[118]

Further, from the language of Section 312, it is clear that voluntarily causing a miscarriage is an offence in two situations, (a) when a woman is with a child, and (b) when the woman is quick with the child. As per judicial interpretation, a woman is considered to be in the former situation as soon as gestation begins, and the second one is true when the motion is felt by the mother. The term 'quick with child' is the name applied to the peculiar sensation experienced by a woman about the 4th or 5th month of pregnancy. The first perception of 'quickening' or foetus movement occurs between 18 and 20 weeks. Thus, it obviously refers to an advanced stage of pregnancy. Taking into account the nature and gravity of the offence with regard to the age or stage of the foetus, in case of causing miscarriage when the woman is 'quick with child', that is, in advance stage of pregnancy, the Act provides severe punishment of imprisonment which may extend to seven years and fine, whereas in case of, causing miscarriage when the woman is 'with child', that is, in the early stage of pregnancy, a lesser punishment of three years imprisonment or fine or both, has been provided under the Code.[119] Moreover, a perusal of section 312 reveals that a person may be punished for causing miscarriage if the same is not caused in good faith for the purpose of saving the life of the woman.[120]

Further, Section 313 provides that, when the termination of pregnancy is caused without the consent of the woman, punishment may extend to imprisonment for life or imprisonment for a term that may extend to ten years and a fine. It is important to note that such imprisonment may be rigorous or simple in nature. According to Section 314, if the death of the woman is caused by an act done with intent to cause miscarriage with her consent then the punishment may extend to ten years of imprisonment and fine, and if it is done without her consent, punishment may extend imprisonment for life or ten years and fine.

---

[118] *Jacob George v. State of Kerala*, (1994) 3 S.C.C. 430.

[119] K.D. Gaur, *Abortion and Law in Countries of Indian Subcontinent, ASEAN Region, United Kingdom Ireland and United States of America*, 37(3) JILI 293, 296 (1995).

[120] *Nargish Paul v. State of Jharkhand*, 2015 (2) J.L.J.R. 295.

Thus, in *Surendra Chauhan v. State of M. P.*,[121] the Supreme Court held that the doctor was not competent to terminate the pregnancy of the deceased woman nor his clinic had the approval of the Government. Even basic facilities required for abortion were not available in his clinic. The petitioner took the deceased to the clinic of the doctor with the intent to cause her miscarriage and then her death was caused by the doctor while causing abortion, which act was done by the doctor in furtherance of the common intention of both the doctor and the petitioner. As a result, there is no escape from the conviction under Sections 314 read with 34 of the Code. Moreover, if an act is done with intent to prevent a child from being born alive or to cause it to die after birth then it is punishable with imprisonment that may extend to ten years or fine, or both.[122] Again Section 316 states that 'whoever does any act under such circumstances that if he thereby caused death he would be guilty of culpable homicide, and does by such act cause the death of a quick unborn child, shall be punished with imprisonment of either description for a term which may extend to ten years, and shall also be liable to fine'. Thus, in *Dal Chand v. State of Haryana*,[123] the Punjab and Haryana High Court clarified the application of Section 316 and held that from the perusal of Section 316 the Code, it reveals that this Section is attracted only when by the act of the accused, death of a quick unborn child is caused. These legal provisions are very strict in terms of punishment, but these are very difficult to implement, due to lack of evidence and non-availability of witnesses.[124]

ii. Medical Termination of Pregnancy Act, 1971

a. Background of the Act

As the traditional law has made medical termination of pregnancy a Penal offence, there was always a tendency to breach these provisions rather than honoured it. As a result, a large number of women

---

[121] A.I.R. 2000 S.C. 1436.

[122] IPC 1860, Section 315.

[123] 2011 (3) R.C.R. (Criminal) 173.

[124] Mukesh Yadav, *Medical Termination of Pregnancy (Amendment) Act, 2002 An Answer to Mother's Health and 'Female Foeticide'*, 27(1) JIAFM 46, 48 (2005).

died attempting illegal abortions. To address this issue, the Central Government constituted a Committee known as the 'Abortion Study Committee'. By highlighting the real status of abortion in India the Committee submitted its report in December 1966. The committee further pointed out that[125]:

> It is felt, that legalising abortions with a view of obtaining demographic results is unpractical and may even defeat the constructive and positive practice of family planning through contraception.

Based upon that report and after inviting objections and suggestions, subsequently, the Medical Termination of Pregnancy Act (MTP Act) was enacted in 1971.[126] India was one of the progressive countries to pass legislation for combating illegal abortions. It is very progressive legislation towards realizing the reproductive rights of women.[127] The MTP Act provides the legal method of abortion by registered medical practitioners under certain specified circumstances.[128] It is enacted by considering the Abortion Act, 1967 of the United Kingdom as model legislation.[129] As a whole, this is a liberal law that enables registered medical practitioners to terminate a pregnancy for social and socio-medical reasons and saves women from 'inflicted pregnancy' and 'forced motherhood'.[130] Thus, by citing *Suchita Srivastava v. Chandigarh Administration*,[131] in *Suresh Kumar Koushal v. NAZ Foundation*,[132] the Supreme Court observed that the legislative intent was to provide a qualified 'right to abortion' and the termination of pregnancy has never been recognized as a normal recourse for expecting mothers.

---

[125] Bhavish Gupta & Meenu Gupta, *The Socio-Cultural Aspect of Abortion in India: Law, Ethics and Practise*, 2 ILI L. REV. 140, 144 (2016).

[126] Act No. XXXIV of 1971. It was enacted on 10 August 1971.

[127] Singh, *supra* note 4, at 51.

[128] MTP Act 1971, Preamble.

[129] Joseph Minattu, *Medical Termination of Pregnancy and Conscientious Objection*, 16(4) JILI 704 (1974).

[130] Memchoubi Phanjoubam, *Proposed Amendments in the Medical Termination of Pregnancy Act in a Nutshell*, 31(1) J. MED. SOC. 1 (2017).

[131] A.I.R. 2010 S.C. 235.

[132] A.I.R. 2014 S.C. 563.

The objects of this Act are (a) to eliminate the high incidence of illegal abortions, (b) to confer on the woman the right to privacy, which includes the right to space and limit pregnancies,[133] (c) to confer on the woman the right to decide about her own body, and (d) to encourage a reduction in the rate of population growth by permitting termination of unwanted pregnancy of a married woman on the ground that a contraceptive device failed.

b. When Pregnancy May Be Terminated?

The MTP Act provides that a pregnancy may be terminated (a) with the satisfaction of one registered medical practitioner regarding the preconditions in case the length of the pregnancy does not exceed twelve weeks, and (b) with the satisfaction of two registered medical practitioners regarding the preconditions in case the length of the pregnancy exceeds twelve weeks but does not exceed twenty weeks. In both these cases abortion can only be done when the opinion, formed in good faith, confirms that (a) the continuance of the pregnancy would involve a risk to the life of the pregnant woman or of grave injury to her physical or mental health, or (b) there is a substantial risk that if the child were born, it would suffer from such physical or mental abnormalities as to be seriously handicapped.[134] By explaining this provision in Z v. the *State of Bihar*,[135] the Supreme Court held that ordinarily a pregnancy can be terminated only when a medical practitioner is satisfied that a continuance of the pregnancy would involve risk to the life of the pregnant woman or of grave injury to her physical or mental health or when there is a substantial risk that if the child born, there is a high chance that it would suffer from such physical or mental abnormalities as to be seriously handicapped. While the satisfaction of one medical practitioner is required for terminating a pregnancy within twelve weeks of the gestation period, two medical

---

[133] The US Supreme Court in two landmark decisions, *Roe v. Wade*, 41 U.S.L.W. 4233 (1973), and *Deo v. Bolton*, 41 U.S.L.W. 4233 (1973), has upheld the right of a woman to an abortion for the first three months of pregnancy as being an element in the right of privacy given by the Fourteenth Amendment of the US Constitution.

[134] MTP Act 1971, Section 3(2).

[135] A.I.R. 2017 S.C. 3908.

practitioners must be satisfied with either of these grounds in order to terminate a pregnancy between twelve to twenty weeks of the gestation period. Therefore, from the literary analysis of this Section, it is clear that it provides certain limitations to the induced abortion services. Moreover, a bare reading also would show that a medical practitioner would be punished under the penal section only when there is reliable evidence that the medical practitioner had terminated a pregnancy violating the provisions thereof and mere agrees to do abortion is not an offence.[136] Thus, it provides all kinds of protection to medical practitioners and allows them to perform termination of pregnancy within the purview of the 1971 Act. Moreover, Section 3(2) also specified the time i.e. maximum up to twenty weeks within which pregnancy can be terminated under the abovementioned circumstances. Thus, in *Chandrakant Jayantilal Suthar v.* the *State of Gujarat*,[137] the Gujarat High Court specifically stated that there is nothing in Section 3 of the MTP Act which provides for the termination of a pregnancy, where the length of pregnancy exceeds twenty weeks. If the Legislature had intended so, it would have been so enacted. Section 3 of the MTP Act is a clear-cut provision of law that specifically provides for the termination of a pregnancy, clearly specifying the length of such pregnancy, not exceeding twenty weeks. However, the provision has been criticized for its 'doctor-centric approach' where the medical practitioner has a greater role than the woman in deciding the question of abortion. Further, Explanations I and II describe two occasions that can be constituted as a grave injury to the mental health of the pregnant woman. Thus, Explanation I states 'Where any pregnancy is alleged by the pregnant woman to have been caused by rape, the anguish caused by such pregnancy shall be presumed to constitute a grave injury to the mental health of the pregnant woman' and Explanation II states

> Where any pregnancy occurs as a result of the failure of any device or method used by any married woman or her husband for the purpose of limiting the number of children, the anguish caused by such unwanted pregnancy may be presumed to constitute a grave injury to the mental health of the pregnant woman.

[136] *Sushma Trivedi v. State of M. P.*, 2018 (I) M.P.J.R. (SC) 219.

[137] 2016 (4) R.C.R. (Criminal) 876.

Thus, by explaining the relevance of mental injury of women in continuation of pregnancy in *Ayesha Khatoon v. Union of India*,[138] the Bombay High Court observed:

> [T]he freedom of a pregnant woman of making choice of reproduction which is integral part of 'personal liberty', whether to continue with the pregnancy or otherwise cannot be taken away. It shall also be taken into consideration that besides physical injury, the legislature has widened the scope of the termination of pregnancy by including 'an injury' to mental health of the pregnant woman. Thus, if continuance of pregnancy is harmful to the mental health of a pregnant woman, then that is a good and legal ground to allow termination of pregnancy if all the conditions incorporated in legal provision are met.

Moreover, Explanation II described 'unwanted pregnancy' as a ground of injury to the mental health of the pregnant woman. The Bombay High Court in *High Court on Its Own Motion v. State of Maharashtra*,[139] explained the reason for considering 'unwanted pregnancy' as a ground of abortion and held that a woman irrespective of her marital status can be pregnant either by choice or it can be an unwanted pregnancy. To be pregnant is a natural phenomenon for which woman and man both are responsible. Wanted pregnancy is shared equally, however, when it is an accident or unwanted, then the man may not be there to share the burden but it may only be the woman on whom the burden falls. Under such circumstances, a question arises why only a woman should suffer. There are social, financial and other aspects immediately attached to the pregnancy of the woman and if pregnancy is unwanted, it can have serious repercussions. It undoubtedly affects her mental health. The lawmakers have taken care of the helpless plight of a woman and have enacted Section 3(2)(b)(i) by incorporating the words 'grave injury to her mental health'. It is mandatory for the registered medical practitioner while forming an opinion regarding the necessity of termination of pregnancy to take into account whether it is injurious to the physical or mental health of that particular woman. While

---

[138] 2018 (3) Bom C.R. 399.

[139] 2017 Cri. L.J. 218.

doing so, the woman's actual or reasonably foreseeable environment may be taken into account.[140]

c. Consent Mechanism and Women Autonomy

Autonomy and the right to informed consent are considered fundamental ethical principles in providing reproductive health services.[141] The MTP Act also puts importance on the consent of the woman or her guardian in case the woman is below 18 years of age or mentally ill. Thus, Section 3(4) states that

> (a) no pregnancy of a woman, who has not attained the age of eighteen years, or, who, having attained the age of eighteen years, is a mentally ill person, shall be terminated except with the consent in writing of her guardian, (b) no pregnancy shall be terminated except with the consent of the pregnant woman.

Therefore, in *X v. State (N.C.T. of Delhi)*,[142] the Delhi High Court observed that a plain reading of provision in the MTP Act clearly indicates that consent is an essential condition for performing an abortion on a woman who has attained the age of majority and does not suffer any mental illness. The Explanations to Section 3 have contemplated the termination of pregnancy when the same is the result of a rape or a failure of birth control methods since both of these eventualities have been equated with a 'grave injury to the mental health' of a woman. In such circumstances, consent of the pregnant woman is an essential requirement for proceeding with the termination of the pregnancy under Section 3 of the Act.[143] It is also important to note that the MTP Act does not fix any importance to the express or implied consent of the husband. The woman is the best judge and is to see whether she wants to continue the pregnancy or to get it aborted.[144] Hence, the

---

[140] MTP Act 1971, Section 3(3).

[141] Rajalakshmi, *Reducing Reproductive Rights: Spousal Consent for Abortion and Sterilisation*, 4(3) IJME 102, 102 (2007).

[142] 2013 (2) J.C.C. 1068.

[143] *X v. State*, 2013 (2) R.C.R. (Criminal) 430.

[144] *Mangla Dogra v. Anil Kumar Malhotra*, 2012 (2) J.C.C. 1440.

consent of the woman is enough to do the abortion procedure by the registered medical practitioner.

Any dilution of this requirement of consent would amount to an arbitrary and unreasonable restriction on the reproductive rights of the woman. There is a high chance that if dilution is permitted then it is liable to be misused in our society where sex-selective abortion is a pervasive social evil.[145] The only exception is found in Section 5(1) of the MTP Act which permits a registered medical practitioner to proceed with a termination of pregnancy when he or she is of an opinion formed in good faith that the same is 'immediately necessary to save the life of the pregnant woman'. Thus, Section 5 of the MTP Act carves out an exception for carrying out the termination of pregnancy required immediately to save the life of the pregnant women irrespective of the length of pregnancy. The opinion in good faith can be made even by a single doctor too. It strictly restricts to the cases where the life of the pregnant woman would be in danger and does not refer to any other circumstances.[146] However, from the detailed analysis of Section 3 certain specific questions have been raised time and again: (a) whether the husband's consent is required in cases of abortion of the married women? and (b) how far the consent of the guardian is important in the case of a mentally retarded major pregnant woman?

Husband's Consent and Its Importance in Abortion: The importance of consent of the husband in the case of abortion of a married woman is always a question that has been linked with marital rights and grounds of divorce. Studies have shown that the insistence on a husband's consent often prevents women from accessing safe abortions. Therefore, the question arises whether a woman can terminate her pregnancy without the consent and against the wishes of her husband and if so, whether such actions on her part would amount to cruelty under Section 13(1)(ia) of the Hindu Marriage Act, 1956 and would entitle the aggrieved husband to obtain a decree of divorce against her. This question came for consideration in *Satya v. Sri Ram*,[147]

---

[145] *Janak Ramsang Kanzariya v. State of Gujarat*, 2011 Cri. L.J. 1306.

[146] *Suchita Srivastava v. Chandigarh Administration*, A.I.R. 2010 S.C. 235.

[147] A.I.R. 1983 P and H 252. Manisha Gupte et al., *Abortion Needs of Women in India: A Case Study of Rural Maharashtra*, 5(9) RHM 77, 78 (1997).

in which the Punjab and Haryana High Court by citing *Forbes v. Forbes*,[148] observed that:

> [I]f a wife deliberately and consistently refuses to satisfy her husband's natural and legitimate craving to have children, and the deprivation reduces him to despair and affects his mental health, the wife is guilty of cruelty.

Further, the Delhi High Court in *Deepak Kumar Arora v. Sampuran Arora*,[149] observed that if a wife undergoes an abortion with a view to spite the husband then it may in certain circumstances, be contended that the act of getting herself aborted has resulted in an act of cruelty. Further, the Supreme Court also added confusion to consent requirements in *Samar Ghosh v. Jaya Ghosh*,[150] by declaring that when a wife terminates a pregnancy without her husband's knowledge or consent, it may amount to mental cruelty and recognized it as a ground for divorce. While this judgment does not have any impact upon the requirement of consent to perform an abortion, it does assume a spousal 'stake' in a woman's reproductive health. Further, it is important to note that this decision does not create a requirement for spousal consent under the MTP Act. Thus, in *Dr. Mangla Dogra v. Anil Kumar Malhotra*,[151] the Punjab and Haryana High Court, by applying the MTP Act, held that the right of a woman to give birth to a child is a personal right and the husband has no right to compel her wife to give birth to a child. No doubt the judicial precedents are there, where the courts have considered the termination of pregnancy by the wife as mental cruelty and gave divorce to the husband on this ground; however, that was done by the Courts by considering the unique facts and circumstances of those cases. The Punjab and Haryana High Court also highlights that nobody can interfere in the personal decision of the wife to carry on her pregnancy or to abort her pregnancy. The woman does not act as a machine in which raw material is put and a finished product comes out. The woman should be mentally prepared to conceive, to continue with the same and to give birth to a child.

---

[148] (1955) 2 All E.R. 3111.

[149] (1983) 1 D.M.C. 182.

[150] (2007) 4 S.C.C. 511.

[151] 2012 (1) R.C.R. (Civil) 976.

Thus, unwanted pregnancy would naturally affect the mental health of pregnant women. The Court further observed that:

> The Medical Termination of Pregnancy Act 1971 does not empower the husband, far less his relations, to prevent the concerned woman from causing abortion if her case is covered under section 3 of that Act.

Guardian Consent and Its Importance in Abortion of Mentally Ill Women: Another important aspect of Abortion is the aspect of guardian's consent in cases of abortion of mentally ill women. By analysing this aspect, in *Chandigarh Administration v. Nemo*,[152] the Punjab and Haryana High Court observed that since the expression 'mentally ill person' does not include a person who is in need of treatment by reason of mental retardation, the purposive construction of Section 3(4)(a) of the MTP Act cannot be stretched to include 'mentally retarded persons' also. It means that ordinarily, a mentally retarded pregnant woman who is more than eighteen years of age has a right of self-determination regarding the continuation or otherwise of her pregnancy. This literal interpretation completely falls short of achieving the legislative object of not only the MTP Act; it may also tinker with the object of the UN Declaration on the Rights of the Mentally Retarded Persons. As the object of the MTP Act is to permit the termination of pregnancy on humanitarian grounds when it is caused by a sex crime like rape or intercourse with a lunatic woman any interpretation with regard to that end should always lean towards liberalizing medical termination of pregnancy.[153] Thus, the Court declined to accept the interpretation of Section 3(4) of the MTP Act that in the case of a mentally retarded major pregnant woman, the medical termination of her pregnancy shall always depend upon her own decision, rather preferred to appoint a guardian in case of mentally retarded major pregnant woman also to uphold her benefit in true sense. The Court observed that the exclusion of mentally retarded persons from the category of mentally ill persons under the MTP Act is not absolute in the sense. Hence, the Court finally held that:

---

[152] 2009 (3) R.C.R. (Civil) 766.

[153] R.V. Kelkar, *Impact of The Medical Termination of Pregnancy Act, 1971: A Case Study*, 16(4) JILI 593 (1974).

[N]otwithstanding the plain and literal meaning of sub-section [4] of Section 3 of the 1971 Act, every Court while exercising its parents-patriae jurisdiction is competent to act or appoint guardian ad-litem of a mentally retarded major pregnant woman for the purpose of deciding the retention or termination of her pregnancy in her best interest, though depending upon the individual facts and circumstances of each case. Such a guardian may consult or seek consent of the pregnant woman concerned for the purpose of formation of his final decision as to whether or not the pregnancy be medically terminated.

d. Place Where Pregnancy May Be Terminated

According to Section 4 of the MTP Act pregnancy can be terminated: (a) in a hospital established or maintained by Government, and (b) in any other place as approved by the Government or a District Level Committee constituted by the Government.

e. Defence Available to the Medical Practitioners

In the case where termination of pregnancy is immediately necessary to save the life of the pregnant woman, the MTP Act permits the medical practitioners to terminate the pregnancy even though that is in contravention to Section Sections 3(2) and 4. However, it is required that medical practitioners should perform such termination under the opinion which is formed in good faith. Thus, in *X v. Union of India*,[154] the Supreme Court after considering the provisions of Section 5 of the MTP Act, permitted termination of pregnancy through the duration of pregnancy twenty-three to twenty-four weeks and observed that Section 3 leaves no room for doubt that it is not permissible to terminate the pregnancy after twenty weeks, however, Section 5 of the Act lays down an exception to Section 3. Therefore, it must be noted that Section 5 of the Act is not controlled by the limitation in respect of the duration of pregnancy contained in Sections 3 and 4 of the Act. If in the opinion of medical experts, formed in good faith, the termination of pregnancy is immediately necessary to save the life of the pregnant woman, such a pregnancy can be terminated.[155]

---

154 A.I.R. 2016 S.C. 3525.

155 *X v. Union of India*, 2018 (5) ALLMR 245.

B. The Pre-conception and Pre-natal Diagnostic Techniques (Prohibition of Sex Selection) Act, 1994

i. Background of the Act

The advancement in medical science and technology with regard to the prenatal sex determination technique has been widely and grossly misused rather than abused in the Indian orthodox and conservative society. Even in the 21st century the blessing of a female baby hardly brings cordial happiness in the majority of Indian families. As a result, to date, the prenatal sex determination technique is used by many in a negative way to kill the female foetus in the mother's womb. This Hippocratic procedure of killing the female child is popularly known as female infanticide.[156] This evil practice had been prohibited in the pre-independence period, however, that Act sadly remained toothless with few or no convictions under the law. Certain specific provisions were also included in the Indian Penal Code which provides punishment for causing miscarriage and other like offences but unfortunately, these provisions were rarely resorted to. Apart from this, the first legislative initiative was taken with the enactment of the Female Infanticide Prevention Act, 1870.[157] With the rise of prenatal diagnostic techniques, especially amniocentesis, the Government in 1978 issued a directive banning the misuse of amniocentesis in Government hospitals or laboratories. Thereafter, due to the relentless efforts of activists, a law to prevent sex determination tests, known as the Maharashtra Regulation of Pre-natal Diagnostic Techniques Act, 1988 was passed in Maharashtra.[158] Finally, to form the Central legislation, the Pre-natal Diagnostic Techniques (Regulation and Prevention of Misuse) Bill, 1991 was introduced in the Lok Sabha.

---

[156] S.C. Tripathi & Vibha Arora, Law Relating to Women and Children 331 (Central Law Publications 2015).

[157] Upma Gautam & Deeksha B. Tewari, *Equal Right to Life for 'Never Born' and Pre-Conception and Prenatal Diagnostic Act in India: Mapping the Regional Disparities and Socio - Economic Correlates*, 2 (Winter Issue) ILI L. Rev. 180, 194 (2019).

[158] R.P. Kataria & S.K.P. Sriniwas, The Pre-Conception and Pre-Natal Diagnostic Techniques (Prohibition of Sex Selection) Act, 1994 35 (Orient Publishing 2016).

The Parliament after deliberations adopted a motion for reference of the said Bill to a Joint Committee of both the Houses of Parliament in September 1991. Ultimately, the Parliament passed the Pre-Natal Diagnostic Techniques (Regulation and Prevention of Misuse) (PNDT) Act in 1994[159] which came into force on January 1, 1996. By highlighting the background of the PNDT Act, in *Saksham Foundation Charitable Society v. Union of India*,[160] the Allahabad High Court observed:

> The enactment of the legislation is to prevent the use of pre-natal diagnostic techniques which were being and continue to be misused for sex determination. The rapid decline in the ratio of females to the male population is widely attributed to the prevalent practice of sex selection. The prevalence of female foeticide constitutes the most egregious violation of human rights in our society. The Act has been enacted in this background.

Ultimately in 2003, the PNDT was amended to the Pre-Conception and Pre-Natal Diagnostic Techniques (Prohibition of Sex Selection) Act (PCPNDT Act) to improve the regulation with regard to the technology used in sex selection.[161] The amendments have brought techniques of preconception sex selection within the ambit of the Act and have also brought the use of ultrasound machines under its umbrella.[162] As a result, now the Act proposes to control the use of these selection techniques both prior to conception as well as its misuse after conception.[163]

ii. Objective Scheme of the Act

The PCPNDT Act was enacted to prohibit sex selection, before or after conception, and to regulate the use of prenatal diagnostic techniques for the purposes of detecting anyone the genetic abnormalities, chromosomal abnormalities, metabolic disorders, certain congenital malformations, sex-linked disorders and for the prevention of their

---

[159] Act No. LVII of 1994. It was enacted on 20 September 1994.

[160] 2015 1 A.W.C. 574 All.

[161] Amended through Amendment Act 14 of 2003.

[162] *Supra* note 33.

[163] *District Appropriate Authority v. Prakash Patel*, (2013) 3 G.L.R. 1881.

misuse for sex determination leading to female foeticide. By stating that Pre-natal diagnostic techniques include prenatal diagnostic tests and prenatal diagnostic procedures,[164] the Allahabad High Court in *Anil Kumar Mishra v. State of U.P.*[165] observed that procedures are defined as all gynaecological or obstetrical or medical procedures such as ultrasonography, fetoscopy, taking or removing samples of amniotic fluid, chorionic villi, embryo blood or any other tissue or fluid of a man, or of a woman, before or after conception, for being sent to a Genetic Laboratory or Genetic Clinic for conducting any type of analysis or prenatal diagnostic tests for selection of sex before or after conception. Tests are defined as ultrasonography or any test or analysis of amniotic fluid, chorionic villi, blood or any tissue or fluid of a pregnant woman or conceptus conducted to detect genetic or metabolic disorders or chromosomal abnormalities or congenital anomalies or haemoglobinopathies or sex-linked disease.

Thus, 'sex-section' includes any procedure, technique, test or administration or prescription or provision of anything for the purpose of ensuring or increasing the probability that an embryo will be of a particular sex. Further, when any diagnostic technique is used against the female sex, it affects the dignity and status of the woman. The PCPNDT Act prescribes that no qualified person shall conduct or cause any prenatal diagnostic technique, to be conducted in any place other than a place registered under this Act. Henceforth, the PCPNDT Act provides the modes of using the techniques and also the regularization for using such techniques. The diagnosis is possible only under certain conditions and only by registered institutions. Punishment is provided for violation of these provisions.[166]

iii. Regulation of Genetic Counselling Centres

Section 3 of the PCPNDT Act prevents the Genetic Counselling Centre, Genetic Laboratory or Genetic Clinic from conducting or associating

---

[164] PCPNDT Act 1994, Section 2(j).

[165] 2011 (4) A.D.J. 672.

[166] *Saraswati v. State of Maharashtra*, 2013 (6) A.B.R. 398.

with any activities relating to prenatal diagnostic techniques unless that Centre or Clinic is registered under this Act. Moreover, the Act also prevents the Centres or Clinics from employing any person who does not possess the necessary qualifications as required for conducting prenatal diagnostic techniques. In addition to this preventive approach, the Act also barred the medical geneticist, gynaecologist, paediatrician, registered medical practitioner or any other person from conducting or aiding in conducting any prenatal diagnostic techniques at a place other than a place registered under this Act.

iv. Prohibition of Sex Selection

In terms of newly added Section 3-A,[167] sex selection on a woman or a man or both or on any tissue, embryo, conceptus, fluid or gametes derived from either or both of them is prohibited. This Section has given a wide meaning to sex selection. Sex selection includes not only the determination of sex but also includes anything done from fertilization until birth, which increases the probability that the embryo will be of a particular sex. Thus, the term 'sex selection' is not confined to the determination of the sex of the foetus. The PCPNDT Act also prohibits the sale of an ultrasound machine or imaging machine or scanner to any Genetic Counselling Centre, Genetic Laboratory, Genetic Clinic or any other person not registered under the Act.[168] In *A. A. Usman v. State of Chhattisgarh*,[169] the Chhattisgarh High Court by judging the relevance of the abovementioned provision held that the fact that Section 3-B inserted by Amendment Act 14 of 2003 puts the bar on sale of an ultrasound machine or other machines which are capable of detecting sex of the foetus to any genetic clinic or any other place or to any person not registered under the Act itself should be sufficient to hold the object of the Act, which prohibits the sex determination at the inception and source.

---

[167] Inserted by Pre- Natal Diagnostic Techniques (Regulation and Prevention of Misuse) Amendment Act, 2002, Section 6 (w.e.f. 14.2.2003).

[168] PCPNDT Act1994, Section 3-B.

[169] 2016 (1) C.G.L.J. 148.

v. Regulation of Prenatal Diagnostic Techniques

The 1994 Act also provides the purposes for which prenatal diagnostic techniques can be conducted. The Act specifies that for the purposes of detection of (a) chromosomal abnormalities, (b) genetic metabolic diseases, (c) haemoglobinopathies, (d) sex-linked genetic diseases, (e) congenital anomalies, (f) any other abnormalities or diseases as may be specified by the Central Supervisory Board, prenatal diagnostic techniques can be conducted.[170] Further, the 1994 Act also prescribes the required preconditions of conducting prenatal diagnostic techniques for the detection of the abovementioned abnormalities. Thus, Section 4(3) states:

> No pre-natal diagnostic techniques shall be used or conducted unless the person qualified to do so is satisfied for reasons to be recorded in writing that any of the following conditions are fulfilled, namely:- (i) age of the pregnant woman is above thirty-five years; (ii) the pregnant woman has undergone two or more spontaneous abortions or foetal loss; (iii) the pregnant woman had been exposed to potentially teratogenic agents such as drugs, radiation, infection or chemicals; (iv) the pregnant woman or her spouse has a family history of mental retardation or physical deformities such as, spasticity or any other genetic disease; (v) any other condition as may be specified by the Board.

Thus, in the absence of fulfilment of the aforesaid conditions and in the absence of abnormality no similar test, which can be used for determining the sex of the foetus, can be performed. However, the Act has not clarified the term 'person qualified to do as mentioned in Section 4(3). Under the Act, through its rulemaking power, the Central government has the authority to specify minimum qualifications for persons to be employed at genetic counselling centres, laboratories and clinics. Thus, the specification of qualifications should be read in a purposive sense which will fulfil the object of the law.[171] It includes the power to prescribe training. The training would sensitize the person concerned to the salutary object and purpose of the legislation which has been enacted by Parliament to deal with a serious social evil

---

[170] PCPNDT Act 1994, Section 4(2).

[171] *Union of India v. Indian Radiological and Imaging Association*, A.I.R. 2018 S.C. 1422.

and be conscious of the misuse of sex-selection tests. Moreover, the person conducting ultrasonography on a pregnant woman has a duty to keep a complete record thereof in the clinic. No encouragement to perform a sex-selection procedure from the relatives should be entertained by the medical practitioner. In case of any contravention in record keeping, the onus of proving not guilty is on the radiologist or the sonologist and not on the authorities. This provision is similar to cases related to dowry or rape where the accused has to prove that he is not guilty. In other criminal cases, the prosecution has to prove that the accused is guilty.[172]

vi. Consent of Pregnant Woman

The consent of women and its implication on the procedure of sex selection is provided under Section 5 which specifies a duty on the registration holder or the Doctor conducting sonography at the hospital to obtain written consent in the language which she understands.[173] According to Section 5, the prenatal diagnostic procedure can be conducted only where all known side and after-effects of such procedures have been explained to the woman and her consent is obtained in writing in the language that she understands and a copy of the written consent so obtained is given to her. The consent of the woman has to be obtained in Form G. A translated version of this form should be available in all local languages. If it is not available, then the clinic has a duty to make a translated version available.[174] The Act also further states that no person should communicate the sex of the foetus to the pregnant woman or her relatives or any other person by words, signs or in any other manner.[175] This Section clearly prohibits communication to anyone, which will also include the physician of the pregnant woman or anyone else. Further, displaying photographs of Gods and Goddesses in the room where prenatal diagnostic procedures

---

[172] Prashant Onkar & Kajal Mitra, *Important Points in the PC-PNDT Act*, 22(2) IJRI 141 (2012).

[173] *Amita R. Patel v. State of Gujarat*, 2009 G.L.H. (1) 584.

[174] ANUBHA RASTOGI, THE LITTLE HANDBOOK ON PC AND PNDT 14 (HRLN 2006).

[175] PCPNDT Act 1994, Section 5(2).

are conducted is not permissible, as the same gives the opportunity to convey the sex of the foetus by signs or in other manners.[176] Sub-section (2) of Section 5 of the Act consequently contains a whole-some prohibition to the effect that no person shall communicate to a pregnant woman or her relatives or to any other person the sex of the foetus in any manner whatsoever including while conducting prenatal diagnostic procedures.

vii. Prohibition of Determination of Sex

Section 6 strictly prohibits the determination of sex. It states that no place should be used to conduct any prenatal diagnostic procedure for the purpose of determining the sex of the foetus. It further lays down that no prenatal diagnostic procedure will be used to determine the sex of the foetus and finally it lays down that no person shall cause or allow to be caused sex selection before or after conception.[177] Thus, in *Kalpesh J. Patel v. State of Gujarat*,[178] the Gujarat High Court observed that Section 6 provides that no prenatal diagnostic techniques, including Sonography, can be conducted for the purpose of determining the sex of the foetus and that no person shall conduct or cause to be conducted any prenatal diagnostic techniques including ultrasonography for the purpose of determining the sex of a foetus. No doubt the bare perusal of the Act indicates that it is a draconic Act from the point of its effect on radiologists or sonologists. The Act does not offer any escape to the erring radiologist or sonologist. Section 10(1A) casts mandatory duty that radiologist or sonologist shall give a declaration on each report on ultrasonography or image scanning that he or she has neither detected nor disclosed the sex of the foetus to anybody and even the pregnant women before undergoing ultrasonography/image scanning has to declare that she does not want to know the sex of her foetus. Thus maintenance and preservation of records and conditions

[176] *Dattatraya v. State of Maharashtra*, 2014 ALLMR (Cri) 3977.

[177] *Saksham Foundation Charitable Society v. Union of India*, 2015 (1) R.C.R. (Criminal) 404.

[178] MANU/GJ/0994/2011.

for conducting prenatal diagnostic procedures are absolutely mandatory in nature.[179]

VI. CONCEPTUAL ORIENTATION OF CHILD'S RIGHT TO HEALTH

Childhood transcends all nationalities and it has no artificial boundaries. While the right to health is regarded as part of human rights and applicable to all, children constitute the most neglected segment having been denied adequate realization of the right to health. One of the reasons behind the negligence towards child health is the lack of control over adverse health events, sanitation and the environment. They are totally dependent upon adults for their needs. The betterment of children is firmly rooted in the social, political, economic, cultural and environmental determinants of health.[180] Under the legal framework, in case of lack of adequate parental care, the State must be responsible to provide medical care by making child-centric policies and sufficient allocation of funds. Moreover, the family as the fundamental group of society plays a substantial role in nurturing children and it provides the required environment for the growth and well-being of all its members and particularly to the children. Thus, children should get necessary preconditions and assistance for the harmonious development of their personalities.[181] The nutritional aspect is another important sphere that has a direct implication on the health of children. Every year the lives of around 50 million children are put at risk as they are dangerously thin and suffering from acute undernutrition, while the long-term health of more than 40 million children is threatened because they are suffering from obesity.[182] Moreover, the provision of proper sanitation is also important in the

---

[179] *Amita R. Patel v. State of Gujarat*, 2009 G.L.H. (1) 584.

[180] Jeffrey Goldhagen & Raul Mercer, *Child Health Equity: From Theory to Reality*, in The Human Rights of Children: From Visions to Implementation 307–326, 307 (Antonella Invernizzi ed, Ashgate Publishing 2011).

[181] Bhupinder Singh, Child Health Law 35 (Satyam Law International 2016).

[182] Francesco Branca et al., *Nutrition and Health in Women, Children, and Adolescent Girls*, 351(Suppl 1) BMJ 27 (2015).

protection of the health of children. The right to health of children, thus, includes (a) promotion of healthy lives by addressing survival, nutrition, health care services, (b) provision for quality education, and (c) protection against abuse, exploitation and violence by combating child labour, child trafficking and sexual abasement of the child.[183]

VII. RIGHT TO HEALTH OF CHILDREN UNDER CHILD-CENTRIC INTERNATIONAL INSTRUMENTS

The international human rights framework is very much concerned about the right of children from its inception. In general, various international instruments such as ICESCR 1966, MDGs 2000, Sustainable Development Goals 2015 (which are already discussed in Chapter 2) contain various provisions relating to the rights of Children in general and the right to health in particular. However, apart from these, there are certain child-centric instruments under international law that also contain various provisions relating to the right to health of the children. Among these instruments, the United Nations Convention on the Rights of the Child is the most prominent one. Thus, to understand the right to health of children within these child-centric instruments, detailed deliberation is required.

A. Convention on the Rights of the Child, 1989

The international aspiration to recognizes various human rights available to children took a concrete form with the adoption of the United Nations Convention on the Rights of the Child (CRC) on November 20, 1989.[184] It is the most widely accepted human rights treaty ever. An unprecedented 62 States signed the Convention on January 26, 1990, the day on which it opened for signatures,[185] and till date, 191

---

[183] R.N. Srivastava, *Right to Health for Children*, 52 INDIAN PEDIATR. 15–18 (2015).

[184] *Shilpa Mittal v. State of NCT of Delhi*, A.I.R. 2020 S.C. 405. India acceded to the Convention on the Rights of the Child on the 11 December 1992.

[185] In September 1990, another 20 States had ratified the Convention and it entered into force on 2 September 1990. The same month UNICEF and six countries convened the World Summit for Children in New York, which made a strong plea to all states to ratify the convention.

countries have already ratified it.[186] It brought into a single international document many of the notions formerly separated into the ICCPR and the ICESCR.[187] The substantive provisions of the CRC reflect a new way of thinking about human rights because they affirm rights that fall into all of the traditional categories -civil, political, economic, social and cultural- with no formal distinctions among these categories.[188] Thus, it addresses children's rights with respect to a vast array of issues from infant mortality and sexual exploitation to freedom of association and religion.[189] In particular, the CRC calls the State parties to take all appropriate measures to ensure that children receive special rights, including the right to access to healthcare.[190] It complemented and anchored the moral obligations with regard to children, already enshrined in the 1924 Geneva Declaration and the 1959 Declaration on the Rights of the Child, in a legally binding international human rights document. The Preamble of the CRC recognizes that in all countries around the world there are children living in exceptionally difficult conditions and thus, children need special consideration and by reason of physical and mental immaturity of a child, there is a need for special safeguards and care.[191] Article 3(3) casts a responsibility upon State parties to ensure that the institutions, services and facilities responsible for the care and protection

---

[186] Somalia and the United States are the only countries that have not ratified the Convention. *See*, Kathryn Libal et al., *The United Nations Convention on the Rights of the Child: Children Can Wait No Longer for Their Rights*, 56(4) Social Work 367 (2011); Ann Marie Pennegard & Anne Franzen, *The Convention on the Rights of the Child From Swedish Perspective*, 25(1–3) IJLI 105, 106 (1997).

[187] Susan O'Rourke, *Violence, Exploitation and Children: Highlights of the United Nations Children's Convention and International Response to Children's Human Rights*, 18 Suffolk Transnat'l L. Rev. 589–590 (1995).

[188] Lawrence J. LeBlanc, *The Convention on the Rights of the Child*, 4(2) LJIL 281, 288 (1991).

[189] Lisa Pilnik, *The United Nations Convention on the Rights of the Child and Its Implementation in Japan and Sweden*, 3(5) JILP 5.1, 5.2 (2006).

[190] The CRC was adopted by the U.N. General Assembly after a decade of negotiations on 20 November 1989, and entered into force on 2 September 1990. Currently 193 countries are party to the Convention, making it the most widely ratified human rights treaty. *See*, Luisa Blanchfield, The United Nations Convention on the Rights of the Child 2 (Congressional Research Service 2013).

[191] CRC 1989, Preamble.

of children shall conform to the standards established by competent authorities, particularly in the areas of safety, health, etc.

By highlighting the special needs of a disabled child, the CRC states that State parties shall provide assistance free of charge, taking into account the financial resources of the parents or others caring for the child and that assistance shall be designed to ensure that the disabled child has effective access to education, training, health care services, rehabilitation services, etc.[192] The participants also agreed that States parties shall promote, in the spirit of international cooperation, the exchange of appropriate information in the field of preventive health care and medical, psychological, and functional treatment of disabled children.[193] Article 24(1) of the CRC specifically recognized the right to health of the child to its fullest extent. The Article states:

> States Parties recognize the right of the child to the enjoyment of the highest attainable standard of health and to facilities for the treatment of illness and rehabilitation of health. States Parties shall strive to ensure that no child is deprived of his or her right of access to such health care services.

The CRC has explained the right to health of the child in a similar way to the Constitution of WHO explains the right to health. The CRC not only secures the right to health but also spills out obligations of State parties to adopt measures that, if implemented, will ensure the highest attainable standard of health taking into account the genetic and other biological predisposition of each child. The aims of these appropriate measures are: (a) to diminish infant and child mortality, (b) to ensure the provision of necessary medical assistance and health care to all children with an emphasis on the development of primary health care, (c) to combat disease and malnutrition by providing adequate nutritious, foods, clean drinking water and pollution-free environment, (d) to ensure appropriate prenatal and postnatal health-care for mothers, (e) to ensure that all segments of society, in particular parents and children, are informed about the requirement of access to education and are supported in the use of basic knowledge regarding

---

[192] *Ibid.* Article 23(3).

[193] *Ibid.* Article 23(4).

the advantages of breastfeeding, child health and nutrition, hygiene and environmental sanitation and the prevention of accidents, (f) to develop preventive health care, guidance for parents and family planning education and services,[194] and (g) to abolish traditional practices prejudicial to the health of children.[195]

The newborn child's biological preconditions are determined partly genetically and partly through other factors, including the conditions of the mother during pregnancy. Prenatal care is, therefore, of vital importance for the health of the child after birth.[196] To achieve these aims and for the full realization of the right to health of children, the CRC also wants to build and promote international cooperation among the State parties by giving special attention to the needs of developing nations.[197] Thus, all these provisions prescribe a set of standards to secure the best interests of the child.

B. Other International Instruments

i. Geneva Declaration of the Rights of the Child, 1924

Historically, the right of the child relating to health is another new dimension formed after the creation of the WHO and recognition of the right to health in other international instruments. The right to health, as it is generally referred to, is a right of assurance and it is more important to children than adults.[198] One of the first international attempts to recognize the right to health of children was the Geneva Declaration of the Rights of the Child, the first international children's rights document adopted by the League of Nations in 1924, while the 1989 Convention on the Rights of the Child (CRC)

---

[194] *Ibid.* Article 24(2).

[195] *Ibid.* Article 24(3).

[196] W.B. Eide & A. Eide, *A Commentary on the United Nations Convention on the Rights of the Child, Article 24: The Right to Health*, in A COMMENTARY ON THE UNITED NATIONS CONVENTION ON THE RIGHTS OF THE CHILD 9–51, 9 (A. Alen et al., eds, Nijhoff 2006).

[197] CRC 1989, Article 24(4).

[198] ELVIS M. FOKALA, IMPLEMENTING CHILDREN'S RIGHT TO PARTICIPATION IN FAMILY DECISION-MAKING PROCESSES IN AFRICA 136 (Abo Akademi University Press 2017).

is the most accepted international treaty dealing with the right of the children including right to health of the children in the global arena. The Geneva Declaration of the Rights of the Child, 1924[199] pushed social work for childhood into an official object of international cooperation.[200] It was also the first document to highlight the responsibility of adults towards children. In a similar line, Eglantyne Jebb put forward a notion of the child which required to be protected, both as a 'resource' and as an isolated 'victim'.[201] However, notably, there is no direct recognition of the right to health of the child under the Geneva Declaration of the Rights of the Child, 1924.[202] It aims to secure the development of children, both materially and spiritually.[203] Along with this, Article 2 categorically specified that 'the child who is sick must be nursed'. Thus, it assures the right to healthcare to needy children.

ii. International Code of Marketing of Breast-milk Substitutes, 1981

Subsequently, in the last part of 1978, the WHO and the United Nations Children's Fund (UNICEF) announced their intention to organize jointly a meeting on infant and young child feeding, and finally from 9 to 12 October 1979 the meeting of 150 representatives of governments and organizations under UN was held in Geneva. The discussions occurred on five main themes: (a) the encouragement and support of breastfeeding, (b) the promotion and support of appropriate and timely complementary feeding (weaning) practices with the use of local food resources, (c) the strengthening of education, training

---

[199] The League of Nations adopted the Geneva Declaration of the Rights of the Child on 26 September 1924.

[200] D. Marshall, *The Construction of Children as an Object of International Relations: The Declaration of Children's Rights and the Child Welfare Committee of League of Nations, 1900–1924*, 7(2) Int. J. Child. Rights 103, 104 (1999).

[201] Lara Bolzman, *The Advent of Child Rights on the International Scene and the Role of the Save the Children International Union 1920–45*, 27(4) Refug. Surv. Q 26, 31 (2009).

[202] Geneva Declaration was adopted on 26 September 1924.

[203] Geneva Declaration, 1924, Article 1.

and information on infant and young child feeding, (d) the promotion of the health and social status of women in relation to infant and young child health and feeding, and (e) the appropriate marketing and distribution of breast-milk substitutes.[204] This approach was taken by recognizing the failure to promote breastfeeding, which has resulted in increasing the risk of gastrointestinal disease, acute otitis media and acute lower respiratory tract infection in infancy.[205] Finally, in January 1981, the Executive Board of the WHO at its sixty-seventh session considered the fourth draft of the code, endorsed it, and accordingly on May 21, 1981, the Health Assembly adopted the International Code of Marketing of Breast-milk Substitutes to ensure the proper use of breast milk substitutes.[206] It recognizes that the health of infants and young children cannot be isolated from the health and nutrition of women, their socioeconomic status and their roles as mothers.[207] The code was based on adequate information and appropriate marketing and distribution practices.

Article 6 of the Code casts a duty upon the health authorities of the Member States for taking appropriate measures to encourage and protect breastfeeding.[208] Further, the facilities of health care systems should not be used for the display of substituted products.[209] Feeding with infant formula, whether manufactured or home-prepared, should be demonstrated only by health workers, or other community workers if necessary; and only to the mothers or family members who need to use it; and the information given should include a clear explanation of the hazards of improper use.[210]

---

[204] WHO, INTERNATIONAL CODE OF MARKETING OF BREAST-MILK SUBSTITUTES 4–5 (WHO 1981).

[205] June Pauline Brady, *Marketing Breast Milk Substitutes: Problems and Perils Throughout the World*, 97(6) ADC 529, 531 (2012).

[206] It was passed by 118 in favour votes to 1 against vote. United States casted the sole negative vote.

[207] Geneva Declaration, 1924, at 6.

[208] International Code of Marketing of Breast-milk Substitutes, Article 6.1.

[209] *Ibid*. Article 6.3.

[210] *Ibid*. Article 6.5.

iii. World Summit for Children, 1990

However, on 29–30 September 1990, World Summit for Children (WSC) [211] was held to address issues like health, nutrition, education of the children and finally adopted a Declaration on the Survival, Protection and Development of Children and a Plan of Action for the implementation of the Declaration. The WSC undertakes a joint commitment to make an urgent appeal to give every child a better future[212] and highlights various challenges that are required to be overcome. In its Declaration 6, the WSC attracts attention by stating that each day, 40,000 children die from malnutrition and disease, including AIDS, from the lack of clean water and inadequate sanitation and the effects of drug problems. In the 'Task' portion of the Declaration, the WSC assumes enhancement of children's health and nutrition by accessing the available means as the most important duty to save the child and to decrease the infant mortality rate.[213] Through Declaration 20(2), the WSC agrees to make a solid effort of national and international action to enhance children's health, to promote prenatal care and to lower infant and child mortality in all countries and among all peoples and also to secure provision for clean water and universal access to sanitation in all communities for all their children. After the CRC, the WSC gave more emphasis on the right to health of the children and expand its ambit to a large extent.

iv. Comprehensive Implementation Plan on Maternal, Infant, and Young Child Nutrition, 2012

The Comprehensive Implementation Plan on Maternal, Infant, and Young Child Nutrition, was adopted on May 26, 2012, by the 65th World Health Assembly (WHA) which includes a range of global targets for children along with the mothers. The objective was to end all forms of malnutrition which is also a critical message in the SDGs, which was adopted in 2015. Finally, in 2014, it was published by the

---

[211] The UN World Summit for Children was held in the UN Headquarters in New York City on 29–30 September 1990.

[212] World Declaration on the Survival, Protection and Development of Children, Declaration 1.

[213] *Ibid.* Declaration 10.

WHO.[214] The WHO Global Nutrition Targets were established for six malnutrition indicators to be achieved by 2025: (a) 40 per cent reduction in children younger than 5 years who are stunted, (b) 30 per cent reduction in the annual incidence of low-birth-weight, (c) no increase in childhood overweight, (d) increase rate of exclusive breastfeeding until 6 months post-partum to at least 50 per cent,[215] and (e) reduce and maintain childhood wasting to <5 per cent.[216] The full realization of these targets requires both nutrition-specific interventions, such as support for breastfeeding, and nutrition-sensitive interventions across a range of sectors. The goals aid to recognize priority areas for action and foster global change.[217] Thus, WHO put forth 5 priority actions for realization of these targets: (a) create a supportive environment for the implementation of comprehensive food and nutrition policies, (b) include all required effective health interventions with an impact on nutrition in national nutrition plans, (c) stimulate development policies and programs outside the health sector that recognize and include nutrition, (d) provide sufficient human and financial resources for the implementation of nutrition interventions, and (e) monitor and evaluate the implementation of policies and programs.

VIII. SPECIFIC CHILD-CENTRIC LEGISLATIVE FRAMEWORK OF RIGHT TO HEALTH IN INDIA

Children are the greatest asset of humanity and thus, the protection of children is one of the basic duties of every nation. In India, the importance of children as potential human resources for the future is

[214] WHO, COMPREHENSIVE IMPLEMENTATION PLAN ON MATERNAL, INFANT, AND YOUNG CHILD NUTRITION (WHO 2014).

[215] Indicators for breastfeeding practices included early initiation of breastfeeding, exclusive breastfeeding, and continued breastfeeding at 1 or 2 years in some specific cases. *See*, Tuan T. Nguyen et al., *National Nutrition Strategies That Focus on Maternal, Infant, and Young Child Nutrition in Southeast Asia Do Not Consistently Align with Regional and International Recommendations*, 12 MATERN. CHILD NUTR. 1, 5 (2019).

[216] Shelley McGuire, *World Health Organization. Comprehensive Implementation Plan on Maternal, Infant, and Young Child Nutrition. Geneva, Switzerland, 2014*, 6(1) ADV. NUTR. 134 (2015).

[217] Marianella Anzola & Jp Pena-Rosas, *World Health Organization's Global Targets on Maternal, Infant and Young Child Nutrition*, 27(1) AN VENEZ NUTR. 26 (2014).

being realized immensely and efforts have been made to strengthen child health through the enactment of various legislations. To have a clear idea about the legislative protection to the right to health of children, a detailed discussion about these legislations is required.

A. Child Labour (Prohibition and Regulation) Act, 1986

Child labour is a vital global issue linked with poverty, inadequate educational opportunities, gender inequality, and a range of health risks. Childhood is the period of rapid growth in a young person's life[218] and thus, children could be at particularly high risk of injuring their muscles and bones. To curtail that chance, employment in the hazardous sector needs to be regulated. In India, the 1986 Child Labour (Prohibition and Regulation) Act[219] was enacted to regulate the issues of child labour. It aims to prohibit the engagement of children in certain employments and to regulate the conditions of work of children in certain harmful employment. This 1986 Act repealed the Employment of Children Act of 1938. The 1986 Act intends to i) ban the employment of children, that is, those who have not completed their fourteenth year, in specified occupations and processes, ii) lay down a procedure to decide modifications to the Schedule of banned occupations or process, iii) to regulate the conditions of work of children in employments where they are not prohibited from working, iv) lay down enhanced penalties for employment of children in violation of the provisions of this Act, and other Acts which forbid the employment of children, and v) to obtain uniformity in the definition of 'child' in the related laws.[220] Thus, this Act aims to identify, prosecute and stop child labour in India.[221] Further, according to the 1986 Act 'child' means a person who has not completed his 14 years of age.[222] Section

---

[218] Kapil Goel et al., *The Social and Occupational Health Problems of Child Labour: A Challenge the World Is Facing*, 24(1) IJCH 53, 55 (2012).

[219] Act No. LXI of 1986. It was enacted on 23 December 1986.

[220] *Ramachander Rao P. v. State of A. P.*, 2006 (2) A.L.T. (Cri) 271.

[221] Niti Nagar & Bindu Roy, *A Critical Analysis of Child Labour in India*, 5(1) IJCRM 7, 16 (2017).

[222] Child Labour (Prohibition and Regulation) Act 1986, Section 2(ii).

3 prevents the employment of a child in an occupation related to transport, railways, catering establishment at a railway station or in a train, construction or port, biddi-making, carpet-making, cement factory, cloth printing, dyeing, weaving, mica-cutting and splitting, soap tanning, wood-clearing, matches, explosives and firework. The 1986 Act also stipulates that any child should not work for more than six hours per day and there should be an interval of one hour after continuous work for three hours. Moreover, he should neither be allowed to work between 7 p.m. and 8 a.m. nor allowed to do overtime.[223] The child has a right to get a weekly full-wage holiday. Further, if any establishment has children as the workers then that establishment should inform the Inspector who will inspect the conditions and nature of work and also certify the age of the child.[224]

Further, the Central Government has a duty under the Act to form a 'Child Labour Technical Advisory Committee' to felicitate the implementation of the Act. The Committee has the responsibility to advise the Central Government with regard to the requirement of adding any other occupations or processes within the ambit of the Act.[225] Thus, the 1986 Act prohibits the entry of children under the age of fourteen into hazardous occupations or processes and regulates the services of children in non-hazardous occupations to protect the health of the children.[226]

B. Infant Milk Substitutes, Feeding Bottles and Infant Foods Act, 1992

Breast Feeding is important for babies or infants to keep them healthy and also for the feeding mothers.[227] On May 21, 1981, the WHO International Code of Marketing Breast-Milk Substitutes was passed

[223] *Ibid.* Section 7.

[224] *Ibid.* Section 9.

[225] *Ibid.* Section 5.

[226] Veronica Pala, *Combating Child Labour: The Need for a Holistic Approach*, 12(2) NEHU J. 27, 32 (2014).

[227] U. Ishwarya v. Director of Medical Education, Directorate of Medical Education, 2018 (2) C.T.C. 654.

by 118 votes to 1, similar to the CRC the USA casting the sole negative vote. In parity with this, the 1992 Infant Milk Substitutes, Feeding Bottles and Infant Foods (Regulation of Production, Supply and Distribution) Act[228] was enacted in India to regulate the production, supply and distribution of infant milk substitutes, feeding bottles and infant foods and to encourage breastfeeding and ensure the proper use of infant foods. The 1992 Act defines 'infant food' as any food being marketed or represented as a complement to a mother's milk to meet the growing nutritional needs of the infant from the age of six months to two years.[229] Moreover, as per Section 2(g) 'infant milk substitute' means any food being marketed or represented as a partial or total replacement for mother's milk for an infant up to the age of two years. In *T. Johnson v. State of Kerala*,[230] the High Court of Kerala observed that from the definition itself it is clear that if any food is marketed as a partial or total replacement for mother's milk, it is an infant milk substitute. On the other hand, if any food is marketed as a complement to the mother's milk to meet the growing nutritional needs of the infant it would be infant food. In both cases, one aspect is common. The food must either be marketed or represented as a complement to the mother's milk or partial or total replacement for the mother's milk. Unless it is as a complement to or replacement, partial or total for mother's milk it will not be an infant food or infant milk substitute.

To control the use of milk substitutes and to promote breastfeeding, the 1992 Act prevents the advertisement for the distribution, sale or supply of infant milk substitutes, feeding bottles or infant foods and strictly checks the creation of impression or belief in any manner that feeding of infant milk substitutes and infant foods are equivalent to, or better than mother's milk.[231] Even the donation of infant milk substitutes or feeding bottles or infant foods to any person is also barred by the Act. Only this donation can be done to an orphanage and for

---

[228] Act No. XLI of 1992. It was enacted on 29 December 1992.

[229] Infant Milk Substitutes, Feeding Bottles and Infant Foods Act 1992, Section 2(f).

[230] 2010 Cri. L.J. 1788.

[231] *Supra* note 229, Section 3.

any specific purpose by the health care system.[232] Further Section 6 specifies that every container of infant milk substitute or infant food should indicate in a clear, conspicuous and in an easily readable and understandable manner, the words 'important notice' in capital letters in such language as may be prescribed and also indicate thereunder (a) a statement 'mother's milk is best for your baby' in capital letters, (b) a statement that infant milk substitute or infant food can be used only on the advice of a health worker, (c) a warning that infant milk substitute or infant food is not the sole source of nourishment of an infant, (d) the instructions for its appropriate preparation, (e) a warning against the health hazards of its inappropriate preparation, (f) the ingredients used, (g) conditions required for the storage, and (h) the batch number, date of its manufacture and the date before which it is to be consumed, taking into account the climatic and storage conditions of the country.

The 1992 Act also prevents the use or sale of infant milk substitutes or feeding bottles or infant foods by displaying placards or posters in any health care system. Further, only the institution or organization, engaged in health care for mothers, infants or pregnant women, has the authority to distribute infant milk substitutes or feeding bottles to a mother who does not have the resources of breastfeeding and who cannot afford to purchase infant milk substitutes or feeding bottles.[233] However, this distribution can be done only if the specific infant milk substitutes or feeding bottles or infant foods conform to the required standards specified for such substitute or food under the Food Safety and Standard Act 2006 and the container thereof has the relevant standard mark specified by the Bureau of India Standards.[234] It is important legislation to promote the benefits of breastfeeding to infants that is important for the proper physical and mental health growth of the infants and to protect the early stage of human life from chemical intakes.

---

[232] *Ibid.* Section 5.

[233] *Ibid.* Section 8.

[234] *Ibid.* Section 11.

C. Prohibition of Child Marriage Act, 2006

The 2006 Prohibition of Child Marriage Act[235] was enacted to prevent child marriage so that children can get an opportunity to develop fully before getting the responsibility of marriage in their adulthood. Child marriage is also linked with health issues as reproductive health always has a connection with marriage in Indian society and that is why there is a necessity to prevent child marriage. Thus, in *Independent Thought v. Union of India*,[236] the Supreme Court expressed its concern on the consequence of early marriage and sexual intercourse at an early age as it could have detrimental effects on the girl child not only in terms of her physical and mental health but also in terms of her nutrition and her general well-being. Carrying the burden of motherhood at an immature age shatters the health of women.[237] In early maternity, there are grave chances of foetal deformities in case of its survival and high risk is posed to the lives of the baby as well as the mother. By considering the object of the Prohibition of Child Marriage Act 2006 and the impact of early marriage on health, the Gujarat High Court in *Yunusbhai Usmanbhai Shaikh v. State of Gujarat*,[238] observed that the Act is to enhance the health of children and the status of women in the society; hence, marriage should not be performed below the age of 18 years for a girl child. Similarly, in *Court on its Own Motion (Lajja Devi) v. State*,[239] the Delhi High Court held that child marriage is such a social evil which has the potentialities of dangers to the life and health of a female child and plays havoc in their lives, who cannot withstand the stress and strains of married life and it leads to early deaths of such minor mothers. However, Section 3 of the Act provides that child marriage is voidable at the option of any one of the parties to the child marriage. Thus, child marriage is not void, but only voidable. Interestingly, even though child marriage is only void-able, Parliament has made child marriage an offence and has provided

---

[235] Act No. VI of 2007. It was enacted on 10 January 2007.

[236] A.I.R. 2017 S.C. 4904.

[237] R. Kalaivani, *Child Marriage Restraint Act (1929) - A Historical Review*, 4(1) IJHSSI 14, 17 (2015).

[238] 2016 (1) R.C.R. (Criminal) 690.

[239] 2013 Cri. L.J. 3458.

punishments for contracting a child marriage. Hence, it is quite clear from the above that Parliament is not in favour of child marriages per se but is somewhat ambivalent about it.[240] Thus, the health and development of two generations of children- the child mother and the newborn baby, suffer as a consequence of early pregnancy.[241] Thus, to prevent these ill effects the 2006 Act defines a Child as a person who, if male, has not completed 21 years of age and if a female, has not completed 18 years of age.[242] Further, the Act provides that being a male adult above eighteen years of age, if anyone contracts a child marriage shall be punishable with rigorous imprisonment which may extend to two years or with fine which may extend to one lakh rupees or with both.[243] The 2006 Act also specified rigorous imprisonment for abetting and promoting child marriage.[244] However, the 2006 Act does not make any provision for punishing a female adult who marries a male child.[245] Though this practice is very rare in Indian society, the legislative approach should consider this aspect also.

D. Juvenile Justice (Care and Protection of Children) Act, 2015

The 2015 Juvenile Justice (Care and Protection of children) Act[246] was passed by the Union legislatures for the care, protection, treatment, development and rehabilitation of neglected or delinquent juveniles, and for the adjudication of certain matters relating to it. This Act repealed the Juvenile Justice (Care and Protection of Children) Act, 2000. This 2015 Act is the result of discussions in the Chief Justice Conference held in 2006, 2009, 2013, 2015 and 2016.[247] The 2015

---

[240] *Independent Thought v. Union of India*, A.I.R. 2017 S.C. 4904.

[241] Vandana, *Child Marriage Under Hindu Personal Law: Factum Valet or An Issue for Protection of Human Rights of Women*, 1 ILI L. REV. 175, 176 (2017).

[242] Prohibition of Child Marriage Act 2006, Section 2(a).

[243] *Ibid.* Section 9.

[244] *Ibid.* Sections 10 and 11.

[245] *Hardev Singh v. Harpreet Kaur*, A.I.R. 2020 S.C. 37.

[246] Act No. II of 2016. It was enacted on 31 December 2015.

[247] *Sampurna Behura v. Union of India*, (2018) 4 S.C.C. 433.

Act defines a child as a person who has not completed eighteen years of age[248] and a juvenile as a child below the age of eighteen years.[249] From the literature of the definitions, it is clear that the child has been defined with the negative concept whereas the juvenile has been defined as a limiting concept. By explaining the importance of the definition of child with respect to the 2015 Act, the Supreme Court in *Re: Exploitation of Children in Orphanages in the State of Tamil Nadu v. Union of India*,[250] observed:

> Since the Juvenile Justice (Care and Protection of Children) Act, 2015 (JJ Act) is intended for the benefit of children and is intended to protect and foster their rights, the definition of a child in need of care and protection must be given a broad interpretation. It would be unfortunate if certain categories of children are left out of the definition, even though they need as much care and protection as categories of children specifically enlisted in the definition.

The children in need of care and protection may be placed in foster care or in a family to provide foster care. The foster family shall be responsible for providing education, health and nutrition to the child and shall ensure the overall wellbeing of the child.[251] As per Section 53, the Child Care Institution has a duty to provide rehabilitation and re-integration of children which includes (a) basic requirements such as food, shelter, clothing and medical attention as per the prescribed standards, (b) equipment such as wheel-chairs, prosthetic devices, hearing aids, braille kits, or any other suitable aids and appliances as required, for children with special needs, (c) mental health interventions, including counselling specific to the need of the child, (d) referral services for the treatment of diseases where required, (e) case management including preparation and follow up of individual care plan, and (f) birth registration along with other facilities. Further, if any child kept in homes is mentally ill or addicted to alcohol or other drugs which lead to behavioural changes in a person, then the Child Welfare Committee or the Juvenile Justice Board will remove such

---

[248] Juvenile Justice Act 2015, Section 2(12).

[249] *Ibid.* Section 2(35).

[250] A.I.R. 2017 S.C. 2546.

[251] Juvenile Justice Act 2015, Section 44(6).

child to a psychiatric hospital or psychiatric nursing home.[252] The State Government has the authority to make rules regarding the health facilities provided by the foster family.[253]

The 2015 Act also provides the constitution of the Child Welfare Committee[254] for exercising the powers and to discharge the duties conferred on such Committees in relation to children in need of care and protection under this Act and Juvenile Justice Board[255] for exercising the powers and discharging functions relating to children in conflict with law with respect to this Act. Collective responsibility for dealing with both these categories of children lies with the District Child Protection Unit. All these abovementioned three institutions are activated under the Integrated Child Protection Scheme which is a centrally sponsored scheme by the Ministry of Social Justice and Empowerment of the Government of India.[256] Thus, the Juvenile Justice (Care and Protection of Children) Act, 2015 is a medium for the State to honour the Directive Principles of State Policy particularly, Article 39(f) which provides for giving opportunities to children to develop in a healthy manner and in conditions of freedom and dignity.[257] However, the 2015 Act till now fails to attain the objective of providing a holistic environment to deter crimes among children[258] and lack of awareness and implementation is causing hindrance in the path of the Act. The 2015 Act has also ignored the concepts of victimology and restorative justice.[259]

---

[252] *Ibid.* Section 93.

[253] *Ibid.* Section 110(2)(xxviii).

[254] *Ibid.* Section 27.

[255] *Ibid.* Section 4.

[256] S. Selvi Nithya & P.B. Shankar Narayan, *Gaps and Challenges in Implementing Juvenile Justice (Care and Protection of Children) Act 2015 - A Critical Analysis*, 5(7) SIJASH 71 (2018).

[257] *Exploitation of Children in Orphanages in the State of Tamil Nadu v. Union of India*, A.I.R. 2017 S.C. 2546.

[258] Smita Agarwal & Nishant Kumar, *Juvenile Justice (Care and Protection of Children) Act 2015: A Review*, 3(3) SPACE CULT. 6, 9 (2016).

[259] Ved Kumari, *The Juvenile Justice Act 2015: Critical Understanding*, 58(1) JILI 84, 103 (2016).

Right to Health in Context of Persons with Disabilities

A healthy body is a very foundation for all human activities and this proverb is also true for persons with disabilities.[1] As per the WHO Manual of 1976, 'disability' includes any restriction or lack of ability to perform any activity in the manner or within the range considered normal for a human being.[2] Disability can be described from different historical and social aspects. As a result, various models to conceptualize disability arose over time, such as (a) religious model, (b) medical model, (c) social model, and (d) rights base model. Among these, the medical approach is the oldest, most conventional and dominant approach towards disability considering medical treatment, physical rehabilitation, charity, welfare and public assistance as the basis of the determination, whereas the human rights approach is the most modern and considers equal rights and equal status as determinants against the discriminating actions towards persons with disabilities. Along with these, under international law, various rights are recognized to secure the right to live with human dignity for disabled people and under the domestic legal framework in India, various legislative and policy orientations are there to address the needs of disabled people. However, the reply to the question of the fullest realization of these rights and protections through the implementation of the international and national standards is not still on a strong footing. Thus, this chapter makes an effort to understand the international recognition of

---

[1] *Tamil Nadu Medical Officers Association v. Union of India*, (2020) 7 M.L.J. 564.

[2] F. Megret, *The Disabilities Convention: Human Rights of Persons with Disabilities or Disability Rights?* 30(2) HRQ 494 (2008).

the human rights to health of disabled persons along with the Indian legislative and policy protection to that end.

I. CONCEPTUAL ORIENTATION OF DISABILITY AND HUMAN RIGHTS

Disability is a complex, dynamic, multidimensional and contested issue of human physical and mental aspects. It is part of the human condition which can make everyone temporarily or permanently impaired and cause difficulties in daily functioning. Apart from other issues of disability, people who survive old age experience increasing difficulties in functioning and maintaining a lifestyle. Historically, the major way of addressing issues related to people with disabilities was the process of isolation and segregation through residential institutions and special schools.[3] Thus, these people have been treated differently from those who remain fit by societal norms. In ancient times, one section of society considered a disability, whether physical or mental, as a punishment from God for one's sin or that of one's ancestors. On similar lines, while in ancient Rome the deformed newborn was killed immediately by means of suffocation or drowning,[4] in ancient Greece, the sick were considered inferior. Plato recommended that the deformed offspring be put away in some mysterious unknown places.[5] This approach to describing disability is based on the religious model of disability. G. Henderson and W. Bryan explained this model and stated that[6]:

> [S]ome people, … believe that some disabilities are the result of lack of adherence to social morality and religious proclamations that warn against engaging in certain behaviour. To further explain this model, some beliefs are based upon the assumption that some disabilities are the result of punishment from an all-powerful entity.

---

[3] WHO & WORLD BANK, WORLD REPORT ON DISABILITY 3 (WHO 2011).

[4] Massimo Fioranelli & Maria Grazia Roccia, *Historical Evolution of Disability Concept*, 1(1) JMEHM 1, 2 (2015).

[5] G.N. Viljoen, *Plato and Aristotle on the Exposure of Infants at Athens*, 2 ACTA CLASSICA 58, 64 (1959).

[6] G. HENDERSON & W. BRYAN, PSYCHOSOCIAL ASPECTS OF DISABILITY 7 (Charles C. Thomas 2011).

The impact of viewing disability in this form sometimes leads to entire families being excluded from social participation in their local communities.[7] On the other hand, early Christian doctrine introduced the view that being disabled is neither a disgrace nor a punishment for sin but, on the contrary, a means of purification and a way of grace. Thus, the study of attitudes of different societies towards people with disabilities suggests that societal perceptions and treatment of persons with disabilities are neither homogeneous nor static.[8]

From the mid-1800s onwards, people with disabilities have been regarded from a medical point of view, where disability has been narrowly equated with an individual's health impairment or capacity limitation. Under this Medical Model, 'disability is seen as a medical problem that resides in the individual. It is a defect in or failure of a bodily system and as such is inherently abnormal and pathological. The goals of intervention are the cure, amelioration of the physical condition to the greatest extent possible, and rehabilitation'.[9] As this Model defines disability in a fundamentally negative way, it is also known as the 'personal tragedy' model.[10] During the 1960s, the Social Model of disability developed as a reaction to the limitations of the medical model of disability,[11] in which people are viewed as being disabled by society rather than by their bodies. Thus, the role of social barriers is emphasized over physical discomfort. Therefore, any meaningful solution to the disability must be directed at societal change rather than individual adjustment and rehabilitation.[12] In order to understand the social model in detail, it is crucial to distinguish between 'disability' and 'impairment'. An impairment is any loss or

---

[7] A. RIMMERMAN, SOCIAL INCLUSION OF PEOPLE WITH DISABILITIES 24 (CUP 2013).

[8] Chomba WaMunyi, *Past and Present Perceptions Towards Disability: A Historical Perspective*, 32(2) DSQ 29 (2012).

[9] R. OLKIN, WHAT PSYCHOTHERAPISTS SHOULD KNOW ABOUT DISABILITY 26 (Guilford Press 1999).

[10] D. THOMAS & H. WOODS, WORKING WITH PEOPLE WITH LEARNING DISABILITIES 15 (Jessica Kingsley 2003).

[11] Marno Retief & Rantoa Letsosa, *Models of Disability: A Brief Overview*, 74(1) THEOL. STUD. 1, 3 (2018).

[12] C. Barnes et al., *The Social Model of Disability*, in SOCIOLOGY: INTRODUCTORY READINGS 161, 163 (A. Giddens & P. Sutton eds, Polity Press 2010).

abnormality of a psychological, physiological, or anatomical structure or function,[13] whereas, a disability is any restriction or lack (resulting from an impairment) of ability to perform an activity in the manner or within the range considered normal for a human being.[14]

However, with the development of human rights after World War II, 'disability' as a concept has started to take a path-breaking shift from an isolation approach to an accommodating approach. Under the international human rights regime, the UN Declaration on Rights of Disabled Persons, 1975 defines the term 'disabled person' as any person who is unable to ensure by himself or herself, wholly or partly, the necessities of a normal individual and/or social life, as a result of deficiency, either congenital or not, in his or her physical or mental capabilities.[15] Parenthetically, even though persons with disabilities constitute a significant statistical minority in the world, they are not considered to be a minority for the purposes of securing effective enforcement of human rights through United Nations law and policy.[16] Finally, the Rights Base Model of Disability has evolved after the adoption of the UN Convention. The Rights Base Model of Disability focuses on anti-discrimination law rather than on welfare programmes. As per the Rights Base Model, (a) disability is a natural part of human diversity that must be respected and supported in all its forms, (b) people with disabilities have the same rights as everyone else in society, and (c) impairment must not be used as an excuse to deny or restrict people's rights. Thus, while the social model supports anti-discrimination policy as to civil rights reforms, the human rights model is more comprehensive in that sense. It encompasses both sets of human rights, civil and political as well as economic, social and cultural rights within its ambit.[17]

---

[13] WHO, INTERNATIONAL CLASSIFICATION OF IMPAIRMENT, DISABILITIES AND HANDICAPS 27 (WHO 1980).

[14] *Ibid.* at 28.

[15] UN Declaration on Rights of Disabled Persons 1975, Declaration 1.

[16] THERESIA DEGENER & YOLAN KOSTER-DREESE, HUMAN RIGHTS AND DISABLED PERSONS 12 (Martinus Nijhoff 1995).

[17] Theresia Degener, *Disability in a Human Rights Context*, 5(3) LAWS 35–38 (2016).

II. CONCEPTUAL ORIENTATION OF MENTAL HEALTH AND ITS RECOGNITION UNDER HUMAN RIGHTS JURISPRUDENCE

The concept of mental health is another component of health besides the physical one which is evident from the WHO's definition of health. Mental health can be described as a cognitive and effective tool for processing and making decisions about the surroundings and it is one of the most meaningful resources to maximize well-being.[18] It can also be identified as a state of well-being in which the individual realizes his or her own abilities, can work productively, can cope with the normal stresses of life, and can make a contribution to his or her community.[19] Thus, mental health can be defined as a state of well-being or a resource to make the most of well-being. The World Health Federation of Mental Health has suggested that to understand the concept of mental health, the following three questions need to be answered: (a) are you comfortable within yourself? (b) Are you comfortable with other people? and (c) Are we able to meet life's demands? If the answer to all these three questions is 'yes' then one can assume himself or herself to be mentally healthy.[20] Further, according to WHO's Report in 1981[21]:

> 'Mental health' is the capacity of the individual, the group and the environment to interact with one another in ways that promote subjective well-being, optimal development and use of mental abilities (cognitive, effective and rational), achievement of individual and collective goals consistent with justice and the attainment and preservation of conditions of fundamental equality.

This definition has several advantages, such as (a) it stresses the complex web of inter-relationships that determine mental health and the

---

[18] Jill Krueger et al., *Promoting Mental Health and Well-Being in Public Health Law and Practice*, 45(S1) JLME 37 (2017).

[19] Venkatashiva Reddy et al., *Mental Health Issues and Challenges in India: A Review*, 3(2) IJSRP 1 (2013).

[20] Virupaksha Dattatreya Gouda, *Mental Health Services - Need for Expansion*, 6 ALT 39 (2007).

[21] WHO, WOMEN'S MENTAL HEALTH: AN EVIDENCE BASED REVIEW 11 (WHO 1981).

factors that determine health operate at multiple levels, (b) it goes beyond the biological and individuals, (c) it acknowledges the crucial role of the social context, and (d) it highlights the importance of justice and equality in determining mental well-being.[22] Later on Rowling, Martin and Walker conceptualized 'mental health' as the capacity of individuals and groups to interact with one another and with the environment in ways that promote subjective wellbeing, the optimal development and use of cognitive, affective and relational abilities, the achievement of individual and collective goals consistent with justice.[23] Nevertheless, the most important emphasis on mental health comes from the WHO with the famous saying, 'there is no health without mental health'.[24]

III. RIGHT TO HEALTH OF PERSONS WITH DISABILITIES UNDER INTERNATIONAL LAW

A. UN Declaration on the Rights of Mentally Retarded Persons, 1971

One of the first overt efforts of the international community to address the needs of disabled people was the UN Declaration on the Rights of Mentally Retarded Persons, 1971.[25] Although the 1971 Declaration was not legally binding on the UN member States, as it is a soft law under the international legal regime, it did has powers of moral and political suasion, which was used effectively by lobby groups in the 1970s to secure important national policy changes with regard to the mentally retarded persons.[26] This Declaration sought to elaborate earlier human rights standards to provide a set of minimum guidelines

---

[22] Madhu Nagla, *Women and Mental Health: Disposition, Narratives and Treatment*, 63(1) Soc. Action 76, 77 (2013).

[23] L. Rowling et al., eds, Mental Health Promotion and Young People: Concepts and Practice 13 (Roseville 2002).

[24] WHO, Mental Health: Facing the Challenges, Building Solutions (WHO 1996).

[25] Proclaimed by the United Nations General Assembly Resolution 2856 (XXVI) of 20 December 1971.

[26] Douglas Hodgson, *The Educational Rights of Persons with Disabilities: International Human Rights Law and Australian Law Perspectives*, 12(4) IJDL 183, 187 (2012).

to inform national policy-making. the declaration secured that the mentally retarded person has, to the maximum degree of feasibility, the same rights as other human beings[27] and hence, that person also has the right to economic security and a decent standard of living.[28]

With respect to health and medical care for these people, the 1971 Declaration stated that 'the mentally retarded person has a right to proper medical care and physical therapy and to such education, training, rehabilitation and guidance as will enable him to develop his ability and maximum potential'.[29] Further, by highlighting the need for family support to these people, the 1971 Declaration stated that the mentally retarded person should live with his own family or with foster parents and participate in different forms of community life. If care in an institution becomes necessary, it should be provided in surroundings and other circumstances as close as possible to those of normal life.[30] These rights cannot be restricted without due process that must contain proper legal safeguards against every form of abuse. However, the 1971 Declaration provides only a limited understanding of the nature of mental health prevailing at the time and failed secure right-based approach in solving the problems faced by mentally retarded persons.[31]

B. UN Declaration on Rights of Disabled Persons, 1975

The United Nations, through its General Assembly, adopted the Declaration on the Rights of Disabled Persons in 1975[32] with an aim to protect the rights and assuring the welfare and rehabilitation of the physically and mentally disadvantaged people. Like the Declaration

---

[27] Declaration on the Rights of Mentally Retarded Persons, 1971, Declaration 1.

[28] *Ibid.* Declaration 3.

[29] *Ibid.* Declaration 2.

[30] *Ibid.* Declaration 4.

[31] Stephen P. Marks et al., *Mental Health and Human Rights: International Standards and Clinical Practice*, in Cambridge Handbook on Psychology and Human Rights 1–20, 5 (Neal S. Rubin & Roseanne Flores eds, CUP 2019).

[32] Proclaimed by General Assembly Resolution 3447 (XXX) of 9 December 1975.

on Mentally Retarded Persons, 1971 this Declaration also stresses that disabled persons have the inherent right to respect for their human dignity and the right to enjoy a decent life, as normal and full as possible.[33] State parties were guided by this Declaration to take appropriate measures designed to enable physically and mentally disadvantaged people to become as self-reliant as possible.[34] The 1975 Declaration also suggested considering the special needs of disabled people at all stages of economic and social planning.[35] Specifically, Declaration 6 dealt with the healthcare needs of disabled persons and defined the path that is needed for their social integration. It states:

> Disabled persons have the right to medical, psychological and functional treatment, including prosthetic and orthetic appliances, to medical and social rehabilitation, education, vocational training and rehabilitation, aid, counselling, placement services and other services which will enable them to develop their capabilities and skills to the maximum and will hasten the processes of their social integration or reintegration.

In a sense, the 1975 Declaration added disability as a protected class and remained silent on exactly how the entitlement will be realized.[36]

C. World Programme of Action Concerning Disabled Persons, 1982

The revolutionary outcome of the observance of the International Year of Disabled Persons in 1981 was the formulation of the World Programme of Action concerning Disabled Persons in 1982.[37] As a part of the observation, the First Founding International Congress of Disabled People held in Singapore from November 30 to December 06, 1981, made the background events for the adaptation of the 1982 World Programme of Action. At the time of its adoption, the

---

[33] Declaration on Rights of Disabled Persons, 1975, Declaration 3.

[34] *Ibid.* Declaration 5.

[35] *Ibid.* Declaration 8.

[36] Charles D. Siegal, *Fifty Years of Disability Law: The Relevance of the Universal Declaration*, 5(2) ILSAJICL 267, 270 (1999).

[37] Proclaimed by the United Nations General Assembly Resolution 37/52 of 3 December 1982.

Programme of Action was marked as a milestone in the eventual rec-ognition of the human rights of disabled persons because it added a human rights component to traditional disability policy.[38] It restruc-tured the disability policy into three distinct areas: (a) prevention, (b) rehabilitation and (c) equalization of opportunities. Prevention means measures aimed at preventing the onset of mental, physical and sen-sory impairments or at preventing impairment, when it has occurred, from having negative physical, psychological and social consequences.

Further, under this Programme of Action, National governments and international organizations were asked to initiate activities by assuring disabled people what they need for their full participation in society, investing in the prevention of disability and educating and informing the public of the rights of disabled persons to participate in and contribute to various aspects of economic, social and political life.[39] It is further notable that the 1982 Programme of Action provided (a) better nutri-tional practices, (b) improvement of health services, (c) early detection and diagnosis, (d) prenatal and postnatal care, (e) proper health care instruction, including patient and physician education, and (f) family planning as preventive measures to secure better access to healthcare to disabled people.[40] Thus, the Programme of Action emphasized equal opportunity rights for disabled people, as well as equal access for them to improved living conditions resulting from economic and social development.[41]

D. Mental Illness Principles, 1991

The United Nations Principles for the Protection of Persons with Mental Illness and the Improvement of Mental Health Care, 1991(MI

---

[38] Degener, *supra* note 17, at 45.

[39] Paul van Trigt, *Equal Reproduction Rights? The Right to Found a Family in United Nations' Disability Policy Since the 1970s*, 25(2) Hist. Fam. 202–206 (2020).

[40] UN, Report of the Secretary-General on World Programme of Action Concerning Disabled Persons, 21 (UN 1982).

[41] Marcia Rioux & Anne Carbert, *Human Rights and Disability: The International Context*, 10(2) J. Dev. Disabil. 1, 4 (2003).

Principles)[42] were the broadest human rights rules concerning mental health treatment and assistance in comparison to its earlier instruments. Such principles are particularly useful as guidelines for the interpretation of the rights established in various human rights treaties. They established minimum standards of practice in the mental health field and have served as models to mental health legislation for UN State parties. It defines 'Mental health care' as the analysis and diagnosis of a person's mental condition, and treatment, care and rehabilitation for a mental illness or suspected mental illness. The MI Principles established standards for treatment and living conditions in psychiatric institutions and for creating protections against arbitrary detention in such facilities.[43] These principles recognized the enjoyment of the highest attainable standard of physical and mental health as the right of every human being.[44] Principle 1 deals with fundamental freedoms and basic rights available to persons with a mental illness. There should be no discrimination on the grounds of mental illness.[45]

It also provided that a determination of mental illness has to be made in accordance with internationally accepted medical standards.[46] A background of past treatment or hospitalization as a patient with mental illness cannot justify any present or future determination of mental illness.[47] With regard to the Standard of care, the MI Principles prescribed that every patient has the right to receive such health and social care as is appropriate to his or her health needs and is entitled to care and treatment in accordance with the same standards as any other ill person.[48] The principles further provided that the treatment and care of every patient have to be based on an individually pre-

---

[42] MI Principles, 1991 was adopted by UN General Assembly Resolution 46/119 of 17 December 1991.

[43] Neil Rees, *International Human Rights Obligations and Mental Health Review Tribunals*, 10(1) PSYCHIATR. PSYCHOL LAW 33 (2003).

[44] D. NAGARAJA & PRATIMA MURTHY, MENTAL HEALTH CARE AND HUMAN RIGHTS 18 (NHRC 2008).

[45] *Ibid.* Principle 1(4).

[46] *Ibid.* Principle 4(1).

[47] *Ibid.* Principle 4(4).

[48] *Ibid.* Principle 8(1).

scribed plan, discussed with the patient, reviewed regularly, revised as necessary and provided by qualified professional staff.[49] Thus, the 1991 United Nations Principles was important not only for its specific provisions but also for its acknowledgement of a particular need to protect the rights of persons with a mental disorder, especially persons with enduring mental disorders whose rights have been significantly ignored in the past.[50]

E. UN Standard Rules on the Equalization of Opportunities for Persons with Disabilities, 1993

The most revolutionary outcome of the Decade of Disabled Persons was the adoption of the Standard Rules on the Equalization of Opportunities for Persons with Disabilities, 1993.[51] Although the Standard Rules is not a legally binding instrument, it represents a strong moral and political commitment of UN State parties to take action to attain equalization of opportunities for persons with disabilities.[52] The rules served as an instrument for policy-making and as a basis for technical and economic cooperation. It requested UN State parties to apply these Equalization Rules in developing national disability programmes.[53] The Rules consist of four parts: (a) preconditions for equal participation, (b) target areas for equal participation, (c) implementation measures, and (d) Monitoring mechanism.[54] Thus, as a 'rights-based' instrument, the purpose of the Standard Rules is to ensure that girls, boys, men and women

---

[49] *Ibid.* Principle 9(2).

[50] Brendan D. Kelly, *Mental Health, Mental Illness, and Human Rights in India and Elsewhere: What Are We Aiming for?* 58(Suppl 2) INDIAN J. PSYCHIATRY S168 (2016).

[51] Adopted by the UNGA Resolution 48/96 of 20 December 1993.

[52] Equalization of Opportunities for Persons with Disabilities, 1993, Paragraph 14.

[53] Hodgson, *supra* note 26, at 92.

[54] Gerard Quinn & Theresia Degener, *The Application of Moral Authority: The Shift to the Human Rights Perspective on Disability through United Nations 'Soft' Law,* in HUMAN RIGHTS AND DISABILITY: THE CURRENT USE AND FUTURE POTENTIAL OF UNITED NATIONS HUMAN RIGHTS INSTRUMENTS IN THE CONTEXT OF DISABILITY 29–46, 34 (Gera d Quinn & Theresia Degener eds, UN, 2002).

with disabilities, as members of their societies, may exercise the same rights and obligations as others.[55] Within the framework for preconditions for equal participation under Section I, Equalization Rules provide (a) awareness-raising, (b) medical care, (c) rehabilitation and (d) support services. The States has the duty to take action to raise awareness in society about persons with disabilities, their rights, their needs, their potential and their contribution.[56] With regard to medical care, the States have to ensure the provision of effective medical care to persons with disabilities.[57]

In concurrence to this, the States should work towards the provision of programmes to prevent, reduce or eliminate disabling effects and ensure the full participation of persons with disabilities and their families at the individual level, and of organizations of persons with disabilities at the planning and evaluation level.[58] Furthermore, the States have to ensure that persons with disabilities, particularly infants and children are provided with the same level of medical care within the same system as other members of society.[59] States also have the duty to ensure that medical, paramedical and related personnel are adequately trained so that they do not give inappropriate advice to parents[60] and these personnel should have the access to relevant treatment methods and technology to secure appropriate healthcare support to persons with disabilities.[61] The Equalization Rules called on every State to engage in a national planning process to bring legislation, policies and programmes into conformity with international human rights standards.[62]

---

[55] Equalization of Opportunities for Persons with Disabilities, 1993, Paragraph 15.

[56] *Ibid.* Rule 1.

[57] *Ibid.* Rule 2.

[58] *Ibid.* Rule 2(1).

[59] *Ibid.* Rule 2(3).

[60] *Ibid.* Rule 2(5).

[61] *Ibid.* Rule 2(4).

[62] WHO, WHO Resource Book on Mental Health, Human Rights and Legislation 14 (WHO 2005).

F. Convention on the Rights of Persons with Disabilities, 2006

Moreover, to address the recent right-based development under international law the Convention on the Rights of Persons with Disabilities (CRPD)[63] was adopted in 2006 which is the first comprehensive human rights treaty of the 21st century and before the CRPD, there was no international binding treaty specifically dealing with the human rights of disabled persons.[64] The CRPD sought to address the widespread discrimination against people living with disabilities in education, healthcare, politics, employment, and other areas. It assures the full participation of people with disabilities[65] and puts an interpretive weight on the aspirations of the broader disability community.[66] At the time of fixing the objectives of the Convention, the importance of accessibility to the physical, social, economic and cultural environment is recognized as a precondition to enable full enjoyment of all human rights including the right to health and fundamental freedoms to the persons with disabilities.[67] Thus, the CRPD recognizes accessibility as the enabler for securing human rights for people with disabilities.[68]

Under the health sector of persons with disability, the CRPD - as the first treaty tackling disability from a rights perspective - distinguishes itself from its earlier instruments by abandoning the medical disability model. Hence, it bifurcates itself from the historical paradigm that

---

[63] The CRPD and its Optional Protocol (A/RES/61/106) was adopted on 13 December 2006 at the United Nations Headquarters in New York, and was opened for signature on 30 March 2007. There were 82 signatories to the Convention, 44 signatories to the Optional Protocol, and 1 ratification of the Convention.

[64] Jayna Kothari, *The UN Convention on Rights of Persons with Disabilities: An Engine for Law Reform in India,* 45(18) EPW 65 (2010).

[65] Anna Lawson, *The United Nations Convention on the Rights of Persons with Disabilities: New Age or False Dawn?* 34(2) SJILC 563 (2007).

[66] Amita Dhanda, *Legal Capacity in the Disability Rights Convention: Stranglehold of the Past or Lodestar for the Future?* 34(2) SJILC 429, 430 (2007).

[67] CRPD 2006, Preamble, para (v). *See,* Alison Bisset (ed.), Blackstone's International Human Rights Documents 200 (OUP 2020).

[68] Simon Darcy, *Accessibility as a Key Management Component of the Paralympics,* in Managing the Paralympics 49–92, 49 (Simon Darcy et al., eds, Springer 2017).

portrayed individuals with disabilities as incapable and in need of protection. Articles 25 and 26 of the CRPD can be addressed together because they have direct relevance to the achievement of the various health indicators referenced in the Millennium Development Goals, as well as to the achievement of education and poverty reduction goals.[69] The Convention also addresses the need to prevent secondary disabilities. Article 25 prohibits discrimination against persons with disabilities in the provision of health insurance[70] and prevents discriminatory denial of health care or health services or food and fluids on the basis of disability.[71] The main focus of these Articles is not on providing disability-specific or segregated health services, rather on ensuring that persons with disabilities have access 'to the same range, quality and standard of free or affordable health care programmes as provided to other persons',[72] and to provide these health services as close as possible to people's own communities, including rural areas.[73] Thus, the CRPD recognizes that persons with disabilities have the right to the enjoyment of the highest attainable standard of health without discrimination on the basis of disability. States Parties have the duty to take all appropriate measures to ensure access for persons with disabilities to health services that are gender-sensitive, including health-related rehabilitation.[74] In addition, the State parties have to provide specific health services needed by persons with disabilities because of their disabilities, including early identification and intervention as appropriate, and services designed to minimize and prevent further disabilities, including the children and older persons.[75] Furthermore, for securing needed healthcare facilities to persons with a disability there should be a required number of health professionals to provide health care on the basis of free and informed consent by, *inter alia*,

---

[69] KATHERINE GUERNSEY et al., CONVENTION ON THE RIGHTS OF PERSONS WITH DISABILITIES: ITS IMPLEMENTATION AND RELEVANCE FOR THE WORLD BANK 14 (World Bank 2007).

[70] CRPD 2006, Article 25(e).

[71] *Ibid.* Article 25(f).

[72] *Ibid.* Article 25(a).

[73] *Ibid.* Article 25(c).

[74] *Ibid.* Article 25.

[75] *Ibid.* Article 25(b).

raising awareness of the human rights, dignity, autonomy and needs of persons with disabilities through training and the promulgation of ethical standards for public and private health care.[76] Hence, the CRPD supports a strict limitation on the provision of involuntary medical treatment and reconciles that through an emphasis on autonomy, self-determination and supported decision making.[77] To achieve all these, States parties have the duty to organize, strengthen, and extend comprehensive habilitation and rehabilitation services and programmes, particularly in the areas of health, employment, education and social security.[78]

IV. SPECIFIC LEGISLATIVE FRAMEWORK OF RIGHT TO HEALTH: DISABLED PERSONS PERSPECTIVE IN INDIA

In our society, disabled persons are one of the most vulnerable sections whose rights require to be protected. The Planning Commission of India defines a disabled person as a person who is (a) blind, (b) deaf, (c) having orthopaedic disability, (d) having a neurological disorder, and (e) mentally retarded.[79] So these persons have certain physical or mental issues and the physical and mental health of these people is required to be protected through specific legislations.

A. Rehabilitation Council of India Act, 1992

The 1992 Rehabilitation Council of India Act[80] was enacted to constitute the Rehabilitation Council of India for regulating and monitoring the training of rehabilitation professionals and personnel, to promote research in rehabilitation and special education, and to maintain the Central Rehabilitation Register. Thus, the Act provides a guarantee to

---

[76] *Ibid.* Article 25(d).

[77] Penelope Weller, *The Convention on the Rights of Persons with Disabilities and the Social Model of Health: New Perspectives*, 21 J. MENT. HEALTH 74, 75 (2011).

[78] CRPD 2006, Article 26.

[79] RATHIN BANDYOPADHYAY & SANGEETA ROY MAITRA, LAW AND THE DISABLED 29 (R. Cambray 2011).

[80] Act No. XXXIV of 1992. It was enacted on 1 September 1992.

the good quality of services rendered by various rehabilitation person-nel.[81] The term 'Rehabilitation' refers to a process aimed at enabling persons with disabilities to reach and maintain their optimal physi-cal, intellectual, sensory, psychiatric or social functional levels.[82] In general, rehabilitation involves the combined and coordinated use of medical, social, educational and vocational measures for training or retraining the individual to the highest possible level of functional ability. The three most popular strategies for rehabilitation of the disabled are institution-based, outreach, and community-based.[83] Hence, the Act defines rehabilitation in the same line. The Act defines 'handicapped' as a person who is (a) visually handicapped; (b) hearing handicapped; (c) suffering from locomotor disability; or (d) suffering from mental retardation.[84] Thus, it includes both the physical and mental aspects of infirmity within its ambit.

To regulate the working of these rehabilitation professionals, the 1992 Act empowers the Central Government to constitute the Rehabilitation Council of India,[85] which has the power to give (a) recognition of qualifications granted by a University in India for rehabilitation professionals,[86] (b) recognition of qualifications granted by institutions outside India,[87] (c) enrolment of persons possessing required qualifications,[88] and (d) detail about the minimum standards of education.[89] Thus, the 1992 Act is clearly a regulative Act to control the functions and treatment of the rehabilitation professionals, which is an important aspect to bring disabled persons into normal social life. In other words, the 1992 Act brought about a major advancement

---

[81] Rajib Bhattacharyya, *Disability Laws in India: A Study*, 1(4) IJR 99, 111 (2014).

[82] Rehabilitation Council of India Act 1992, Section 2(ma).

[83] R. Jose & Sandeep Sachdeva, *Community Rehabilitation of Disabled with a Focus on Blind Persons: Indian Perspective*, 58(2) IJO 137 (2010).

[84] Rehabilitation Council of India Act 1992, Section 2(c).

[85] *Ibid.* Section 3.

[86] *Ibid.* Section 11.

[87] *Ibid.* Section 12.

[88] *Ibid.* Section 13.

[89] *Ibid.* Section 18.

in human resource development in the area of tackling the issues of persons with disabilities.[90]

B. National Trust for Welfare of Persons with Autism, Cerebral Palsy, Mental Retardation and Multiple Disabilities Act, 1999

The 1999 National Trust for Welfare of Persons with Autism, Cerebral Palsy, Mental Retardation and Multiple Disabilities Act[91] aims to constitute a body at the national level for the welfare of persons with autism, cerebral palsy, mental retardation and multiple disabilities and other allied diseases. The 1999 National Trust proposes to create an enabling environment that will allow as much independent living as possible for persons with Autism, Cerebral Palsy, Mental Retardation and Multiple Disabilities.[92] The Act includes any person suffering from any of the conditions relating to autism, cerebral palsy, mental retardation or a combination of any two or more of such conditions and includes a person suffering from severe multiple disabilities within the definition of 'Persons with disability'.[93] The definition of mental retardation under the 1999 Act is the same as the definition of mental retardation under the Rehabilitation Council of India Act 1992. It is interesting to note that persons who are in a condition of 'mental retardation' should ordinarily be treated differently from those who are found to be 'mentally ill'. While a guardian can make decisions on behalf of a 'mentally ill person', the same cannot be done on behalf of a person who is in a condition of 'mental retardation'.[94]

Further, Section 3 empowers the Central Government to constitute the National Trust for Welfare of Persons with Autism, Cerebral

---

[90] Vijay Khare, *Status of Persons with Intellectual Disabilities in India*, 7(8) IJCR 19210, 19211 (2015).

[91] Act No. XLIV of 1999. It was enacted on 30 December 1999.

[92] Aadil Bashir & Zahoor Ahmed Ganie, *Critical Appraisal of the Disability Programs in Jammu and Kashmir with Special Reference to Children*, 2(10) IJSR 223, 225 (2013).

[93] National Trust for Welfare of Persons with Autism, Cerebral Palsy, Mental Retardation and Multiple Disabilities Act 1999, Section 2(j).

[94] *Eera through Manjula Krippendorf v. State*, A.I.R. 2017 S.C. 3457.

Palsy, Mental Retardation and Multiple Disabilities. This National Trust should be a body corporate, having perpetual succession and a common seal, with power to contract for the benefit of the persons with these infirmities.[95] The Act also specifies the objects of the Trust as to (a) enable and empower persons with disabilities to live independently within the community, (b) provide support to disabled persons to live within their own families, (c) extend support to registered organizations to provide need-based services during period of crisis in the family of disabled persons, (d) deal with problems of persons with disability who do not have family support, (e) promote measures for the care and protection of persons with disability in the event of death of their parents or guardians, (f) evolve procedure for the appointment of guardians and trustees for persons with a disability requiring such protection, and (g) facilitate the realization of equal opportunities, protection of rights and full participation of persons with disability.[96] Further, for the working of the Trust, the Board has the power to constitute Local Level Committee(LLC) for such area as may be specified by it from time to time.[97] The primary function of these LLC is to verify and appoint a guardian for persons with disability. A parent of a person with disability or his relative or any registered organization can make an application for the appointment of a guardian to the LLC.[98] While considering the application for the appointment of a guardian, the LLC has to consider (a) whether the person with disability needs a guardian; and (b) the purposes for which the guardianship is required for person with disability.[99] After considering these, the LLC may recommend the name of the guardian for a disabled person to the Board. Every person appointed as a guardian has the duty to provide care to such persons of disability and his property or to maintain that person with disability.[100] Thus,

[95] *Ibid.* Section 3(1).

[96] *Ibid.* Section 10.

[97] *Ibid.* Section 13(1).

[98] *Ibid.* Sections 14(1) and 14(2).

[99] *Ibid.* Section 14(3).

[100] *Ibid.* Section 15.

in *Pratibha Pande v. Union of India*,[101] the Delhi High Court appointed the petitioner's daughter as the guardian of the person and vested the property of the petitioner to her. The Court further held that the particular guardian has to do all acts, deeds and things for the proper medical treatment, nursing care, welfare and benefit of the petitioner. By analysing the abovementioned objectives and the duties of the guardian, it can be concluded that these are necessary to provide effective healthcare protection to disabled persons and to secure the right to health of disabled persons.

C. Rights of Persons with Disabilities Act, 2016

i. Background and Scope of the Act

The 2016 Rights of Persons with Disabilities Act[102] was passed to (a) respect for inherent dignity, individual autonomy including the freedom to make one's own choices, and independence of persons, (b) upheld non-discrimination, (c) ensure full and effective participation and inclusion in society, (d) respect for difference and acceptance of persons with disabilities as part of human diversity and humanity, (e) guarantee equality of opportunity, (f) secure accessibility, (g) established equality between men and women, and (h) secure capacities of children with disabilities and help them to preserve their identities and came into force on April 10, 2017. This Disabilities Act is premised on the fundamental idea that society creates barriers and oppressive structures which impede the capacities of the person with disabilities.[103] Thus, it emphasized a right-based approach to deal with this social issue. Further, the said 2016 Act has been brought into existence to give effect to the United Nations Convention on the Rights of Persons with Disabilities and for matters connected therewith or incidental thereto.[104] This 2016 Act repealed the Persons with Disability (Equal Opportunity, Protection of Rights and Full Participation) Act of 1995

---

[101] 229 (2016) D.L.T. 512.

[102] Act No. XLIX of 2016. It was enacted on 27 December 2016.

[103] *Disabled Rights Group v. Union of India*, (2018) 2 S.C.C. 397.

[104] *Justice Sunanda Bhandare Foundation v. Union of India*, (2017) 14 S.C.C. 1.

and provides a more detailed scheme about the protection of rights of disabled persons, with regard to health, skill development, national fund, offences and penalties as added features.[105]

ii. Specific Provisions Relating to Health and Rehabilitation

Chapter V of the 2016 Act specifically deals with health and rehabilitation along with social security and recreation. Section 24(1) directs the appropriate Government to formulate necessary schemes and programmes to safeguard and promote the right of persons with disabilities to enable them to live independently or in the community. Whereas Section 24(3) explains the areas to which those schemes and programmes as mentioned in Section 24(1) have to be applied. It directs to establish community centres by considering safety, sanitation, health care and counselling as basic conditions of good living. The Act also directs the appropriate Government and the local authorities to provide healthcare facilities to disabled persons. Thus, Section 25(1) states:

> The appropriate Government and the local authorities shall take necessary measures for the persons with disabilities to provide (a) free healthcare in the vicinity, especially in rural areas subject to such family income as may be notified; (b) barrier-free access in all parts of Government and private hospitals and other healthcare institutions and centres; (c) priority in attendance and treatment.

Thus, the 2016 Act denotes that the appropriate Government and the local authorities have to take measures to promote healthcare and prevent the occurrence of disabilities. To attain such purposes the Government and the local authorities has to (a) undertake surveys, investigations and research concerning the cause of occurrence of disabilities, (b) promote various methods for preventing disabilities, (c) screen all the children at least once in a year for the purpose of identifying 'at-risk' cases, (d) provide facilities for training to the staff at the primary health centres, (e) sponsor awareness campaigns and

---

[105] Raj Kumari Gupta, *Rights of Persons with Disabilities Act 2016: A Critique*, 3(1) JDS 17, 19 (2017).

disseminate information for general hygiene, health and sanitation, (f) take measures for prenatal and postnatal care of mother and child, (g) educate the public through the preschools, schools, other educational institutions, primary health centres, village level workers and anganwadi workers, (h) create awareness amongst the masses through television, radio and other mass media on the causes of disabilities and the preventive measures to be adopted, (i) assure healthcare during the time of natural disasters and other situations of risk, (j) assure essential medical facilities for life saving emergency treatment and procedures, and (k) secure sexual and reproductive healthcare especially for women with disability.[106]

Moreover, the appropriate Government has a duty to make insurance schemes for their disabled employees.[107] Further Section 27 provides for rehabilitation services and programmes by the appropriate Government and the local authorities, particularly in the field of health, education and employment of disabled persons. It is important to note that all these duties of the government depend upon economic capacity and development. This is against the idea of providing 'Rights' and allows the 'State' to absolve from its duties.[108] Thus, it leaves ample room for denial of justice and non - fulfilling the duties by specified institutes as well as other authorities.[109] Further, the 2016 Act empowers the Government and local authorities like Municipality, Panchayat or Cantonment Board to grant financial assistance to non-governmental organizations.[110] Along with the empowerment, the 2016 Act also cast a duty on the appropriate Government and the local authorities to consult the non-governmental organizations working for the cause of persons with disabilities at the time of formulating rehabilitation policies for persons with disabilities.[111] The appropriate Government

---

[106] *Ibid.* Section 25(2).

[107] *Ibid.* Section 26.

[108] Suresh Bada Math et al., *The Rights of Persons with Disability Act, 2016: Challenges and Opportunities*, 61 (Suppl. 4) INDIAN J. PSYCHIATRY S809, S810 (2019).

[109] Banti Rani, *The Rights of Persons with Disabilities Act, 2016 Promoting Inclusive Education*, 3(2) IJARD 798–800 (2018).

[110] Rights of Persons with Disabilities Act 2016, Section 27(2).

[111] *Ibid.* Section 27(3).

also has to initiate research and development through individuals and institutions for enhancing habilitation and rehabilitation and on such other issues which are necessary for the empowerment of persons with disabilities.[112]

iii. Access to Healthcare and Other Provisions

Along with securing of healthcare delivery system for disabled persons, the 2016 Act is also concerned with the accessibility of healthcare.[113] Section 45 casts a duty upon the appropriate Government and the local authorities to provide space for primary health centres, civil hospitals and to make a plan to confirm the accessibility of the disabled persons to such establishments. Every person, who wants to establish or maintain an institution for persons with disabilities, has to register for the same under the competent authority appointed by the State Government and has to obtain a certificate of registration.[114] The Act also provides for the constitution of Central and State Advisory Boards on Disability and District Level Committee for recommending steps and suggestions to ensure accessibility, reasonable accommodation, non-discrimination, monitoring and review the implementation of the Act.

D. Mental Healthcare Act, 2017

i. Background

In the early days of Indian medical history, Ayurveda played a vital role in respect of mental disorder patients. During the British regime in India, various laws were enacted in quick succession such as (a) the Lunacy (Supreme Courts) Act, 1858; (b) the Lunacy (District Courts) Act, 1858; (c) the Indian Lunatic Asylum Act, 1858; and (d) the Military Lunatic Acts, 1877 for controlling the process of care

---

[112] Ibid. Section 28.

[113] The issue of 'Accessibility' is always a primary concern for disabled persons and it has been interpreted as a part of right to life. Thus, in State of Himachal Pradesh v. Umed Ram Sharma, [A.I.R. 1986 S.C. 847], the Supreme Court held that the right to life under Article 21 is broad enough to incorporate the right to accessibility.

[114] Rights of Persons with Disabilities Act 2016, Section 50.

and treatment of mentally ill persons. These Acts gave primitive legal guidelines for the establishment of mental asylums and procedures to take in the custody of mental patients.[115] After independence, in 1987, Mental Health Act was enacted with a view to change the attitudes of the society towards mentally ill persons and to treat them as normal sick person.[116] The 1987 Act provides enormous changes in various fields with respect to its predecessors. It provides (a) an advanced concept of mental illness and treatment, (b) primacy of the role of medical officers, (c) simplification of the rules of admission and discharge, (d) providing for supervision of the standard of care by creating the Mental Health Authority, and (e) provision of penalties in case of breach of laws in connection with the welfare of the patients.[117] However, this 1987 Act is criticized as it overstressed the theoretical aspects and utopian process and the implementation of which is to some extent impossible in the Indian scenario.[118] This act also paving the way for isolating mentally ill patients, which is a very primitive approach to deal with this problem. Consequently, India has recently revised its mental health legislation with a new law that has been greatly anticipated *i.e.* the Mental Healthcare Act 2017 that was enacted by the Parliament on April 7, 2017.[119] The need for the new Act is clear from the Statement of Objects and Reasons of the 2017 Act[120] which states that:

> The United Nations Convention on the Rights of Persons with Disabilities, which was ratified by the government of India in October, 2007, made it obligatory on the Government to align the policies and laws of the country with the Convention. The need for amendments to the Mental

[115] O. Somasundaram, *The Indian Lunacy Act, 1912: The Historic Background*, 29(1) INDIAN J. PSYCHIATRY 3 (1987).

[116] Mental Health Act 1987, Preamble.

[117] Sougata Talukdar, *The Mental Healthcare Bill, 2013: A Critical Appraisal*, (March) WJJP 1, 2 (2017).

[118] Jaydip Sarkar, *A New Mental Health Act for India: An Ethics Based Approach*, 46(2) INDIAN J. PSYCHIATRY 104, 109 (2004).

[119] Richard M. Dufy & Brendan D. Kelly, *Concordance of the Indian Mental Healthcare Act 2017 with the World Health Organization's Checklist on Mental Health Legislation*, 11 IJMHS 48, 50 (2017).

[120] Act No. X of 2017. It came into force on 29 May 2018.

Health Act, 1987 was felt by the fact that the related law, i.e., the Persons with Disabilities (Equal Opportunities, Protection of Rights and Full Participation) Act, 1995 was also in the process of amendment.

ii. Object and Definitional Scheme

The Mental Healthcare Act 2017 was enacted to provide for mental healthcare and services for persons with mental illness and to protect, promote and fulfil the rights of such persons during delivery of mental healthcare and services and for matters connected therewith or incidental thereto.[121] By explaining the extent of application of this Act, in *Accused 'x' v. State of Maharashtra*,[122] the Supreme Court observed that the Act aspires to provide mental health care facilities for those who are in need, including prisoners. The State Governments are obliged under this Act to set up a mental health establishment in the medical wing of at least one prison in each State and Union Territory,[123] and prisoners with mental illness may ordinarily be referred to and cared for in the said mental health establishment. Thus, the ambit of the Act includes rights to prisoners to have access to mental healthcare within its purview.

The Act defined mental illness as:

[A] substantial disorder of thinking, mood, perception, orientation or memory that grossly impairs judgment, behaviour, capacity to recognise reality or ability to meet the ordinary demands of life, mental conditions associated with the abuse of alcohol and drugs, but does not include mental retardation which is a condition of arrested or incomplete development of mind of a person, specially characterised by subnormality of intelligence.[124]

iii. Advance Directive and Its Impact on Treatment of Persons with Mental Illness

This 2017 Mental Healthcare Act also empowers a mentally ill person to have the right to make an advance directive toward the way he or

---

[121] Mental Healthcare Act 2017, Preamble.

[122] A.I.R. 2019 S.C. 3031.

[123] Mental Healthcare Act 2017, Section 103.

[124] *Ibid*. Section 2(s).

she wants to be treated for the requisite illness and who shall be his nominated representative.[125] In the case of a minor, the legal guardian has the right to make an advance directive in writing for securing required treatment.[126] An advance directive may be made by a person irrespective of his past mental illness or treatment for the same. This directive has to be examined by a qualified medical practitioner. An advance directive shall have effect only when such person does not have the capacity to make decisions regarding his treatment and shall remain effective until such person regains the capacity to make such decisions. Any decision made by a person, while he has the capacity to make decisions regarding mental healthcare and treatment, always has an over-riding effect on any previously written advance directive by such person.[127] An advance directive may be revoked, amended or cancelled by the person who made it at any time.[128]

For proper implementation of advance directives, the 2017 Mental Healthcare Act has imposed a duty over every medical officer in charge of a mental health establishment and the psychiatrist in charge of a person's treatment to propose or give treatment to a mentally ill person, in accordance with his valid advance directives.[129] Whereas Section 11 provides that if there is any objection on the part of the mental health professional or a relative or a caregiver of such mentally ill person, they can apply to the Review Board to cancel that advance directive. Thus, mental health professional or a relative or a care-giver cannot supersede the will of the mentally ill person about his treatment arbitrarily. Thus, the Supreme Court in *Common Cause v. Union of India*[130] has dealt with the working of advance directives and observed that the Mental Healthcare Act, 2017 recognizes the validity of advance directives for the treatment of mental illness. An advance directive

---

[125] Abhisek Mishra & A. Galhotra, *Mental Healthcare Act 2017: Need to Wait and Watch*, 8 IJABMR 67, 68 (2018).

[126] Mental Healthcare Act 2017, Section 11(4).

[127] *Ibid.* Section 5.

[128] *Ibid.* Section 8(1).

[129] *Ibid.* Section 10.

[130] A.I.R. 2018 S.C. 1665.

is to be in writing and signed by two witnesses attesting to the fact that the directive was executed in their presence. A directive is to be registered with the Mental Health Review Board. It may be changed as many times as desired by the person executing it and the treating mental health professional must be informed of such change. Further, under this legislative framework, the Central Authority is empowered to review the use of advance directives regularly and periodically and make recommendations in respect thereof. It can also examine whether the existing procedure protects the rights of persons with mental illness. Even, the Central Authority has the power to modify or to make additional regulations regarding the procedure for the advance directive to protect the rights of these persons.[131] Moreover, to protect the medical practitioners from the consequence of the following advance, Section 13(1) of the Act states that a medical practitioner or a mental health professional is not liable for any unforeseen consequences which occurred due to a valid advance directive. Even, when a copy of the valid advance directive is not given to the medical practitioners, they are not liable to be held responsible for not following the advance directives.[132]

iv. Role of Nominated Representative in Securing Treatment to Persons with Mental Illness

Every person, except the minor, has the right to appoint a nominated representative of his choice.[133] In the case of a minor, the legal guardian is his nominated representative, unless the Mental Health Review Board orders otherwise. Thus, if the Board is of the opinion that (a) the legal guardian is not acting in the best interests of the minor, or (b) the legal guardian is otherwise not fit to act as the nominated representative of the minor, the Board may appoint, any suitable individual as the nominated representative of the minor with mental illness.[134] In addition to this, the 2017 Act is also concerned about

---

[131] *Ibid.* Section 12.

[132] *Ibid.* Section 13(2).

[133] *Ibid.* Section 14(1).

[134] *Ibid.* Section 15.

the competence of the nominated representative. Thus, it provides that the person appointed as the nominated representative should be competent to discharge the duties or perform the functions assigned to him under this Act and give his consent in writing to the mental health professional to discharge his duties and perform the functions assigned to him under this Act. Further, such nominated representative cannot be a minor. However, this choice of the nominated representative may not be permanent in nature. Under the framework, the 2017 Act allows a person, who has appointed any person as his nominated representative, to revoke or alter such appointment at any time. Similar power is also provided to the Mental Health Review Board when it is in the interest of the person with mental illness to do so.[135] However, along with this, the individual and the board also have the power to nominate another as the representative for future medical assistance.

v. Rights of Persons with Mental Illness

The rights of persons with mental illness, during the delivery of mental health care services, have found express recognition for the first time in the Mental Healthcare Act, 2017 in India. Chapter V of the 2017 Act enumerates these rights which are a penumbra of hope and reflects the ultimate right of health.[136] Among these some rights are directly connected to the health right of persons suffering from mental illness such as (a) right to access mental healthcare, (b) right to confidentiality, (c) restriction on the release of information in respect of mental illness, and (d) right to access mental health records. Other rights can be categorized as incidental to the above-mentioned rights such as (a) right to community living, (b) right to protection from cruel, inhuman and degrading treatment, (c) right to equality and non-discrimination, (d) right to information, (e) right to personal contacts and communications, and (f) right to make complaints about deficiencies in the provision of services.

---

[135] *Ibid.* Section 14.

[136] *Ibid.* Sections 18–28.

Section 18 of the Act ensures the right of everyone to have access to mental health care services and treatment from mental health services run or funded by the appropriate Government. The Act also specifies that every person with mental illness should be treated as equal to persons with physical illness and there should be no discrimination on the basis of gender, sex, religion, caste, sexual orientation, culture, social or political beliefs, class or disability.[137] Thus, Sections 18(1) and (2) read with 21(1)(a) provide for the right to access mental health-care and equal treatment of people with physical and mental illnesses without discrimination, *inter alia*, on the basis of 'sexual orientation'.[138] Further, the 2017 Act mandates the appropriate government to make sufficient provisions for the services required by persons with mental illness including, the provision of acute mental healthcare services, halfway homes, sheltered accommodation and supported accommodation.[139] Section 18(5) requires the appropriate government to integrate mental health services into general healthcare services at all levels of healthcare including primary, secondary and tertiary healthcare and in all health programmes run by it. Section 18(7) again states that persons with mental illness living below the poverty line whether or not in possession of a below poverty line card, or who are destitute or homeless are entitled to mental health treatment and services free of any charge and at no financial cost at all mental health establishments run or funded by the appropriate Government and at other mental health establishments designated by it. Thus the 'right to access mental healthcare and treatment' for the purpose of the Act includes mental health services (a) of affordable cost, (b) of good quality, (c) available in sufficient quantity, (d) accessible geographically, (e) without discrimination on the basis of gender, sex, sexual orientation, religion, culture, caste, social or political beliefs, class, disability or any other basis, and (f) provided in a manner that is acceptable to persons with mental illness, their families and care-givers.[140]

---

[137] *Ibid.* Section 21.

[138] *Navtej Singh Johar v. Union of India*, A.I.R. 2018 S.C. 4321.

[139] Mental Healthcare Act 2017, Sections 18(3) and 18(4).

[140] Kirandeep Kaur, *Implications of the Mental Healthcare Act, 2017 on the Rights of Women with Mental Illnesses in India*, 19(4) JIWS 3, 5 (2018).

A person with mental illness shall have the right to confidentiality with regards to the treatment and condition of illness including mental healthcare and physical healthcare.[141] No photograph or any other information relating to a person undergoing treatment at a mental health establishment shall be released to the media without the consent of such person.[142] All persons with mental illness have the right to access their basic medical records.[143] Every mentally ill person should be protected from cruel, inhuman or degrading treatment in any mental health establishment. These persons also have the right (a) to live in a safe and hygienic environment, (b) to have adequate sanitary conditions, (c) to privacy, and (d) to have proper clothing so as to protect such person from exposure of his body to maintain his dignity along with other necessary rights.[144] This Act assures the right to have mental health insurance similar to those with physical illnesses and mandates the government and private insurance companies to provide mental health insurance on par with physical illnesses.[145] In accordance with this, the Insurance Regulatory and Development Authority of India has already issued a welcome directive to health insurers to include mental illnesses in medical insurance policies.[146]

V. NATIONAL MENTAL HEALTH PROGRAMME

India was one of the first few countries around the world to formulate a National Mental Health Programme (NMHP) in 1982. The objectives of this programme were (a) to ensure the availability and accessibility of mental healthcare for all in the foreseeable future, particularly to the most vulnerable and most underprivileged sections of the population, (b) to encourage the application of mental health knowledge in

---

[141] Mental Healthcare Act 2017, Section 23.

[142] *Ibid.* Section 24.

[143] *Ibid.* Section 25.

[144] *Ibid.* Section 20.

[145] *Ibid.* Section 21(4).

[146] A. Jagadish et al., *Mental Healthcare Act 2017 - The Way Ahead: Opportunities and Challenges*, 41(2) INDIAN J. PSYCHOL. MED. 113, 114 (2019).

general health care and social development, (c) to promote community participation in mental health services.[147] Thus, the basic strategy of NMHP was to integrate the mental health care service with general health care services. Further in 1996, the National Institute of Mental Health and Neuro Sciences developed a new District Mental Health Program to operationalize and implement the NMHP in a district.

During the Eleventh Five Year Plan, the NMHP aimed to establish centres of excellence in mental health, increase intake capacity and start postgraduate courses in psychiatry. It also modernized the mental hospitals and upgraded the medical college psychiatry departments, and secured the participation of non-government organizations (NGOs) and the public sector in mental healthcare programmes.[148] However, though funds have been made available by the Central Government in a phased manner the State Governments fail to utilize them for proper implementation of the NMHP. Further, the lack of confidence in treating mental disorders by medical officers trained under the programme and lack of confidence on the part of beneficiaries are also concerning for the policy.

---

[147] Sarbjeet Khurana & Shweta Sharma, *National Mental Health Program of India: A Review of the History and the Current Scenario*, 3(10) IJCMPH 2696, 2698–2699 (2016).

[148] NIRAJ AHUJA, A SHORT TEXTBOOK OF PSYCHIATRY 236 (Jaypee Brothers 2011).

Right to Health in Context of Epidemic Diseases

The previous chapter deals with the human right to health of disabled people within the international and national legislative framework of India. However, like disabled people, people's suffering from epidemic diseases, including HIV/AIDS in particular, is also a major concern for realizing the right to health in general. Primitively, separation and isolation were the popular ways to treat epidemic diseases. Growth of human rights assures the anti-discrimination and de-stigmatization efforts in combating epidemic diseases. Today, human rights advocates are demanding life-saving treatment and specific legislative and policy approaches to deal with these issues. Under international law, epidemic diseases, including HIV/AIDS, continue to be the primary driver of global concern and action about health[1] and, thus, attempts have been made to secure healthcare access and other allied issues in the last few decades. Similarly, across the globe, judicial authorities are holding that claims to treatment articulate a justiciable right that is grounded in domestic law and is supported by international human rights commitments.[2] Within the national legal framework in India, specific attempts through legislative enactments and policy orientation are made to secure various human rights aspects including the right to health for people affected by epidemic diseases including HIV/AIDS. This chapter is primarily devoted to giving a detailed deliberation of all these efforts.

[1] Laurie Garrett, *The Challenge of Global Health*, 86(1) FOREIGN AFF. 14, 23 (2007).

[2] Noah Novogrodsky, *The Duty of Treatment: Human Rights and the HIV/AIDS Pandemic*, 12(1) YHRDLJ 1, 5 (2009).

I. CONTEMPORARY INTERNATIONAL GUIDELINES IN COMBATING EPIDEMIC AND PROTECTION OF HUMAN RIGHT TO HEALTH

In recent times, the world has faced various infectious disease emergencies, such as anthrax attacks in 2001, the rapid global spread of severe acute respiratory syndrome (SARS) in 2003, the 2009 influenza A (H1N1) pandemic, the emergence and international spread of the Middle East respiratory syndrome coronavirus (MERS-CoV), the largest Ebola epidemic on record and the emergence and spread of Zika virus and lastly the most devastating one, COVID-19.[3] The outbreak of all these epidemics and pandemics again highlights not only the importance of 'global health governance' in which states are not the only actors but also of a more observative approach of 'global public goods for health' from which all states would benefit.[4] Under Article 12 of the ICESCR, the States Parties are required to take steps to secure prevention, treatment and control of epidemic, endemic and other diseases. Thus, the obligation to report epidemic outbreaks forms a part of the minimum core obligations under the ICESCR.[5] The Committee on Economic, Social and Cultural Rights in its General Comment Number 14, 'The Right to the Highest Attainable Standard of Health (Article 12)' articulates that[6]:

> The right to treatment includes the creation of a system of urgent medical care in cases of accidents, epidemics and similar health hazards, and the provision of disaster relief and humanitarian assistance in emergency situations. The control of diseases refers to States' individual and joint efforts to, *inter alia*, make available relevant technologies, using and improving epidemiological surveillance and data collection on a disaggregated basis, the implementation or enhancement of immunization programmes and other strategies of infectious disease control.

[3] Jennifer B. Nuzzo & Matthew P. Shearer, *International Engagement Is Critical to Fighting Epidemics*, 15(1) HEALTH SECUR. 31, 33 (2017).

[4] D.P. Fidler, *SARS: Political Pathology of the First Post-Westphalian Pathogen*, 31(4) JMLE 485, 489 (2003).

[5] L.O. GOSTIN & ZITA LAZZARINI, HUMAN RIGHTS AND PUBLIC HEALTH LAW IN THE AIDS PANDEMIC 29 (OUP 1997).

[6] CESCR General Comment No. 14, Paragraph 16.

Moreover, the comment specified that some diseases are easily transmissible beyond the frontiers of a state and, thus, the international community has a collective responsibility to address this problem. Along with these, the WHO is playing a pivotal role in proposing a global concern for combating epidemic diseases. After the Second World War, the newly created WHO emphasized its work to unify the separate international sanitation treaties in a single code.[7] As a result, WHO adopted International Sanitary Regulations in 1951, which later on in 1969 was renamed as International Health Regulations. These 1969 Regulations are a legally binding set of regulations and are one of the earliest multilateral regulatory mechanisms strictly focusing on global surveillance for communicable diseases.[8] In 1995, the WHO, through the WHA, adopted a resolution on Communicable Diseases Prevention and Control: New, Emerging and Re-emerging Infectious Diseases[9] which urged (a) to strengthen national and local programmes of active surveillance for infectious diseases, ensuring that efforts are directed to early detection of outbreaks and prompt identification of new, emerging and re-emerging infectious diseases, (b) to improve routine diagnostic capabilities for common microbial pathogens so that outbreaks due to infectious diseases may be more easily identified and accurately diagnosed, (c) to enhance and to participate actively in communications between national and international services involved in disease detection, early notification, surveillance, control and response, etc.[10] In 1997, the WHO established a mechanism by working closely with its collaborating centres, governments and governmental agencies, as well as relevant non-governmental organizations and other partners in the global outbreak alert and response network to seek, collect and verify information on reported epidemics.[11]

---

[7] D.P. Fidler, *The Role of International Law in the Control of Emerging Infectious Diseases*, 95(2) Bull. Inst. Pasteur 57, 59 (1997).

[8] Obijiofor Aginam, *International Law and Communicable Diseases*, 80(12) BWHO 946, 947 (2002).

[9] Adopted by Forty-Eighth WHA on 22 February 1995.

[10] WHO, Communicable Diseases Prevention and Control: New, Emerging and Re-emerging Infectious Diseases 2 (1995), Document No. WHA 48.13.

[11] WHO, Global Health Security - Epidemic Alert and Response 2 (2001), Document No. A/54/9.

Thereafter, since the early 2000, WHO has actively promoted the idea of 'Global Health Security',[12] seeking to forward a vision of collective security in which the national security of each member State rests on the security of the whole, and in which international cooperation is key.[13] It sets the relationship between infectious diseases and globalization, arguing that 'infectious disease events in one country are potentially a concern for the entire world'.[14] Further, in 2005 the WHA adopted new the International Health Regulations (IHR) with the aim to 'prevent, protect against, control and provide a public health response to the international spread of disease in ways that are commensurate with and restricted to public health risks, and which avoid unnecessary interference with international traffic and trade'.[15] It engages State and non-State actors in addressing public health threats and draws together objectives found in multiple international legal regimes concerning infectious disease control, human rights, trade, environmental protection and security and configure them in a way that has no precedent in international law on public health.[16]

The revised IHR outline specific minimum core public health capacities and implementation processes that nations need to adequately address in combating acute public health threats. The new IHR embodies the strategy of global health security which has to be implemented through a new approach of global health governance.[17] It also emphasizes the importance of global communications and cooperation for early detection and mitigation of potential public health emergencies of international concern.[18]

---

[12] Adopted by Fifty-Fourth WHA, 2 April 2001.

[13] Adam Ferhani & Simon Rushton, *The International Health Regulations, COVID-19, and Bordering Practices: Who Gets In, What Gets Out, and Who Gets Rescued?* 41(3) CONTEMP. SECUR. POLICY 458, 462 (2020).

[14] WHO, *supra* note 11, at 1.

[15] IHR 2005, Article 2.

[16] D.P. Fidler, *From international Sanitary Conventions to Global Health Security: The New International Health Regulations*, 4(2) CHIN. J. INT. LAW 325, 325 (2005).

[17] *Ibid.* at 343.

[18] IHR 2005, Article 7.

To that end, every member state has to establish a National IHR Focal Point for communication to and from WHO and meet core capacities for disease surveillance and response.[19] Using these mechanisms, the member State has the duty to notify WHO within 24 hours of a national assessment of any event that may constitute a public health risk to other States requiring a coordinated international response.[20] In return, WHO will coordinate communications across nations, provide technical assistance to responding nations, and work with international scientific experts to develop recommendations for mitigating the consequences of the event.

Along with this, WHO develops global strategies for the prevention and control of epidemic diseases, such as yellow fever, cholera and influenza. The Pandemic Influenza Preparedness (PIP) Framework 2011[21] brings member States, WHO and other stakeholders together to implement a global approach to combat Influenza. It aims to improve pandemic influenza preparedness and response and strengthen the protection against pandemic influenza.[22] Under this scheme, the member States, through their National Influenza Centres and other authorized laboratories, have to provide, in a rapid, systematic and timely manner, PIP biological materials from all cases of H5N1 and other influenza viruses with human pandemic potential, as feasible, to the WHO Collaborating Centre on Influenza or WHO H5 Reference Laboratory.[23] Further, WHO developed the Global Influenza Strategy for 2019–2030 to (a) enhance global and national pandemic preparedness, (b) combat the ongoing threat of zoonotic influenza, and (c) improve seasonal influenza prevention and control in all countries.[24]

In October 2016, WHO's Strategic Advisory Group of Experts on Immunization reviewed existing control tools and outlined a long-term

---

[19] Ibid. Article 4.

[20] Ibid. Article 6.

[21] This document was adopted by Sixty-Fourth WHA, 24 May 2011.

[22] WHO, PANDEMIC INFLUENZA PREPAREDNESS FRAMEWORK FOR THE SHARING OF INFLUENZA VIRUSES AND ACCESS TO VACCINES AND OTHER BENEFITS 6 (WHO 2011).

[23] Ibid. at 12.

[24] WHO, GLOBAL INFLUENZA STRATEGY FOR 2019–2030: PREVENT CONTROL PREPARE 4 (WHO 2019).

and global strategy to 'Eliminate Yellow Fever Epidemics' globally by 2026.[25] WHO in collaboration with UNICEF and Gavi, coordinates member States to prevent yellow fever outbreaks and to prepare for those which might still occur.[26] It consists of three strategic objectives (a) protect at-risk populations, (b) prevent international spread, and (c) contain outbreaks rapidly. It aims to minimize suffering, damage and spread by early and reliable detection and rapid and appropriate response. The strategy highlights the importance of strong surveillance and diagnostic capacities to allow early detection of outbreaks and rapid implementation of control measures that can help to mitigate the risk of spreading of diseases. Further, Ending Cholera: a Global Roadmap to 2030 is the WHO's response towards the Cholera epidem ics. The Global Task Force on Cholera Control came up with this new roadmap on October 4, 2017. It is a new global strategy for cholera control at the country level and provides a concrete path toward a world in which cholera is no longer a threat to public health.[27] The strategy focuses on 47 countries affected by cholera today and on three basic strategic axes (a) early detection and quick response to contain outbreaks, (b) a targeted multi-sectoral approach to prevent cholera recurrence, and (c) an effective mechanism of coordination for technical support, advocacy, resource mobilization, and partnership at local and global levels.

Moreover, the TRIPS Agreement offers a set of legal frameworks to provide the minimum standards for intellectual property protection including patent protection to pharmaceutical products. By inter- preting the provisions of the TRIPS Agreement, in November 2001, World Trade Organization (WTO) Ministerial Conference adopted the Doha Declaration, which recognized the gravity of the public health problems afflicting many developing countries, especially HIV/AIDS,

---

[25] Nedghie Adrien et al., *Differences Between Coverage of Yellow Fever Vaccine and the First Dose of Measles-Containing Vaccine: A Desk Review of Global Data Sources*, 37(32) VACCINE 4511, 4512 (2019).

[26] WHO et al., A GLOBAL STRATEGY TO ELIMINATE YELLOW FEVER EPIDEMICS (EYE) 2017–2026 (WHO 2018).

[27] GLOBAL TASK FORCE ON CHOLERA CONTROL, ENDING CHOLERA: A GLOBAL ROADMAP TO 2030 4 (WHO 2017).

tuberculosis, malaria, and other epidemics. Hence, it assumes that the TRIPs Agreement must be interpreted and implemented in such a way that the WTO member states have the right to protect public health and to promote access to medicine.[28] Thus, international law played a critical role in securing the surveillance and treatment of epidemic diseases.

II. LEGISLATIONS APPLICABLE IN COMBATING EPIDEMIC DISEASES IN INDIA

The legislative scheme for combating the spread of epidemic diseases in India consists of two types of legislations. One set is specifically dealt with procedures in combating the spreading of epidemic diseases. This set includes Epidemic Diseases Act 1897 and Disaster Management Act 2005. The other set comprises the Indian Penal Code 1860, which provides penal sections for spreading infectious diseases and violating quarantine rules.

A. Epidemic Diseases Act, 1897

The 1897 Epidemic Diseases Act[29] was enacted as a response to the plague epidemic in Bombay.[30] Thereafter, it was frequently applied to the containment of epidemics like cholera, malaria and dengue and swine flu.[31] The Act aims to prevent the spread of dangerous epidemic diseases. This Act is one of the shortest Acts in India, comprising just four Sections.[32] It is recently amended in 2020 through an Ordinance dated April 22, 2020. Section 1 describes the title and the extent of

---

[28] Aliasghar Kheirkhah et al., *Investigating the Role of International Law in Controlling Communicable Diseases*, 1(2) IMMI 38, 40 (2016).

[29] Act No. III of 1897. It was enacted on 4 February 1897.

[30] Binod K. Patro et al., *Epidemic Diseases Act 1897, India: Whether Sufficient to Address the Current Challenges?* 18(2) J. MGIMS 109, 110 (2013).

[31] M.Z.M. Nomani et al., *Quarantine Law Enforcement and Corona Virus (COVID-19) Pandemic in India*, 14(4) JXU 536 (2020).

[32] P.S. Rakesh, *The Epidemic Diseases Act of 1897: Public Health Relevance in the Current Scenario*, 1(3) IJME 156 (2016).

the Act and Section 2 empowers the State and Central Government to take special measures and prescribe regulations that are to be observed by the public to prevent the spread of specific diseases. Thus, Section 2 states:

> When the State Government is satisfied that the State or any part thereof is visited by or threatened with an outbreak of any dangerous epidemic disease; and if it thinks that the ordinary provisions of the law are insufficient for the purpose, the state may take, or require or empower any person to take some measures and, by public notice, prescribe such temporary regulations to be observed by the public or by any person or class of persons as it shall deem necessary to prevent the outbreak of such disease or the spread thereof, and may determine in what manner and by whom any expenses incurred (including compensation if any) shall be defrayed.

This empowers the State Governments to arrange services of doctors in districts when there is a shortage of doctors in such districts during the epidemic situation. The application of this provision depends on the satisfaction of the State Government or any person empowered by the State Government.[33] During this COVID-19 situation, some State Governments had declared COVID-19 as an epidemic, in order to invoke the emergency provisions of the Epidemic Diseases Act, 1897.[34] Thus, recently, by issuing a set of guidelines called 'Guidelines for notifying COVID-19 affected persons by Private Institutions', the Government had clearly applied its mind to the provisions of the 1897 Act which permit the Government 'to take measures necessary to prevent the outbreak and spread thereof' by permitting private laboratories and hospitals to be involved in preventing the spread of the epidemics. By giving approval to this fact, the Telangana High Court in *Ganta Jai Kumar v. State of Telangana*,[35] held that in a case where there is a dangerous epidemic disease for which the ordinary provisions of the law are insufficient, the State may take, require or empower any person to take 'such measures' and by public notice such 'temporary regulations' to be observed by the public or by any person or class of

---

[33] *Shakuntala P. Devlekar v. Surat Municipal Corporation*, (2003) 4 G.L.R. 154.

[34] In Re: Contagion of Covid-19 Virus in Prisons, (2020) 5 S.C.C. 313.

[35] A.I.R. 2020 NULL 139.

persons as it shall deem necessary to prevent the outbreak of disease or the spread thereof. Thus, during 1897 the concept of private sector participation in health care was hardly there in India, though there is no power in Section 2 of the Epidemic Diseases Act, 1897 to prevent private hospitals from testing suspected victims of an epidemic such as COVID-19 patients or from treating confirmed infected patients. The Act empowers the Central Government to inspect any ship or vessel when the ship or vessel is leaving or arriving at any port and detain in any port. The Central Government also has the power to inspect any person intending to sail from or arriving at any port.[36] The Epidemic Diseases (Amendment) Ordinance, 2020 expands these powers of inspection to any bus, train, goods vehicle, and aircraft leaving or arriving at any land port, port or aerodrome.[37] Section 3 prescribes a penalty as per Section 188 of the Indian Penal Code for disobeying any order or regulation made under this Act. It is noteworthy that Section 188 of the Penal Code provides six months of imprisonment or 1,000 rupees fine or both as punishment for violating the rules made under the Epidemic Diseases Act, 1897. Thus, by the combined effect of these provisions along with the other provisions of criminal law, police are empowered to arrest the person who is violating the quarantine rules.[38] Further, the 1897 Act provides that an act done in good faith can be considered as a defence under the Act.[39]

The 2020 Ordinance specifies the inclusion of Section 2B in the original Act of 1897 to provide security to the healthcare personnel. It provides that no person should indulge in any act of violence against a healthcare service personnel, or cause damage or loss to any property during an epidemic.[40] Contravention of this provision is punishable with imprisonment for a term which shall not be less than three months and may extend to five years, and with a fine between fifty thousand rupees and two lakh rupees. Moreover, if such act of violence

[36] Epidemic Diseases Act 1897, Section 2A.
[37] Epidemic Diseases (Amendment) Ordinance, 2020, Section 4.
[38] *Siddharth Varadarajan v. State of U. P.*, 2020 (2) A.C.R. 2026.
[39] *Supra* note 36, Section 4.
[40] *Supra* note 37, Section 5.

against a healthcare service personnel causes grievous hart, the person committing the offence is punishable with imprisonment for a term which shall not be less than six months and may extend to seven years, and a fine between one lakh rupees and five lakh rupees.[41] All the offences under this provision are cognizable and non-bailable.[42] Thus, for the first time under the Indian legislative system-specific provision is provided to secure the safety of the healthcare personals. Thus, this new ordinance provides a broader ambit to apply the Epidemic Diseases Act. However, this age-old Act overtime has accumulated various loopholes with regards to the changing priorities in the field of public health.[43] The 1897 Act has not defined 'dangerous epidemic disease'. Apart from the isolation or quarantine measures, the Act is also silent about the availability and distribution of vaccines and drugs and the implementation of response measures. Further, it is not in line with the contemporary scientific understanding of outbreak prevention and response, but only reflects the scientific and legal standards that prevailed at the time when it was framed.[44]

B. Disaster Management Act, 2005

Disaster Management is an age-old concern for the revival of human civilization after any kind of disaster. After prolonged discussions and pursuant to the recommendations of the High Power Committee on Disaster Management, the parliament enacted the Disaster Management Act[45] in 2005 to act as the foundational legislation of disaster management in the country.[46] The primary approach of post-disaster management has been changed with the enactment of the Disaster Management Act of 2005 and the paradigm shifts from response and

---

[41] *Ibid.* Section 6.

[42] *Ibid.* Section 7

[43] T.J. John et al., *Continuing Challenge of Infectious Diseases in India*, 377 LANCET 252 (2011).

[44] Rakesh, *supra* note 32, at 157.

[45] Act No. LIII of 2005. It was enacted on 23 December 2005.

[46] Rajendra Kumar Pandey, *Legal Framework of Disaster Management in India*, (Winter Issue) ILI L. REV. 172, 180 (2016).

relief to mitigation and preparedness.[47] The Act was enacted to provide effective management of disasters.[48] The term 'disaster management' includes prevention of danger/threat of a disaster, mitigation or reduction of risk of a disaster, preparedness to deal with the disaster and prompt response to any threatening disaster situation or disaster etc.[49] While Section 3 articulates the constitution of the National Disaster Management Authority (NDMA) for the purposes of the Act, Section 8 provides for the constitution of the National Executive Committee as the main functional group of the NDMA. The National Executive Committee is to assist the National Authority in the discharge of its functions and has the responsibility for implementing the policies and plans of the National authority and ensure the compliance of the directions issued by the Central Government.[50] In pursuance of these provisions, in *Gurusimran Singh Narula v. Union of India*,[51] the Supreme Court held that these provisions of the Disaster Management Act are not only provisions of empowerment but also cast a duty on different authorities to act in the best interest of the people to sub-serve the objects of the Act. Thus, the framework assures the implementation of the schemes for the benefit of the people.

With respect to the right to health and combating epidemic diseases, the Act concentrates on the issue of providing healthcare support to disaster-affected persons. In the aftermath of a disaster, maintenance of hygiene through a quickly reorganized sanitation system and restoring the supply of potable water becomes absolutely essential.[52] The 2005 Act directed the State Executive Committee to provide shelter, food, drinking water, essential healthcare and services to assist and protect the community affected by disaster or threatening disaster situations.[53] However, the National Authority and State Authority have

---

[47] H. Shivananda & P.K. Gautam, *Reassessing India's Disaster Management Preparedness and the Role of the Indian Armed Forces Focus*, 6(1) JDS 102 (2012).

[48] Statement of Object of the Disaster Management Act, 2005.

[49] *Gurusimran Singh Narula v. Union of India*, (2021) 1 S.C.C. 152.

[50] Disaster Management Act 2005, Section 10.

[51] (2021) 1 S.C.C. 152.

[52] A. Sinha & R. Srivastava, *Concept Objectives and Challenges of Disaster Management*, 6(7) IJSR 418, 422 (2015).

[53] Disaster Management Act 2005, Section 24(d).

the power to specify the standard of all these essential amenities.[54] The same duty is deputed by the 2005 Act upon the District Authority also. By interpreting the responsibility of the National Authority in framing minimum standards of relief with respect to COVID-19, the Supreme Court in *Centre for Public Interest Litigation v. Union of India*,[55] observed that the guidelines brought on record, which were in existence since before the declaration of COVID-19 pandemic, covers all statutory requirement as enumerated in Section 12. Section 12 contemplates minimum standards of relief to be provided to persons affected by the disaster. The word disaster mentioned in Section 12 encompasses all the disasters including the present COVID-19 disaster. Furthermore, Section 12 does not contemplate that there shall be different guidelines for minimum standards of relief for different disasters. Therefore, the Central Government is not obliged to lay down minimum standards of relief under Section 12 of the Act, 2005 for COVID-19 and the earlier guidelines issued under Section 12 providing for minimum standards of relief holds good for pandemic COVID-19 also.

Further, the Act also casts the responsibilities upon the Ministries or Departments of Government of India to make available its resources to the National Executive Committee or State Executive Committee for the purposes of responding promptly and effectively to any threatening disaster situation or disaster.[56] The Supreme Court in *Swaraj Abhiyan v. Union of India*[57] observed the utility of Section 36 of the 2005 Act and held that it places a responsibility on every Ministry or Department of the Government of India to take measures necessary for the prevention of disasters, mitigation, preparedness and capacity building in accordance with the guidelines laid down by the National Authority. It casts a duty to provide drinking water and healthcare services. It is notable that on March 25, 2020, the Disaster Management Act 2005

[54] *Ibid.* Section 12(1). In *Fukan Rabha v. State of Assam*, (2012 (5) G.L.T. 482) the Guwahati High Court held that as per the mandate of the Disaster Management Act, 2005, a National Disaster Management Authority has been set up principally in order to address all aspects of disaster management and mitigation and management of the situations arising out of natural disasters.

[55] A.I.R. 2020 S.C. 5075.

[56] Disaster Management Act 2005, Sections 34(e) and 36(g)(v).

[57] A.I.R. 2016 S.C. 2953.

was invoked in India for the first time since it was passed to tackle the COVID-19 pandemic that was then in its initial stages of spreading. The order directed the ministries and departments of the Government of India and State Governments along with State Disaster Management Authorities to take measures for 'ensuring social distancing so as to prevent the spread of COVID-19 in the country'.[58]

C. Quarantine Laws in IPC

Apart from the specific legislations like the Epidemic Diseases Act, 1897 and Disaster Management Act, 2005, the Indian Penal Code, 1860[59] (IPC) puts certain criminal liability in cases of violation of quarantine rules and spreading infectious disease. Thus, the IPC is one of the earliest legislations of the country containing provisions relating to offences affecting public health safety convenience, decency and morals.[60] Majorly Sections 269 and 270 deal with the punishment for spreading infectious disease and 271 deals with the punishment for violating quarantine rules. Section 269 provides that whoever unlawfully or negligently spreads infection shall be imprisoned for six months or pay a fine or both. This provision is there to control the spreading of infectious diseases. For the application of this provision, two major perquisites are there: (a) it must be shown that the accused has knowledge that the disease is infectious, and (b) the infection which is likely to be spread must be of disease dangerous to life.[61] Thus the purport of Section 269 of IPC is not pertaining to the cause of infection, but it is about the spread of infection.[62] Further, Section 270 of IPC, prescribes punishment for any person whose malignant act is likely to spread infection and in that case, the person shall be punishable with two years imprisonment or with fine, or both. Thus, a bare reading of Section 270, clearly shows that this provision is applicable only if a person malignantly does any act which is, and which

---

[58] *Rachna v. Union of India*, 2021 (2) S.C.T. 26 (S.C.).

[59] Act No. XLV of 1860. It was enacted on 6 October 1860.

[60] Nomani et al., *supra* note 31.

[61] *Raman Kumar v. State of Jharkhand*, 2006 Cri. L.J. 4496.

[62] *Vikram Singh Chouhan v. State of Rajasthan*, 2018 (184) A.I.C. 495.

he knows or has reason to believe to be, likely to spread infection of any disease dangerous to life.[63] The expression 'malignantly' differentiates this provision from Section 269. The expression 'malignantly' is synonymous with 'maliciously'.[64] The Madhya Pradesh High Court in *State Government, Madhya Pradesh v. Indarsingh Labhsingh*,[65] observed that the word 'malignantly' implies, the doing of a thing with malice or ill-will. In its legal sense, it means a wrongful act done intentionally, without just cause or excuse, which is different than unlawful or negligent.

By applying both these provisions, the Bombay High Court, in *Hla Shwe v. State of Maharashtra*,[66] held that to attract ingredients of Sections 269 and 270, the person must commit any act which he knows is likely to spread infection of any disease which is dangerous to life. The Court further observed that it is not in dispute that the applicants had undergone the COVID-19 test during their period of quarantine and their test report for infection of COVID-19 was negative. It is also not disputed that they were kept in isolation from 24.03.2020 till 31.03.2020. There is no material on record to prove that applicants had indulged in any act which was likely to spread infection of COVID-19. Therefore, from the material produced in the charge sheet, there is no evidence to substantiate the fulfilment of ingredients of Sections 269 and 270 of the IPC. In addition to these, Section 271 IPC, prescribes punishment of imprisonment which may extend to six months or of fine or both for disobeying quarantine rules.

III. NATIONAL POLICY AND PLAN FOR DISASTER MANAGEMENT AND CONTROL OF EPIDEMIC IN INDIA

Efficient management of disasters, rather than a mere response to their occurrence has, in recent times, received increased attention in India and as a result, National Policy on Disaster Management was adopted by the NDMA in 2009. It aims at ensuring an efficient mechanism for

---

[63] *Dipika Saikia v. Mrinaljyoti Bordoloi*, 2013 (1) G.L.D. 255 (Gau).

[64] *Sabhajeet Maurya v. State NCT of Delhi*, 276 (2021) D.L.T. 439.

[65] A.I.R. 1962 M.P. 292.

[66] 2020 (4) Bom C.R. (Cri) 154.

identification, assessment and monitoring of disaster risks, and developing contemporary forecasting and early warning systems backed by responsive and failsafe communication with information technology support.[67] It emphasizes medical preparedness as a crucial component for any disaster management plan. Under the scheme of this policy, the NDMA, in close coordination with the Ministry of Health and Family Welfare, states and premier medical research institutes will formulate policy guidelines to enhance capacity in emergency medical response and mass casualty management. Further, the State and District authorities are responsible to formulate appropriate procedures for the treatment of casualties by private hospitals during disasters. The policy also suggests that disaster management plans have to address the post-disaster disease surveillance systems, networking with hospitals, referral institutions and accessing services and facilities such as the availability of ambulances and blood banks.[68] The 2009 Policy also suggested the creation of mobile surgical teams, mobile hospitals and mobile ambulances for evacuation of patients. It also recommended for proper and speedy disposal of the dead bodies.[69]

Section 11 of the Disaster Management Act 2005 requires the drawing up of a National Plan for disaster management in consultation with State Governments and expert bodies or organizations in the field of disaster management.[70] In parity with this, in 2016 National Disaster Management Plan was adopted by NDMA and the same is revised in 2019. This revised plan within the ambit of Human- Hazards includes the disasters related to biological emergencies and epidemics.[71] The Biological emergency is one which generally causes due to natural outbreaks of epidemics or intentional use of biological agents (viruses and microorganisms) or toxins through the dissemination of such agents in ways to harm the human population, food crops and livestock. Thus, as a result, outbreaks of diseases occur. For biological emergencies, the

---

[67] National Policy on Disaster Management 2009, Paragraph 2.4.1.

[68] *Ibid.* Paragraph 5.2.8.

[69] *Ibid.* Paragraph 5.2.9.

[70] *Gaurav Kumar Bansal v. Union of India,* (2017) 6 S.C.C. 730.

[71] National Disaster Management Plan 2019, Paragraph 2.2.3.3.

Ministry of Health and Family Welfare of the Central Government is the nodal agency under the Plan,[72] thus the primary responsibility to tackle this kind of disaster is vested on it. To secure a long-time solution, the 2019 Plan directed the Ministry of Home and Family Welfare, Central Government to improve coverage of community health and epidemic management.[73] Thus, the National Policy and Plan provide a detailed guideline in combating the outbreak of epidemic diseases.

IV. HUMAN RIGHTS AND PERSONS LIVING WITH HIV/AIDS: GENERAL OVERVIEW

Human Immunodeficiency Virus (HIV) and Acquired Immunodeficiency Syndrome (AIDS) are well-known diseases and gave birth to socio-legal challenges in the contemporary era. The HIV/AIDS epidemic has continued to exaggerate over the last two and half decades and has affected health scenarios in the international as well as a national arena.[74] The susceptibility to HIV/AIDS does not depend upon race, ethnicity, gender, age or even sexual orientation and HIV/AIDS has no short-term solution.[75] In addition to the physical issues, the mental health issue of these infected persons is very vulnerable. The infected persons might feel inferior to others if their HIV-positive status is disclosed. Unauthorized disclosures not only revealed the person's health status but also generated speculation as to his or her sexual orientation or use of injection drugs and thus cause harm to the dignity of the individual.[76]

Moreover, stigmatization from HIV/AIDS deeply degrades the person's personality from a whole to an ordinary and finally to a stigmatized human being, as a result, the person loses social status and gets

---

[72] *Small Scale Industrial Manufactures Association v. Union of India*, 278 (2021) D.L.T. 1.

[73] *Ibid*. Paragraph 7.2.5.

[74] F. Shu-Acquaye, *The Legal Implications of Living with HIV/AIDS in a Developing Country: The African Story*, 32(1) SJILC 51 (2004).

[75] L.O. Gostin et al., *The Public Health Information Infrastructure: A National Review of Health Information Privacy*, 275(24) JAMA 1921 (1996).

[76] L.O. Gostin, The AIDS Pandemic: Complacency, Injustice and Unfulfilled Expectations 9 (University of North Carolina Press 2004).

labels. Thus, the social stigma and its impact on the mental health of the people living with HIV/AIDS are pervasive problems regarding the attempts of HIV prevention, diagnosis, and treatment.[77] As a result, much of the discriminating attitude has resulted purely on the basis of their HIV/AIDS status or association with groups at risk.[78] Moreover, the opposite phenomenon is also true, that is poor mental health or in some cases, mental illness has a critical role in HIV/AIDS acquisition across populations. Apart from social stigma, these people often face other significant individual, biological and structural challenges to accessing and adhering to HIV prevention and treatment modalities. The individual factors include the domains of socio-demographics, neighbourhood and local environmental factors. Socio-demographics factors consist of poverty, unstable housing, low education and food insecurity, and these contribute to increase vulnerability to HIV infection and poor HIV health outcomes. Biological factors, including comorbid communicable diseases (e.g., hepatitis, tuberculosis) and noncommunicable diseases (e.g., diabetes, bone disease, heart disease), contribute to poorer physical and mental health outcomes.[79] Neighbourhood and environmental factors include violence and lack of safety, lack of adequate delivery of medical supplies, and thus, present barriers to healthcare access for the people with HIV/AIDS. Hence, HIV/AIDS are now recognized as an immense challenge to international security, peace and development under international human rights law.

As per the legal recognition to the right of people living with HIV/AIDS, there are prerequisites such as (a) recognition of the right to access of health services, (b) discrimination based on HIV status, which undermines access, should be prohibited, (c) laws against sexual violence and exploitation, which perpetuate the spread of HIV and its negative effects, should be enforced, (d) realization of those rights through human rights framework, and (e) drafting the law

---

[77] Emmanuel N. Kontomanolis et al., *The Social Stigma of HIV-AIDS: Society's Role*, 9 HIV/AIDS - Res. Palliat. Care. 111, 115 (2017).

[78] Gostin, *supra* note 76, at 10.

[79] Robert H. Remiena et al., *Mental Health and HIV/AIDS: The Need for an Integrated Response*, 33(9) AIDS 1411, 1413 (2019).

more effectively to protect the health.[80] As a result of these prerequisites, global health governance has started to consider human rights aspects in framing policy response to HIV/AIDS. Jonathan Mann, the first Director of the WHO's Global Programme on AIDS, identified the international human rights law as a comprehensive framework by which responsibility could be cast upon the State for addressing the underlying causes of HIV/AIDS, trauma and other health threats.[81] Under the human rights jurisprudence, two methods have been evolved for the protection of the right of HIV/AIDS affected persons. These are (a) prevention of discrimination and stigmatization, and (b) access to advance treatment, antiretroviral drugs and hold States accountable for their HIV policies.[82] However, under the present health care system, there is a movement from the negative right of discrimination to the positive right of access for the persons living with HIV/AIDS. In addition to this, the international human rights law sets concrete, time-bound targets for the introduction of national legislation, policy and other measures to ensure the respect of rights of people living with HIV/AIDS in regard to education, inheritance, employment, privacy, legal protection and health care services including prevention, support, and treatment.[83] Moreover, the international human rights regime speaks about the obligations of public health practitioners for the protection and promotion of health at a population level for curbing HIV/AIDS.[84]

V. INTERNATIONAL GUIDELINES ON HIV/AIDS AND PROTECTION OF RIGHT TO HEALTH

Respecting, protecting and fulfilling human rights including the right to health of people affected with HIV/AIDS is a long-time demand

---

[80] L. Gable et al., *HIV/AIDS, Reproductive and Sexual Health, and the Law*, 98(10) AJPH 1779 (2008).

[81] David Patterson & Leslie London, *International Law, Human Rights and HIV/AIDS*, 80(12) BWHO 964, 965 (2002).

[82] Gostin, *supra* note 76, at 8.

[83] General Assembly, *Declaration of Commitment on HIV/AIDS* (UN 2001) Paragraphs 16.

[84] Patterson & London, *supra* note 81, at 967.

under international legal jurisprudence. Though there is no specific mention of HIV/AIDS in Article 12 of the ICESCR, the CESCR in its General Comment Number 14, 'The Right to the Highest Attainable Standard of Health (Article 12)' recognizes that[85]:

> [F]ormerly unknown diseases, such as human immunodeficiency virus and acquired immunodeficiency syndrome (HIV/AIDS) ... have created new obstacles for the realization of the right to health which need to be taken into account when interpreting article 12.

It further suggested to secure health facilities, goods and services within safe physical reach for all sections of the population, especially vulnerable or marginalized groups including persons with HIV/AIDS.[86] As per Article 12(3) of the ICESCR, that is, 'The prevention, treatment and control of epidemic, endemic, occupational and other diseases' the establishment of prevention and education programmes need to be there for behaviour-related health concerns such as sexually transmitted diseases, in particular HIV/AIDS.[87] Core obligations in this context include the provision of essential drugs to treat HIV/AIDS also. Moreover, the State parties have to organize information campaigns in particular with respect to HIV/AIDS as part of the States' obligation under ICESCR.[88]

Thus, the right-based approach to the problems of HIV/AIDS affected people always has been recognized as an essential element of ethical and effective responses to this epidemic. In pursuance of this demand, in 1996, an international expert consultation group was convened by the UN AIDS Committee along with the Office of the High Commissioner for Human Rights to prepare guidelines for State parties regarding the application of international law in the context of HIV/AIDS. The guidelines prepared by this consultation group, namely 'International Guidelines on HIV/AIDS and Human Rights' were tabled at the 53rd

---

[85] CESCR General Comment No. 14, Paragraph 10.

[86] *Ibid.* Paragraph 12.

[87] *Ibid.* Paragraph 16.

[88] *Ibid.* Paragraph 36.

session of the Commission on Human Rights in 1997.[89] The group provides 12 Guidelines for the States to implement an effective, rights-based response to the issues of HIV/AIDS. States should (a) establish an effective national framework to ensure a coordinated, participatory, transparent and accountable approach towards HIV/AIDS affected people and to integrate HIV policy and programmes, (b) ensure community participation through political and financial support, (c) review and reform public health laws to ensure that they adequately address public health issues raised by HIV, (d) review and reform criminal laws and correctional systems to ensure consistency with international human rights obligations and to prevent misuse of the same in the context of HIV, (e) enact or strengthen anti-discrimination and other protective laws, (f) enact national legislation to regulate HIV-related goods, services and information, (g) educate people affected by HIV about their rights, provide free legal services to enforce those rights, develop expertise on HIV-related legal issues, (h) promote a supportive and enabling environment for women, children and other vulnerable groups in collaboration with the community, (i) promote creative education, training and media programmes explicitly designed to change attitudes of towards HIV, (j) ensure that Government and the private sector develop codes of conduct regarding HIV issues, (k) ensure monitoring and enforcement mechanisms to guarantee the protection of HIV-related human rights, and (l) cooperate with the United Nations system, including UNAIDS, to share knowledge and experience concerning HIV related human rights issues.[90]

These Guidelines aim to assist States in translating international human rights norms into practical observance in the context of HIV/AIDS.[91] In 1998 these International Guidelines were adopted by the International Council of AIDS Service Organizations (ICASO), which decided to focus human rights advocacy around these Guidelines at the international level. Thus, the promotion and acceptance of

---

[89] Patterson & London, *supra* note 81, 965.

[90] UNHC on Human Rights and UNAIDS, International Guidelines on HIV/AIDS and Human Rights 17–19 (UNAIDS 2006).

[91] Novogrodsky, *supra* note 2, at 15.

the human rights approach to address the issues of HIV/AIDS have reached their zenith.[92] Furthermore, the UN adopted the Declaration of Commitment on HIV/AIDS on 26 June 2001[93] which constitutes a global commitment to enhancing coordination and intensification of national, regional and international efforts to combat HIV/AIDS comprehensively.[94] This Declaration provides specific objectives for the national level, regional and subregional level and global level. At the national level, it fixes the goal to ensure the development and implementation of multi-sectoral national strategies and financing plans for combating HIV/AIDS which includes promotion and protection of the right to the highest attainable standard of physical and mental health by 2003.[95]

Further, Millennium Development Goals (MDGs) specifies combating HIV/AIDS, malaria and other diseases as Goal 6 to be achieved by 2015. The target is to have halted and begun to reverse the spread of HIV/AIDS by 2015.[96] Moreover, to achieve Goal 6, the MDGs fixe three indicators: (a) HIV prevalence among pregnant women aged 15–24 years,[97] (b) Condom use rate of the contraceptive prevalence rate,[98] and (c) Ratio of school attendance of orphans to school attendance of non-orphans aged 10–14 years.[99] Primarily it was criticized that within the framework of Goal 6, there is no mention of health systems or a call for rights-based universal access to decent health services and medicines.[100] The MDG monitoring framework, to address this issue,

---

[92] Mark Heywood & Dennis Altman, *Confronting AIDS: Human Rights, Law, and Social Transformation*, 5(1) HHR 149, 156 (2000).

[93] Adopted by UN in the Twenty-sixth Special Session. Document No. A/RES/S-26/2.

[94] Declaration of Commitment on HIV/AIDS 2001, Paragraph 1.

[95] *Ibid.* Paragraph 37.

[96] ADAM WAGSTAFF & MARIAM CLAESON, THE MILLENNIUM DEVELOPMENT GOALS FOR HEALTH: RISING OF THE CHALLENGES 2 (World Bank 2004).

[97] MDGs 2000, Goal 6, Indicator 18.

[98] *Ibid.* Indicator 19.

[99] *Ibid.* Indicator 20.

[100] Ashwani Saith, *From Universal Values to Millennium Development Goals: Lost in Translation*, 37(6) DEV. CHANGE 1167, 1189 (2006).

was revised in 2007 to include four new targets agreed on by Member States at the 2005 World Summit. One of them is access to treatment for HIV/AIDS.[101] Thus, the revision specifies the need for treatment for people living with HIV/AIDS, which is one of the human rights paradigms for the protection of people living with HIV/AIDS. Further, though there is no specific mention of HIV/AIDS in the Sustainable Development Goals of 2015, in its document 'Transforming Our World: The 2030 Agenda for Sustainable Development' the United Nations specified that the organization will accelerate the pace of progress made in fighting with HIV/AIDS.[102] Hence, it assures the continuance of working of the international legal regimes in combating and halting HIV/AIDS.

VI. LEGISLATIVE FRAMEWORK RELATED TO HIV/AIDS AFFECTED PERSONS: HIV AND AIDS (PREVENTION AND CONTROL) ACT, 2017

Health, nutrition and education are the three inputs accepted as significant for the development of people with HIV/AIDS. Human Immunodeficiency Virus (HIV) and Acquired Immune Deficiency Syndrome (AIDS) are evolved as a threat to health in recent times. In 1989 for the first time the AIDS Prevention Bill was introduced in the Parliament, but it fails to get assent. However, the Human Immunodeficiency Virus and Acquired Immune Deficiency Syndrome (Prevention and Control) Act[103] finally enacted on April 20, 2017. The 2017 HIV and AIDS (Prevention and Control) Act was enacted to prevent and control HIV/AIDS disease. In detail, it makes an attempt to protect and secure the human rights of persons who are HIV-positive or affected by HIV/AIDS.[104]

---

[101] Other three are: (i) full and productive employment and decent work for all, (ii) access to reproductive health, and (iii) protection of biodiversity.

[102] UN Doc. A/RES/70/1 (2015), Paragraph 26.

[103] Act No. XVI of 2017.

[104] HIV and AIDS (Prevention and Control) Act 2017, Preamble.

A. Prevention of Discrimination in Access to Healthcare

Section 3(c) provides that there should not be discrimination against any person on the ground that he is affected with HIV/AIDS in healthcare services. There should not be any denial or discontinuation of, or, unfair treatment in, healthcare services also. Moreover, no person should, by words, either spoken or written, publish, propagate, advocate or communicate by signs or by visible representation or otherwise the feelings of hatred against any protected persons or disseminate, broadcast or display any information, advertisement or notice, which may reasonably be construed to demonstrate an intention to propagate hatred or which is likely to expose protected persons to hatred, discrimination or physical violence.[105] Thus, in *Ramesh Kumar v. Union of India*,[106] the Patna High Court allowed the complaint under this provision and observed that the factum of the petitioner being HIV positive was disclosed, enable the application of this provision which prevented criticizing or broadcasting the disease of some other person through words either spoken or written, publish, propagate, advocate or communicate by signs. Further, Section 37 of the 2017 Act provides the penalty for contravention of this provision. Section 37 states that whoever contravenes the provisions of Section 4 can be punished with imprisonment for a term which shall not be less than three months but which may extend to two years and with a fine which may extend to one lakh rupees, or with both.

B. Consent for Medical Intervention

Consent of the patients or their relatives is another important aspect related to the rights of HIV/AIDS-affected persons. In this modern medical era concept of consent has two basic components: (a) whether the consent is an informed one? and (b) whether the person who is giving consent can give it? The 2017 Act describes 'informed consent' as a consent given by any individual or his representative specific to a

---

[105] *Ibid.* Section 4.
[106] 2020 (2) S.L.R. 950.

proposed intervention without any coercion, undue influence, fraud, mistake or misrepresentation and such consent obtained after notifying such information, as specified in the guidelines, relating to risks and benefits of the proposed intervention in such manner and in such language as understood by that individual or his representative.[107] Further, a person has the ability to give consent only if he has the capacity to understand and appreciate the nature and consequences of a proposed action and to make an informed decision concerning such action.[108] Section 5 of the Act prevents the performance of HIV tests and medical treatment or medical interventions upon any protected person without the informed consent of such person or his representative. The 2017 Act also provides certain situations when informed consent is not required for doing the medical intervention. Those are (a) where a Court orders to carry out HIV test of any person for the determination of issues in the matter before it, (b) in case of procuring, processing, distribution or use of a human body or any part thereof including tissues, blood, semen or other body fluids for use in medical research or therapy, (c) in case of epidemiological or surveillance purposes where the HIV test is anonymous and is not for the purpose of determining the HIV status of a person, and (d) in case of screening purposes in any licensed blood bank.[109]

C. Disclosure of HIV Status

Privacy of information related to HIV-positive status is another important aspect in connection to a protected person's right to health. The 2017 Act provides that no person should be compelled to disclose his HIV status except by an order of the Court when the disclosure of such information is necessary in the interest of justice. The third-party should not disclose the HIV status or any other private information of another person which he received due to a relationship of a fiduciary nature, except with the informed consent of the person affected by HIV/AIDS or a representative of such person obtained in the manner as

[107] *Ibid.* Section 2(n).
[108] *Ibid.* Section 2(b).
[109] *Ibid.* Section 6.

specified in Section 5 and the fact of such consent has to be recorded in writing.[110] Such informed consent for disclosure is not required in case of (a) disclosure by a healthcare provider to another healthcare provider who is involved in the care, treatment or counselling of such person, when such disclosure is necessary to provide care or treatment to that person, (b) an order of a court that the disclosure of such information is necessary in the interest of justice, (c) suits or legal proceedings between persons where the disclosure of such information is necessary for filing suits or legal proceedings or for instructing their counsels, (d) requirement under Section 9, (e) it relates to statistical or other information of a person that could not reasonably be expected to lead to the identification of that person, and (f) disclosure to the officers of the Central Government or the State Government or State AIDS Control Society for the purposes of monitoring, evaluation or supervision.[111] Section 9 permits the physician or a counsellor to disclose the HIV-positive status of a person to his or her partner. Further Section 10 directs the HIV-positive to take all reasonable precautions to prevent the transmission of HIV to other persons.

D. Welfare Measures

In a welfare State, both the Central and State Governments have to take measures to facilitate better access to welfare schemes to persons affected by HIV/AIDS and also frame schemes to address the needs of all protected persons.[112] Further, Section 17 empowers the Central Government as well as State Governments to formulate HIV and AIDS-related information which is age-appropriate, gender-sensitive, non-stigmatizing and non-discriminatory. The Central Government has the duty to lay down guidelines for the care, support and treatment of children infected with HIV/AIDS. Moreover, in the case of the HIV-positive pregnant woman, sterilization or abortion should not be done without her informed consent.[113] Thus, the 2017 Act procures

---

[110] *Ibid.* Section 8(1).

[111] *Ibid.* Section 8(2).

[112] *Ibid.* Section 15.

[113] *Ibid.* Section 18.

the human rights of the persons infected with HIV/AIDS and specifies the duties of the Governments in securing those rights. Ombudsman has the power to review the implementation and violation of the Act.

VII. NATIONAL AIDS CONTROL PROGRAMME IN INDIA

HIV is a lentivirus of the retrovirus group which may cause HIV infection or AIDS. AIDS has emerged as one of the most serious health problems in India after its first case was reported in 1986. Since then India has made substantial progress in achieving targets related to HIV/AIDS. The National AIDS Control Programme (NACP) was launched in 1987, with a focus on screening high-risk populations, blood donors and carrying out educational programmes for creating awareness. In 1992, the Government launched the first National AIDS Control Programme (NACP-I) with the objective of slowing down the spread of HIV infections so as to reduce morbidity, mortality and the impact of AIDS in the country. The National AIDS Control Board was constituted and an autonomous National AIDS Control Organization (NACO) was set up to implement the project through the States and Union Territories. It is a 100 per cent centrally sponsored scheme.[114] A number of Anti-Retroviral Treatment Centres were established during this period by the NACO to provide a comprehensive package of care, support and treatment services to persons living with HIV/AIDS.[115]

The Second National AIDS Control Project (NACP-II) was launched in November 1999. The strategic shift was reflected in the two key objectives of NACP II: (a) to reduce the spread of HIV infection in India, and (b) to increase the capacity to respond to HIV/AIDS on a long-term basis. Key policy initiatives taken during NACP-II included the adoption of the National AIDS Prevention and Control Policy of 2002, scale-up of targeted interventions for high-risk groups in high prevalence States, adoption of the National Blood Policy, the launch of the National Adolescent Education Programme, the introduction of

---

[114] *Subodh Sarma v. State of Assam*, 2000 (3) G.L.T. 351.

[115] *Kasturi Lal v. National Aids Control Organization*, 2015 (4) S.C.T. 751 (P and H).

counselling, testing and setting up of the National Council on AIDS in the centre and the State AIDS Control Societies in all States. Further, in July 2007 the Third National AIDS Control Project (NACP-III) was launched with the goal of halting and reversing the epidemic by the end of the project period by scaling up prevention efforts among the high-risk groups and the general population and integrating them with care, support and treatment services.[116] The term 'high-risk groups' includes males having sex with males, sex workers, and people who inject drugs.[117] The NACP-III project specified an urgent need for proper HIV/AIDS information and services and sexual and reproductive health programmes targeted specifically at youth. The NACP-IV was launched in 2012 with the aim of consolidating gains made to date, accelerating the process of reversal and further strengthening the response to the epidemic in India. Under NACP-IV, targeted intervention services include needle or syringe exchange programmes and oral-substitution therapy for persons with Immunodeficiency, condom promotion and distribution, and linkage to HIV and sexually transmitted infections testing and treatment services. Along with these, many new HIV prevention initiatives such as interventions for migrant workers and focused strategies for transgender people have been initiated as a strategic part of NACP-IV.[118]

---

[116] Mohammed K. Suhail, *National AIDS Control Program (NACP III) India - Program Evaluation and Comparative Analysis*, 3(4) AIMDR 10, 11 (2017).

[117] Harshal T. Pandve & Purushottam A. Giri, *HIV/AIDS Prevention and Control in India: Achievements and Future Challenges*, 7(12) NAJMS 275 (2015).

[118] Sukarma Tanwar et al., *India's HIV Programme: Successes and Challenges*, 2 (Suppl. 4) J. VIRUS ERAD. 15 (2016).

Right to Health and Protection against Occupational Health Hazards

Occupational health is one of the major aspects of the right to health discussion in this era of industrialization. The realization of workers' health and safety as a fundamental human right is dependent upon revitalizing labour rights in the working environment.[1] Historically, it was the Industrial Revolution in the 19th century and the related movement of ideas that catalysed the evolution of international labour standards in connection with various human rights in general and occupational health and safety in particular. The phrase 'occupational health right' as a whole includes various rights, such as right to just and humane condition of work, right to access to healthcare, right to get compensation, right to maternity benefit including social security measures and welfare facilities.[2] In this background, this chapter is primarily devoted to elaborating the international and Indian legislative framework relating to occupational health and safety.

I. HUMAN RIGHTS ORIENTATION TO OCCUPATIONAL HEALTH AND SAFETY

Occupational health and safety are some of the most important aspects of human concern in this industrial age. In the early days, workers'

---

[1] Jeffrey Hilgertt, *The Future of Workplace Health and Safety as a Fundamental Human Right*, 34(3) CLLPJ 715, 734 (2013).

[2] Constance Thomas & Yuki Horii, *Equality of Opportunity and Treatment in Employment and Occupation*, in Fundamental Rights at Work and International Labour Standards 57–89, 64 (ILO ed, 2003).

health as provided by physicians was a part of general healthcare rather than a part of a complex system built on different assumptions.[3] With the development of the human right to health the multidimensional concept of occupational health and safety evolved. In general, occupational health is defined as the science of the anticipation, evaluation, recognition and control of hazards arising in or from the workplace which could impair the health and well-being of workers. It also takes into account the possible impact of the surrounding communities and the general environment on the health of the workers.[4] Health promotion is a central element of occupational health practice and thus efforts must be made to enhance workers' physical, mental and social well-being. The goals of occupational safety and health programmes include fostering a safe and healthy work environment. Therefore, under the modern human rights jurisprudence, occupational health is an extensive multidisciplinary field, invariably touching on issues related to scientific areas such as medicine—including physiology and toxicology—ergonomics, physics and chemistry, as well as technology, economics, law and other areas specific to various industries and activities.[5] However, as a dimension of right to health, the sphere of occupational health is necessarily vast, encompassing a large number of disciplines and numerous workplace and environmental hazards.

Further, the WHO and the ILO in 1950 jointly stated that

> Occupational health should aim at the promotion and maintenance of the highest degree of physical, mental and social well-being of workers in all occupations; the prevention amongst workers of departures from health caused by their working conditions; the protection of workers in their employment from risks resulting from factors adverse to health; the placing and maintenance of the worker in an occupational environment adapted to his physiological and psychological capabilities.[6]

---

[3] Jerzy A. Kopias, *Multidisciplinary Model of Occupational Health Services. Medical and Non-Medical Aspects of Occupational Health*, 14(1) IJOMEH 23 (2001).

[4] BENJAMIN O. ALLI, FUNDAMENTAL PRINCIPLES OF OCCUPATIONAL HEALTH AND SAFETY vii (ILO 2008).

[5] *Ibid.* at 17.

[6] Kwesi Amponsah-Tawiah & Kwasi Dartey-Baah, *Occupational Health and Safety: Key Issues and Concerns in Ghana*, 12(4) IJBSS 119, 120 (2011).

In summary, the definition of 'the adaptation of work to man, and of each man to his job'[7] is applicable irrespective of any discrimination.

To address all these aspects, employers and Governments must strive to establish and maintain decent working conditions and a working environment. The stakeholders of the occupational health should assure that (a) work should take place in a safe and healthy working environment, (b) work should offer real possibilities for personal achievement, self-fulfilment and service to society, and (c) conditions of work should be consistent with workers' well-being and human dignity.[8] Broadly, the concept of occupational health comprise four broad concepts: (a) occupational health practice, (b) occupational health care, (c) occupational hygiene, and (d) occupational safety and health management.

II. RIGHT TO HEALTH, OCCUPATIONAL HEALTH UNDER INTERNATIONAL HUMAN RIGHTS LAW

A. UN Initiatives in Protecting Occupational Health

The occupational health and workers' rights in securing the same is always a major concern for the international community. The initiatives are prominent in various human rights instruments. The UDHR as proclaimed by the United Nations General Assembly in 1948 states that everyone has the right 'to just and favourable conditions of work',[9] which includes health and safety at work.[10] Further, Article 24 of the UDHR stipulates everyone's 'right to rest and leisure, including reasonable limitation of working hours and periodic holidays with pay'. Though it is soft law, all member-States of the United Nations have an

---

[7] TAKELE TADESSE & MENGESHA ADMASSU, OCCUPATIONAL HEALTH AND SAFETY 4 (Ethiopia Public Health Training Initiative 2006).

[8] ILO, CONCLUSIONS CONCERNING FUTURE ACTION IN THE FIELD OF WORKING CONDITIONS AND ENVIRONMENT, (Adopted by the 70th Session of the International Labour Conference, 6–26 June 1984) Section I, Paragraph 2.

[9] UDHR 1948, Article 23(1).

[10] Alli, *supra* note 4, at 20.

obligation to protect these rights in respect of their citizens.[11] Thus, by understanding the importance of enjoyment of just and favourable conditions of work, Gordon Brown correctly noted this right as a way of securing the dignity of the working individual.[12] Thus, the Supreme Court of India, in *Vishaka v. State of Rajasthan*,[13] emphatically stated that the right to work with dignity is a universally recognized basic human right and that the common minimum requirement of this right has received global acceptance. Later on, the ICESCR, 1966 recognized the right of everyone to the enjoyment of just and favourable conditions of work which ensure 'safe and healthy working conditions',[14] 'rest, leisure and reasonable limitation of working hours and periodic holidays'[15] and 'decent living for themselves and their families'[16]. The CESCR by interpreting the abovementioned clauses observed that[17]:

> People must be afforded minimum conditions of occupational health and safety, and States parties are responsible for adopting policies and laws to that end. A coherent national policy in this regard is incumbent on all States parties. The standards laid down in Article 7 also relate to the duties of State parties to reduce the working week in a progressive manner and to ensure that workers enjoy adequate rest and holidays. For all aspects of this Article, State parties must establish a baseline or minimum standard below which the working conditions of no worker should be allowed to fall; they must also develop enforcement measures guaranteeing these rights.

Thus for decades, there is a clear and shared global understanding that occupational health and safety is a fundamental human rights question.[18] Further, the CEADW, 1979 guarantees women's 'right to protection of health and to safety in working conditions, including

---

[11] *Arun Kumar Bhadoria v. State*, 2018 (3) R.C.R. (Criminal) 146.

[12] GORDON BROWN (ed.), THE UNIVERSAL DECLARATION OF HUMAN RIGHTS IN THE 21ST CENTURY: A LIVING DOCUMENT IN A CHANGING WORLD 35 (Open Book Publishers 2016).

[13] A.I.R. 1997 S.C. 3011.

[14] ICESCR 1966, Article 7(b).

[15] *Ibid.* Article 7(d).

[16] *Ibid.* Article 7(a)(ii).

[17] ESCR Committee, Fact Sheet No.16 (Rev.1). Adopted by the World Conference on Human Rights, 1993 (A/CONF. 157/24 (Part 1), Chap. III).

[18] Hilgertt, *supra* note 1, at 720.

the safeguarding of the function of reproduction'[19] and requires States to provide special protection to pregnant women performing types of work that are harmful to them.[20] Hence, international law requires States to take measures to ensure that formal and informal workers enjoy these rights.

B. ILO Initiatives in Protecting Health Rights of Workers

In the protection of occupational health, the most important contributor is the ILO and it adopted various conventions on occupational health from its early days. However, India is not a party to all those conventions. Thus, the study of the ILO initiatives in protecting the health rights of the worker is confined only to the Convention which has been ratified by India. The Underground Work (Women) Convention, 1935 is the earliest Convention that has been ratified by India. This Convention was adopted by the ILO through its Nineteenth Session of General Conference on June 21, 1935. The Convention strictly prohibited the employment of females, irrespective of their age, on underground work in any mine as this kind of employment may be derogative for the health of the women.[21] However, the Convention allows the member States to make exemption in their national laws with regard to the prohibition for (a) females holding positions of management who do not perform manual work, (b) females employed in health and welfare services, (c) females who, in the course of their studies, spend a period of training in the underground parts of a mine, and (d) any other females who may occasionally have to enter the underground parts of a mine for the purpose of a non-manual occupation.[22]

Later during the Forty-fourth Session of General Conference, the ILO adopted the Radiation Protection Convention (RPC) on June 22, 1960, with certain proposals with regard to the protection of workers

[19] CEDAW 1979, Article 11(1)(f).

[20] *Ibid.* Article 11(2)(d).

[21] Underground Work (Women) Convention 1935, Article 2.

[22] *Ibid.* Article 3.

against ionizing radiations and India ratified this Convention on November 17, 1975. Article 2 of the RPC specifies the ambit of the applicability of the Convention to all activities involving exposure of workers to ionizing radiations in the course of their work. The Convention casts a duty upon the State parties to take all appropriate steps to ensure effective protection of workers, as regard their health and safety, against ionizing radiations[23] and to restrict the exposure of workers to such radiations to the lowest practicable level and barred any unnecessary exposure by all parties concerned.[24] Moreover, before and during such employment, all workers have to be adequately instructed with regard to the precautions to be taken for their protection in connection with their health and safety and the reasons thereof.[25] It also requires that all workers should undergo an appropriate medical examination prior to or shortly after taking up any radiation-related work and subsequently undergo further medical examinations at appropriate intervals. It is also required that workers should not be exposed by contravening qualified medical advice.[26]

Thereafter, through the Fifty-first Session of the General Conference, the ILO adopted certain proposals with regard to maximum permissible weight to be carried by one worker and finally adopted Maximum Weight Convention on June 28, 1967.[27] The Convention ensures that 'no worker shall be required or permitted to engage in the manual transport of a load which, by reason of its weight, is likely to jeopardize his health or safety'[28] and states that States shall take appropriate steps to provide adequate instruction or training in working techniques, prior to assigning the duty of manual transport of loads other than light loads, to the workers with a view to safeguard the health of the workers and to prevent accidents.[29]

---

[23] Radiation Protection Convention 1960, Article 3.

[24] *Ibid.* Article 5.

[25] *Ibid.* Article 9(2).

[26] *Ibid.* Article 14.

[27] Came into force on 10 March 1970. India has ratified on 26 March 2010.

[28] Maximum Weight Convention 1967, Article 3.

[29] *Ibid.* Article 5.

Subsequently, the ILO through its Fifty-sixth Session of General Conference decided to adopt Convention Concerning Protection against Hazards of Poisoning Arising from Benzene on June 23, 1971.[30] Article 1 of the Convention specifies the scope of applicability of the provisions only to the activities involving exposure of workers to (a) the aromatic hydrocarbon benzene (C_6H_6), and (b) products containing benzene. The Convention ensures protection for the workers who may have skin contact with liquid benzene or liquid products containing benzene against the risk of absorbing benzene through the skin.[31] These workers are required to undergo a thorough pre-employment medical examination to prove their fitness for employment including a blood test and also the periodic re-examinations during employment at intervals as may be fixed by national laws or regulations.[32] These medical examinations shall be carried out under the responsibility of a qualified physician and with the assistance of a competent laboratory[33] and they should not incur any expenses from such workers.[34]

In 1973 the Convention Concerning Minimum Age for Admission to Employment was adopted by the ILO through its Fifty-eighth Session of General Conference on June 26, 1973.[35] The Convention requires Member States to draft and implement a national policy to ensure the effective abolition of child labour and to raise the minimum age for admission to employment to a level consistent with the required physical and mental development of young persons.[36] The Convention fixes that the minimum age may not be less than the age of completion of compulsory schooling and, in any case, less than fifteen years.[37] However, if the employment is hazardous in nature

---

[30] Adopted on 23 June 1971 and came into force on 23 July 1971. India has ratified on 11 June 1991.

[31] Convention Concerning Protection against Hazards of Poisoning Arising from Benzene 1971, Article 8(1).

[32] *Ibid.* Article 9(1).

[33] *Ibid.* Article 10(1).

[34] *Ibid.* Article 10(2).

[35] Came into force on 19 January 1976. India has ratified on 13 June 2017.

[36] Minimum Age Convention 1973, Article 1.

[37] *Ibid.* Article 2(3).

to a young person's health, safety or morals, the minimum age is generally not to be less than eighteen years.[38]

III. SPECIFIC LEGISLATIVE FRAMEWORK OF RIGHT TO OCCUPATIONAL HEALTH IN INDIA

A very significant proportion of contemporary health problems in India is originated from work-related issues. Since most of the workers with hazardous jobs are working in unhealthy conditions, they end up disabled for the rest of their lives.[39] However, along with the available medical treatment, there are various legislations to deal with issues of occupational health and to provide proper protection to the workers. The specific provisions of these legislations related to health issues required detailed discussion.

A. Workmen's Compensation Act, 1923

The 1923 Workmen's Compensation Act[40] is one of the earliest labour welfare and social security legislation enacted in India. It stands at the crossroads of fault liability and social insurance.[41] Before the enactment of this statute, the compensation scheme was not unknown to the Indian legal system, though that was at the mercy of the employer. The workers cannot claim it as right.[42] In 1884, for the first time in India, workers in Bombay made a demand for compensation, but it was not fruitful.[43] However, this 1923 Act secured right-based approach to the compensatory claims of the workers. The Act recognizes the fact that if a workman is a victim of an accident or an occupational disease in

---

[38] *Ibid.* Article 3(1).

[39] Ayesha Khan, *Occupational Health and Indian Labour Force*, 4 LAB & IND C. 132, 133 (2012).

[40] Act No. VIII of 1923. It was enacted on 15 March 1923.

[41] Jyotsna Nath Mallik, *Workmen's Compensation Act and Some Problems of Procedure*, 3(2) JILI 131 (1961).

[42] LAW COMMISSION OF INDIA, SIXTY-SECOND REPORT ON THE WORKMEN'S COMPENSATION ACT, 1923 9 (GOI 1974).

[43] NAJMUL HASAN, SOCIAL SECURITY SYSTEM OF INDIA 65 (S. Chand 1972).

the course of his employment, he needs to be compensated.[44] Besides, the Act has a provision of paying compensation to the employees for some occupational diseases contracted by them during the course of their employment.[45] The reason for bringing out such legislation was the strong realization that the complexity of the industry, with the increasing use of machinery, had consequently endangered the health and well-being of the workman leading to penury and deterioration.

Section 3 of the Act provides for the nature of the injury, the extent of liability and relevant grounds for the payment of compensation. The Act explains that if personal injury is caused to a workman by accident arising out of and in the course of his employment, his employer is liable to pay compensation to him.[46] The preconditions for attracting the provisions of Section 3 of the Act are that (a) death or injury must be caused to an employee, (b) the said injury must have been caused by accident, and (c) the accident must have arisen out of and in course of his employment.[47] Thus, an accident may lead to death but that an accident had taken place must be proved. Only because a death has taken place in course of employment will not amount to the accident. In other words, death must arise out of the accident[48] and there must be a causal relationship between the accident and the employment.[49] By analysing this aspect of casual relationship, the Allahabad High Court in *Oriental Insurance Company Ltd. v. Somdatt Sharma*[50] observed that, under this case, the workman was murdered and injury causing the death of workman had no causal connection with the nature of work performed by the deceased, thus the employer is not responsible to pay compensation. A similar approach was there on the part of the

---

[44] Workmen's Compensation Act 1923, Preamble.

[45] Labour Bureau, *Report on the Working of the Employees' Compensation Act, 1923 for the Year 2010*, 54(6) INDIAN LABOUR J. 569 (2013).

[46] Workmen's Compensation Act 1923, Section 3(1).

[47] *Talcher Thermal Station v. Bijuli Naik*, 76 (1993) C.L.T. 699 (Orissa).

[48] *Jai Prakash Agrawal v. Phool Sai*, 2011 A.C.J. 1923.

[49] *Mackinnon Mackenzie and Co. (P) Ltd. v. Ibrahim Mahmmed Issak*, A.I.R. 1970 S.C. 1906.

[50] 2019 A.C.J. 2821.

Supreme Court in *Shakuntala Chandrakant Shreshti v. Prabhakar Maruti Garvali*.[51] In this case, the Supreme Court had occasion to consider a fact where the workman while performing his duty had suffered chest pain and died. The cause of death in the post-mortem was revealed as cardiac arrest due to a ruptured aortic aneurysm. The Court held that the owner is not liable for payment of compensation on the ground that the necessary ingredients of Section 3(1) of the 1923 Act which attracts the liability of the employer to pay compensation were not present in the case. Further, in *Jyothi Ademma v. Plant Engineer, Nellore*[52] the Supreme Court observed that if the workman dies as a natural result of the disease which he was suffering or while suffering from a particular disease he dies of that disease as a result of wear and tear of the employment, no liability would be fixed upon the employer. But if the employment is a contributory cause or has accelerated the death, then the employer is liable.

Further, in determining the causes of accidents arising out of or in course of employment, the judiciary preferred the 'theory of notional extension of entry and exit of working premises or period of the working hour'. In *Saurashtra Salt Manufacturing Co. v. Bai Valu Raja*,[53] the Supreme Court explained that:

> As a rule, the employment of a workman does not commence until he has reached the place of employment and does not continue when he has left the place of employment, the journey to and from the place of employment being excluded. It is now well settled, however, that this is subject to the theory of notional extension of the employer's premises so as to include an area which the workman passes and repasses in going to and in leaving the actual place of work. There may be some reasonable extension in both time and place and a workman may be regarded as in the course of his employment even though he had not reached or had left his employer's premises. The facts and circumstances of each will have to be examined very carefully in order to determine whether the accident arose out of and in the course of employment of a workman keeping in view at all times this theory of notional extension.

---

[51] A.I.R. 2007 S.C. 248.

[52] A.I.R. 2006 S.C. 2830.

[53] A.I.R. 1958 S.C. 881.

Further, in *Mackinnon Mackenzie and Co. (P) Ltd. v. Ibrahim Mohd. Issak*,[54] the Supreme Court held that the expression 'arising out of employment' is not confined to the mere nature of the employment. The expression applies to employment including its nature, its conditions, its obligations and its incidents. If by reason of any of those factors the workman is brought within the zone of special danger in the course of his employment, the injury suffered would be one that arises out of employment. It was further clarified in the aforesaid judgment that if the accident had occurred on account of a risk which is an incident of the employment, the claim for compensation must succeed. In regard to the relationship between death and employment, in *Shakuntala Chandrakant Shreshti v. Prabhakar Maruti Garvali*,[55] the Supreme Court further reiterated that there has to be a proximate nexus between the cause of death and employment instead of a stray mention that death took place during the course of employment. As a result, the Court laid down the following principles to determine the course of employment:

1. There must be a causal connection between the injury and the accident and the accident and the work done in the course of employment.
2. The onus is upon the appellant to show that it was the work and the resulting strain which contributed to or aggravated the injury.
3. If the evidence brought on records establishes a greater probability which satisfies a reasonable man that the work contributed to the causing of the personal injury, it would be enough for the workman to succeed, but the same would depend upon the fact of each case.

However, the employer is not liable to pay the compensation though there is injury arising out of and in the course of his employment to the employee in case of (a) injury which does not result in the total or partial disablement for a period exceeding three days,[56] (b) injury caused due to influence of drink or drug taken by the workman, (c) injury caused due to wilful disobedience to safety rules, and (d) injury caused due to wilful removal of safety guards by the worker.[57] Thus, to hold the

54 A.I.R. 1970 S.C. 1906.

55 A I R 2007 S.C. 248.

56 Workmen's Compensation Act 1923, Section 3(1)(a).

57 *Ibid.* Section 3(1)(b).

liability of the employer, it is not necessary to prove negligence on the part of the employer and as such, the liability of the employer to pay compensation is absolute subject to these three exceptions.[58]

Further, Section 4 of the Act provides a manner for calculating the amount of damages to be paid and in determining that amount the percentage of total disability suffered is an important criterion.[59] In case of death of the workman, an amount equal to 50 per cent of the monthly wages of the deceased employee multiplied by the relevant factor or an amount of one lakh and twenty thousand rupees, which-ever is more, has to be paid to the dependents of that workman. In the case of permanent total disablement, an amount equal to 60 per cent of the monthly wages of the injured employee multiplied by the relevant factor or one lakh and twenty thousand rupees, whichever is more has to be paid to the worker. Where permanent partial disable-ment results from the injury the amount will depend on the loss of earning capacity caused by that injury. Further, in case of temporary disablement, whether total or partial, a half monthly payment of the sum equivalent to 25 per cent of the monthly wages of the employee, has to be paid. The explanation of Section 4 shows that allowance for medical treatment shall not be deemed to be compensation. Further, the Act empowers the Commissioner to be appointed by the provi-sional government[60] to implement the Act to its fullest extent. If any question arises in any proceedings under this Act as to the liability of any person to pay compensation or as to the amount or duration of compensation, the question shall be settled by a Commissioner.[61] However, there was no provision under the Workmen's Compensation Act for payment of medical expenditure incurred by the workmen for treatment.[62] This lacuna of the Workmen's Compensation Act needs to be addressed.

---

[58] *Royal Sundaram Alliance Insurance Co. Ltd. v. Shakuntla*, 2020 (2) A.L.J. 385.

[59] Gaurav Mukherjee, *The 'Disabled' as a Subject of Law: Utopian Discourse or Pragmatic Paradigm?* 3(2) CULJ 1, 13–14 (2014).

[60] Workmen's Compensation Act 1923, Section 20.

[61] *Ibid.* Section 19.

[62] *Beli Ram v. Rajinder Kumar*, A.I.R. 2020 S.C. 4453.

B. Employees State Insurance Act, 1948

i. Scope of the Act

The 1948 Employees State Insurance Act[63] is also one of the earliest legislations in the field of social insurance and includes health facilities within its purview.[64] The Act was enacted to provide certain benefits to employees in case of sickness, maternity and employment injury.[65] It was argued in *Gasket Radiators Pvt. Ltd. v. Employees' State Insurance Corpn.*[66] before the Supreme Court that in pursuance of Directive Principles of State Policy to secure a social order for the promotion of the welfare of the people and Entries 23 and 24 in List III of the Seventh Schedule of the Constitution, the Parliament has enacted the Employees' State Insurance Act. The Act applies to non-seasonal factories or manufacturing units employing ten or more people in a power using factory and twenty or more people in a non-power using a factory.[67] Section 1(5) however empowers the appropriate government to extend the provisions of this statute to other establishments as well.[68] By explaining this Section 1(5) of the ESI Act, in *Bangalore Turf Club Ltd. v. Regional Director, Employees State Insurance Corporation,*[69] the Supreme Court observed that the genus lies in the words 'any other establishment or class of establishment'. The three words industrial, commercial and agricultural represents species. Since the legislature did not want to restrict the operation of the ESI Act to these three species has used the catchwords 'or otherwise'.

By applying this principle, later on, the ambit of the ESI Act extends to other establishments such as road and motor transport undertakings, shops, hotels and restaurants, newspaper establishments, cinema

---

[63] Act No. XXXIV of 1948. It was enacted on 19 April 1948.

[64] A. Ananda Kumar et al., *Fffective Utilization of Employee State Insurance (ESI) Policy at E-Publishing Sector*, 17(5) GJMBR 35 (2017).

[65] ESI Act 1948, Preamble.

[66] A.I.R. 1985 S.C. 790.

[67] ESI Act 1948, Sections 1(4) and 2(12).

[68] *Salesian Province of Kolkata v. State of West Bengal*, 2011 (4) C.H.N. 456.

[69] A.I.R. 2015 S.C. 221.

halls and educational or medical institutions wherein ten or more persons are employed.[70] Further, the Act provides for the establishment of Employees' State Insurance Corporation[71] with the power (a) to promote measures for the improvement of the health and welfare of insured persons, (b) to take measures for the rehabilitation and re-employment of insured persons who have been disabled or injured.[72] Thus, the ESI Corporation has the power to expend the funds of the Corporation within such limits as may be prescribed by the Central Government.[73] The Act provides a scheme under which the employer and the employee must contribute a certain percentage of the monthly wage to this Insurance Corporation.[74] The existing wage limit for coverage under the Act is ₹15,000/- per month.[75]

Another question is that whether parties can, by their consent, contract out of the beneficial provisions of the ESI Act? It is true, in the ESI Act, there does not exist an express prohibition against contracting out of the beneficial provisions. But, at the same time, there is no provision which intends to permit such contracting out of the beneficial provisions of this Act. Thus, to answer this question, it is imperative to see whether this Act is intended to have a more extensive operation as a matter of public policy. It is equally true that everyone has a right to waive and agree to waive the advantage of law or rule or regulation made solely for the benefit and protection of the individual in his private capacity. But such a right cannot be dispensed with if it is likely to infringe any public right or public policy. A democratic society is founded on the rule of law and any practice which seeks to subvert or circumvent the law strikes at its very root.[76] Having regard to the scheme of the ESI Act, it is clear that it was enacted for the

---

[70] Sumitra Pujari, *A Study on Welfare Schemes of ESI*, 5(1) IJETSR 761 (2018).

[71] ESI Act 1948, Section 3.

[72] *Ibid.* Section 19.

[73] *ESI Corporation v. C. Saseendran*, 2001 (7) S.L.R. 16 (SC).

[74] Charulata Kulkanri, *Employee Benefits in Industries*, 1(2) IJRBM 41, 42 (2013).

[75] Shyam Pingle, *Occupational Safety and Health in India: Now and the Future*, 50 IND. HEALTH 167, 168 (2012).

[76] *Rattan Chand Hira Chand v. Askar Nawaz Jung*, (1991) 3 S.C.C. 67.

benefit of industrial workers and the object of this Act is one of public policy. Therefore, the answer to this question is obviously negative since contracting out of the beneficial provisions of this Act would infringe upon public rights or public policies. Any agreement, which tends to be injurious to the public or against the public good, is liable to be invalidated on the ground of public policy.[77]

ii. Beneficial Schemes under the Act

In *Employees State Insurance Corporation v. Bhakra Beas Management Board*,[78] the Supreme Court explained the working of ESI Corporation and observed that the Act has been enacted for the benefit of the workers to give them medical benefits, which have been mentioned in Section 46 of the Act. Hence the principal beneficiary of the Act is the workmen and not the ESI Corporation. The ESI Corporation is only the agency to implement and carry out the object of the Act. Further, with the approval of the State Government, the Corporation may establish and maintain hospitals, dispensaries and other medical and surgical services as it may think fit for the benefit of insured persons and their families.[79] In connection with this, the Act also specifies improvement of the health, welfare, rehabilitation and re-employment of insured persons as the purpose of expenditure from the Employees' State Insurance Fund.[80]

Further, this Act provides for the grant of cash benefits to the employees in the recognized contingencies of sleekness, maternity and employment injury. It is interesting to note that all these benefits have been allowed with the right-based attitude to the employees. Section 46(1) states that the insured persons and their dependents shall be entitled to (a) periodical payments in case of sickness certified by a duly appointed medical practitioner, (b) periodical payments in case of confinement or mis-carriage or sickness arising out of pregnancy,

---

[77] *R.C.C. (Sales) Private Limited v. E.S.I. Corporation*, A.I.R. 2015 A.P. 134.

[78] (2009) 10 S.C.C. 671.

[79] ESI Act 1948, Section 59. V. Jagannadham & K.S.R.N. Sarma, *Employees' State Insurance Scheme: A Critique of the Utilization of Reserves*, 17(19) EPW 786, 787 (1965).

[80] *Ibid.* Section 28(xi).

(c) periodical payments for suffering from disablement as a result of an employment injury sustained, (d) periodical payments to dependants when the insured person dies as a result of an employment injury sustained, (e) payment for medical treatment of insured persons, (f) payment for keeping attendance of an insured person, and (g) payment to the eldest surviving member of the family of an insured person who has died, towards the expenditure on the funeral of the deceased insured person, or, where the insured person did not have a family or was not living with his family at the time of his death, to the person who actually incurs the expenditure of the funeral of the deceased insured person. The qualification, conditions, rates and period of the abovementioned payments have to be fixed by the Central Government.[81] In addition to this, the Act also assures periodical payment to the person who sustains temporary disablement for not less than three days, excluding the day of the accident and the person who sustains permanent disablement, whether the total or partial.[82]

C. Factories Act, 1948

Health and medical facilities for workers in factories assume special significance as the workers are often exposed to occupational risks such as temperature (excessive cold or heat), the humidity of air, dampness including chill, low air movements and defective lighting in their workplaces. Even the external physical exciters like noise, sustain vibration, excessive uncontrolled ionizing radiation, high voltage electronic current and abnormal air pressure produce a damaging effect on certain definite organs of the worker's body. In addition to these, certain substances also cause poisoning diseases in specified industries. As a result, it is essential to take effective measures to protect the workers from such risks and dangers.[83] In India, to address these issues and to provide the required protection to the workers, in 1948, the Factories Act was enacted.[84] The Act aims to ensure

[81] *Ibid.* Sections 49–50.

[82] *Ibid.* Section 51.

[83] SURESH C. SRIVASTAVA, COMMENTARY ON THE FACTORIES ACT, 1948 170 (Universal 2002).

[84] Act No. LXIII of 1948. It was enacted on 23 September 1948.

adequate safety measures, to promote the health and welfare of the workers employed in factories.[85] To ensure this, the Act casts a duty upon every occupier to ensure so far as is reasonably practicable, the health, safety and welfare of all workers while they are at work in the factory.[86] Chapter III of the Act deals with the health issues of the workers, which required detailed discussion.

i. Cleanness and Disposal of Wastes and Effluents

Section 11 of the Act puts emphasis on the cleanness of the factory premise. It states that every factory shall be kept clean and free from effluvia arising from any drain, privy or other nuisance. In particular, accumulations of dirt and refuse should be removed by sweeping or by any other effective methods from the floors, staircases, benches of workrooms and passages, and disposed of in a suitable manner on daily basis. The floor of every workroom has to be cleaned at least once every week by washing. When the floor of the factory premise becomes usually wet due to any manufacturing process, there should be a proper drainage system to keep the floor clean. All inside walls and partitions, all ceilings and all walls, sides and tops of passages and staircases should be maintained. Where these walls are painted otherwise than with washable water paints or varnished, they should be repainted or re-varnished at least once in every five years. The doors and window frames and other wooden or metallic frameworks and shutters should be kept painted or varnished and that painting or varnishing has to be carried out at least once in every period of five years. The Factories Act further provides that when the abovementioned procedures are not possible to maintain by the occupier, the State Government may exempt that occupier from such compliance or may specify alternative methods for keeping the factory clean.

Section 12(1) of the Factories Act makes it obligatory for the occupier of every factory to make effective arrangements for the treatment of wastes and effluents originated due to the manufacturing process to

---

[85] Sapna, *Awareness of Workers to Health, Safety and Welfare Provisions under Factories Act, 1948*, 5(12) IJBMI 75 (2016).

[86] Factories Act 1948, Section 7A(1).

render them innocuous and for their disposal. The State Government may make rules regarding this, if needed, or may require this waste management arrangement to be approved by the appropriate authority.[87] By applying this power, the Effluent Board was constituted. Further, a question arises that whether this provision of the Factories Act is violative of Article 19(1)(g) of the Constitution? In *Synthetics and Chemicals Limited v. State of Uttar Pradesh*,[88] the Allahabad High Court dealt with this question and held that the provisions of Section 12 of the Factories Act constitute a restriction on the right of an owner or occupier of a factory to carry on trade and business as guaranteed by Article 19(1)(g) of the Constitution. Of course, it is always open to the Legislature to impose reasonable restrictions. Therefore, the norm or guideline, which the Effluent Board may adopt for the purpose of approving the arrangements made in a factory for the treatment of waste and effluents, should pass the test of reasonableness as required by the provisions of Article 19(6) of the Constitution. That provision requires that the restrictions should be reasonable and they should be in the interest of the general public. A balance should be drawn between the public interest and the right of the owner or occupier of a factory to carry on its business. It appears that the prime intention of the Legislature in enacting Section 12 is that public health should be allowed to suffer as little as possible as a result of the discharge of wastes and effluents due to the manufacturing process carried on in a Factory. Thus, Section 12 is not violative of Article 19(1)(g) of the Constitution. Adequate ventilation for fresh air and proper temperature in the factory are essential for maintaining the health of the workers.[89] Section 13 of the Factories Act requires that every factory makes effective and suitable provision in every workroom for securing and maintaining (a) adequate ventilation by the circulation of fresh air, and (b) a temperature to secure reasonable conditions of comfort and prevent injury to the health of workers therein.[90]

---

[87] *Ibid.* Section 12(2).

[88] Civil Misc. Writ No. 8888 of 1975, decided on: 11.05.1983.

[89] R.N. DWIVEDI & R.B. SETHI, FACTORIES ACT 97 (Law Book Company 1967).

[90] Factories Act 1948, Section 13.

ii. Access to Drinking Water and Sanitation

In addition to the abovementioned requirements, the Act also contains specific provisions for drinking water and sanitation. Section 18 of the Act provides those effective arrangements should be made to provide and maintain a sufficient supply of wholesome drinking water at suitable points conveniently situated for all workers. For convenient use of such water points, the Act directs to mark them as 'drinking water' in a language understood by the majority of the workers employed in the factory and for maintaining hygiene therein, the Act specifies that water points should not be situated within six metres of any washing place, urinal, latrine, spittoon, open-drain carrying sullage or effluent or any other source of contamination. Further, the Act directs to make provision for cooling drinking water during hot weather and for distribution thereof when more than two hundred and fifty workers are employed in a factory.[91] The use of the word 'cooling' in preference to 'cooled' gave rise to some arguments and it was *inter alia* contended that, whether a drink is cooling or not is entirely subjective, varying with individual taste. It was further urged in this context that for a cooling drink, some would prefer to take plain water; some may like to have a cold beer, and some others would even opt-out for a warm beverage. The concept therefore of what is 'cooling' appears to vary from age to age, place to place, and person to person. In view of this specific provision, one need not enter into the dichotomy of a 'cooling' drink rather it should be observed as 'the felt necessities of the time'.[92] Further, Section 19 makes it obligatory to provide sufficient latrine and urinal accommodation that should be accessible to workers at all times. This sanitation accommodation should be enclosed one and separate for male and female workers. All these latrines or urinals have to be adequately lighted, ventilated, clean and in sanitary condition at all times.[93]

---

[91] *Ibid.* Section 18.

[92] *Superintendent and Remembrancer of Legal Affairs v. Madhablal Mehta*, 1974 Cri. L.J. 1330.

[93] Factories Act 1948, Section 19.

iii. Provisions Related to Overcrowding and Spittoons

Except for these specific provisions, Section 16 provides that room in any factory should not be over-crowded to an extent that is injurious to the health of the workers employed therein. Moreover, the Act secures the provision for a sufficient number of spittoons in convenient places and they shall be maintained in a clean and hygienic condition. If any person spits within the premises of a factory except in the spittoons, then it is punishable with a fine not exceeding five rupees.[94]

iv. Safety Provisions

Like 'Health' in Chapter III, there are 'Safety' provisions in Chapter IV of the Act. Safety is logically one of the preconditions of health and should be understood holistically. Provisions relating to the fencing of machinery,[95] work on or near machinery in motion,[96] striking gear and device for cutting power,[97] self-acting machine,[98] the casing of new machinery,[99] hoist and lifts,[100] lifting machines, chains, ropes and lifting tackles,[101] revolving machinery,[102] pressure plant,[103] excessive weights,[104] protection of eyes,[105] precautions against dangerous fumes, gases,[106] prevention of explosive or inflammable dust, gas,[107]

---

[94] *Ibid.* Section 20(4).

[95] *Ibid.* Section 21. S.N. Mishra, Labour and Industrial Laws 815 (Central Law Publication, Allahabad, 2014).

[96] *Ibid.* Section 22.

[97] *Ibid.* Section 24.

[98] *Ibid.* Section 25.

[99] *Ibid.* Section 26.

[100] *Ibid.* Section 28.

[101] *Ibid.* Section 29.

[102] *Ibid.* Section 30.

[103] *Ibid.* Section 31.

[104] *Ibid.* Section 34.

[105] *Ibid.* Section 35.

[106] *Ibid.* Section 36.

[107] *Ibid.* Section 37.

and precautions in case of fire[108] are there to facilitate better working environment. As per Section 21, the prime-mover and flywheel connected with the prime-mover,[109] in all circumstances, whether it may be in motion or not, are required to be securely fenced and the nature and time of that fencing should be of substantial construction and should be kept in position while the parts of the machinery are in motion or in use. By explaining this provision, in *Sohanlal v. State of Rajasthan*,[110] the Rajasthan High Court held that Section 21 aims at the safety of the workmen who may not come into contact with the dangerous parts of the machinery and that is why it requires that these parts should be securely fenced. The obligation to securely fence the dangerous parts of the machinery is absolute whether those parts may be in motion or use or not. The parts by themselves may be so dangerous as to imperil the lives of those who are likely to come in contact with them. Therefore, the law seems to have imposed the obligation to securely fence them even though machinery may not be in motion.

Where it becomes necessary to examine any part of machinery referred to in Section 21, it can be carried out only by a specially trained adult male worker wearing tight-fitting clothing whose name has been registered in the register prescribed on this behalf.[111] Further, in every factory suitable striking gear or other efficient mechanical appliance has to be provided and maintained and used to move driving belts to and from fast and loose pulleys.[112] Every set screw, bolt or key on any revolving shaft, spindle, wheel or pinion required to be so sunk, encased or otherwise effectively guarded as to prevent danger and all spur, worm and other toothed or friction gearing which does not require frequent adjustment while in motion has to be completely encased unless it is so situated as to be as safe as it would be if it were completely encased.[113] In addition to this, all parts of every lifting

---

[108] *Ibid.* Section 38

[109] The Factories Act 1948, under Section 2(h) defines Prime-mover as 'any engine, motor or other appliance which generates or otherwise provides power'.

[110] (1962) I.L.L.J. 607 Raj.

[111] Factories Act 1948, Section 22(1).

[112] *Ibid.* Section 24(1).

[113] *Ibid.* Section 26.

machine and every chain, rope or lifting tackle has to be (a) of good construction, sound material and adequate strength and free from defects, (b) properly maintained, and (c) thoroughly examined by a competent person at least once in every period of twelve months.[114] Section 34 provides that no person shall be employed in any factory to lift, carry or move any load so heavy as to be likely to cause him injury. Here, the expression 'employed' means nothing more than 'engaged'.[115]Special provisions for women and children like the prohibition of employment of women and children near cotton openers[116] are also of great significance. It provides that no woman or child shall be employed in any part of a factory for pressing cotton in which a cotton opener is at work. Furthermore, for the proper monitoring and enforcement of these provisions, the Act envisages appointment of the Inspector by the State Government.[117]

v. Special Provisions for Young Persons

The Act defines a 'young person' as a person who is either a child or an adolescent[118] and a 'child' as a person who has not completed his fifteenth year of age.[119] Under the general framework, the 1948 Act provides that no child who has not completed his fourteenth year is allowed to work in any factory.[120] Further, Section 68 prohibits the employment of any child who has completed his fourteen years of age without a certificate of fitness granted by a competent medical authority. Sub-section (b) of Section 68 further says that a child or adolescent has to carry with him a token giving reference to such certificate at the time of working in the factory. In this regard, it is important to note that under Section 10 qualified medical practitioners can be appointed

---

[114] *Ibid.* Section 29(1).

[115] *State v. Alisaheb Kashim Tamboli*, A.I.R. 1955 Bom 209.

[116] Factories Act 1948, Section 27.

[117] *Ibid.* Section 8.

[118] *Ibid.* Section 2(d).

[119] *Ibid.* Section 2(c).

[120] *Ibid.* Section 67.

to be Certifying Surgeons for the purpose of the Act. The Certifying Surgeon has to carry out such duties as may be prescribed in connection with the examination and certification of young persons under the Act.[121] The Certifying Surgeon has the duty to medically supervise young persons when they are or are about to be, employed in any work which is likely to cause injury to his or her health.[122] Section 69 deals with the fitness certificates to be issued by the Certifying Surgeon to any young person upon satisfaction that the young person is of more than 14 years of age and has attained prescribed physical standards and he is fit for such work.[123] Sub-Section (2) of Section 70 says that an adolescent who has not been granted a certificate of fitness by a Certifying Surgeon to work as an adult shall be deemed to be a 'child' for all the purposes of this Act.

The Factories Act also concentrates on the working hour of child workers. Under Section 71 it states that children are not allowed to be employed or permitted to work, in any factory: (a) for more than four and a half hours in any day, and (b) during the night. No female child is allowed to work in any factory except between 8 a.m. and 7 p.m.[124] The manager of every factory in which children are employed is responsible to maintain a register of child workers, to be available to the Inspector at all times during working hours or when any work is being carried on.[125] Further, Section 23 directs that no young person shall be allowed to work on dangerous machines.

vi. Welfare Provisions for Maintaining Hygiene

The welfare provisions are important for the protection of the health of the workers as they are very much related to the maintenance of hygiene in the workplace. Chapter V deals with the welfare of the

---

[121] *Delhi Cloth and General Mills Co. Ltd. v. Chief Commissioner, Delhi*, A.I.R. 1971 S.C. 344.

[122] Factories Act 1948, Section 10(4)(iii).

[123] *Subash Kizhakkeveettil v. K.P.S.C.*, 2007 (2) K.L.J. 383.

[124] Factories Act 1948, Section 71(5).

[125] *Ibid.* Section 73.

workers and includes provisions for storing and drying of clothing,[126] sitting,[127] first aid appliances,[128] canteens[129] and creches.[130] Every factory wherein 500 or more workers are ordinarily employed is required to have such number of welfare officers as may be prescribed.[131] Section 42 directs that in every factory: (a) adequate and suitable facilities for washing have to be maintained for the use of the workers, and (b) separate and adequately screened facilities have to be provided for the use of male and female workers. Section 43 empowers the State Government to make rules in respect of any factory or class or description of factories to secure provision for suitable places for keeping clothing not worn during working hours and for the drying of wet clothing. Section 46 empowers the State Government to make rules requiring that in any specified factory wherein more than two hundred and fifty workers are ordinarily employed, a canteen or canteens shall be provided and maintained by the occupier for the use of the workers. Further, Section 47 requires that in every factory, where more than one hundred and fifty workers are employed, adequate and suitable shelters or restrooms and a suitable lunchroom, with the provision of drinking water, where workers can eat meals brought by them is be provided and maintained for the use of the workers.

Section 48 requires when more than fifty women are employed ordinarily in a factory, the provision and maintenance of a suitable room or rooms for the use of children under the age of six years of such women employed in that factory. Therefore, in order that a factory may function in accordance with the law, buildings or parts of buildings have to be provided by the owner or occupier for the use of the workmen for the purposes mentioned in the several provisions mentioned above.[132]

---

[126] *Ibid.* Sections 42 and 43.

[127] *Ibid.* Section 44.

[128] *Ibid.* Section 45.

[129] *Ibid.* Section 46.

[130] *Ibid.* Section 48.

[131] *Ibid.* Section 49.

[132] *State of Punjab v. British India Corporation Ltd.*, A.I.R. 1963 S.C. 1459.

vii. Working Hours of Adults and Maintenance of Strength

Chapter VI deals with the provisions in regulating of working hours of adults. It prescribes that no adult worker is allowed to work in a factory for more man 48 hours a week.[133] Section 52 provides that no adult worker is allowed to work in a factory on the first day of the week which is subject to certain exemptions. Section 53 provides for compensatory holidays. Further, subject to Section 51, no adult worker is allowed to work in a factory for more than nine hours a day.[134] Further, Section 55 states that:

> The periods of work of adult workers in a factory each day shall be so fixed that no period shall exceed five hours and that no worker shall work for more than five hours before he has had an interval for rest of at least half an hour.

By studying Sections 54, 55 and 56, the Supreme Court in *Workmen of Bombay Port Trust v. The Trust of The Port of Bombay*,[135] observed that the hours of work cannot be more than 9 in a day and taken with the intervals for rest these 9 hours may be spread over 10 and 1/2 hours. The only difference is that a worker must not be made to work for more than 5 hours at a stretch before he has had an interval for the rest of half an hour at the least. Thereafter, where a worker in a factory works on a shift that exceeds beyond midnight for the purposes of Sections 52 and 53, in his case, a holiday for a whole day means a period of 24 consecutive hours beginning when his shift ends.[136] Section 58 prohibits overlapping of shifts and Section 59 provides for payment of extra wages over time. Section 61 provides for a notice board being maintained indicating the hours of work, shift, etc. in every factory. Section 62 provides for the maintenance of a register of adult workers. Section 65 enables the State Government to grant exemptions. Thus, by explaining all these provisions, the Supreme Court in *Gujarat Mazdoor Sabha v. State of Gujarat*,[137] observed that the

---

[133] Factories Act 1948, Section 51.

[134] *Ibid.* Section 54.

[135] A.I.R. 1966 S.C. 1201.

[136] Factories Act 1948, Section 57.

[137] A.I.R. 2020 S.C. 4601.

provisions embodied in Chapter VI of the Factories Act reflect hard-won victories of masses of workers to ensure working conditions that uphold their dignity. Moreover, under the framework of the Factories Act, except in Section 66, the restriction or regulation or privileges or obligations imposed are identical in all respects and there is no difference from one worker to another, be it a male or a female. Only in Section 66 of the Act, discrimination is introduced and Section 66(1) (b) of the Act provides that no women are required or allowed to work in any factory except between the hours 6.00 a.m. and 7.00 p.m.

D. Plantation Labour Act, 1951

After independence, in 1951 on the basis of the recommendation of the Labour Investigation Committee, the then Central Legislature enacted Plantation Labour Act[138] to give the plantation workers special treatment in comparison to the other general workers, to provide welfare and regulate the conditions of work of plantation workers. This Act applies to any land used or intended to be used for growing tea, coffee, rubber, cinchona or cardamom if they admeasured 10.117 hectares or more or in which 30 or more persons were employed.[139] By explaining the importance of the 1951 Act in *Tata Tea Limited v. State of Tamil Nadu*,[140] the Madras High Court observed that the agony of plantation workers was sought to be remedied only after India became a republic in the form of the Plantation Labour Act, 1951. The Act for the first time attempted to provide certain minimum safeguards in respect of health and welfare to the plantation workers. The Act provides for certain statutory service conditions including housing, hours of work, weekly holidays, leave including annual leave, maternity leave, etc. Thus, the 1951 Act, in its Chapter III, namely, 'Provisions as to Health' emphasizes certain necessary health requirements of plantation workers. Section 8 of the Act casts an obligation upon the employer to provide and maintain a sufficient supply of drinking water for all workers. A sufficient number of latrines and urinals separately for

---

[138] Act No. LXIX of 1951. It was enacted on 2 November 1951.

[139] Plantation Labour Act 1951, Section 1(4)(a).

[140] (2010) IILLJ 762 Mad.

males and females have to be provided in every plantation area.[141] Both of these are the preconditions of good health. The 1951 Act also emphasizes access to medical care and provides direction upon the employer to secure such medical facilities for the workers and their families as may be prescribed by the State Government. If the employer fails to provide the medical facilities, the State Government upon a request of the Chief Inspector may arrange medical facilities therein and recover the cost thereof from the defaulting employer. Such cost of medical facilities can be recovered as an arrear of land revenue.[142] Where adolescents are employed in any work in any plantation which is likely to cause injury to their health, continuous supervision of the Certifying Surgeon is required.[143]

Section 18 provides for the appointment of welfare officers in plantations wherein 300 or more workers are employed. Moreover, every worker who is exposed to insecticides, chemicals and toxic substances has to go through a periodical medical examination and that the record of the medical examination has to be maintained by the employer. Every worker should also have access to such medical records.[144] Except these, there are provisions for maternity benefit,[145] housing of every worker,[146] creches for children of women workers,[147] which all have direct impacts upon the right to health of the plantation workers.

E. Mines Act, 1952

The Mines Act 1952[148] was enacted to provide law relating to the regulation of labour and safety in mines. This Act was enacted in

---

[141] Plantation Labour Act 1951, Section 9(1).

[142] *Ibid.* Section 10.

[143] *Ibid.* Section 7(2)(b).

[144] *Ibid.* Section 18A.

[145] *Ibid.* Section 32.

[146] *Ibid.* Section 15.

[147] *Ibid.* Section 12.

[148] Act No. XXXV of 1952. It was enacted on 15 March 1952 and came into force on 1 July 1952.

the exercise of power under Entry 55, List I, 'Regulation of labour and safety in mines and oil fields' of the Seventh Schedule of the Constitution.[149] The object of the 1952 Act is to regulate the labour and safety of workers working in the mines.[150] Like all other labour legislations, Section 19 of the 1952 Act directs to provide a sufficient supply of cool and wholesome drinking water for all persons employed in the mine. In addition to this special arrangement has to be made to supply drinking water for persons employed below the ground. Similarly, adequately lighted, ventilated and clean latrines and urinals separately for males and females have to be provided.[151] Further, Section 21(1) provides that:

> In every mine, there shall be provided and maintained so as to be readily accessible during all working hours such number of first-aid boxes or cupboards equipped with such contents as may be prescribed.

This first-aid box should be kept in charge of a responsible person who is trained and always be readily available during the working hours of the mine.[152] Further, there is a statutory direction to arrange conveyance to hospitals for persons who suffer bodily injury or become ill during the working hour within the mine.[153] Wherein more than one hundred and fifty persons are employed, in such mines, there has to be a first-aid room of such size with such equipment and in the charge of such medical and nursing staff as may be prescribed.[154] The Act also prohibits the employment of children below 18 years of age in a mine with the exception that apprentices above 16 years may be allowed to work under proper supervision in a mine.[155] Moreover, no person is allowed to work in a mine for more than six

---

[149] *Tara Prasad Singh v. Union of India*, A.I.R. 1980 S.C. 1682.

[150] *Bagalkot Udyog Ltd. v. Union of India*, 1993 (4) Kar. L.J. 7.

[151] Mines Act 1952, Section 20.

[152] *Ibid.* Section 21(3).

[153] *Ibid.* Section 21(4).

[154] *Ibid.* Section 21(5).

[155] *Ibid.* Section 40. *See*, K.G. Mallikarjuna, *Constitutional Provisions and Legislations for Child Labour in India*, 3(2) IJECR 133, 136 (2013).

days in any one week.[156] Any adult employed above ground in a mine is not allowed to work for more than forty-eight hours in any week or for more than nine hours in any day.[157] Similarly, any adult employed below ground in a mine is not allowed to work for more than forty-eight hours in any week or for more than eight hours in any day.[158] With regard to health and safety standards, this Act gives blanket power to the Central Government to regulate various aspects like prevention of dust, noxious fumes, safe pillars to prevent premature collapse, waterlogging and lighting arrangements. But the nature of mining work is so diverse that the absence of clear-cut specifications poses problems for the implementation of the Act.[159]

F. Maternity Benefit Act, 1961

i. Objective and Application of Act

The 1961 Maternity Benefit Act[160] was passed by the Central Legislature to regulate the employment of women in certain establishments for a certain period before and after child-birth and to provide for maternity benefit and certain other benefits. The Act protects the dignity of motherhood and the dignity of a new person's birth by providing protection for the full and healthy maintenance of the woman and her child at the time of pregnancy or lactation when she is not working.[161] By analyzing the importance of the 1961 Act, the Supreme Court in *Municipal Corporation of Delhi v. Female Workers (Muster Roll)*,[162] observed that:

---

[156] *Ibid.* Section 28.

[157] *Ibid.* Section 30.

[158] *Ibid.* Section 31.

[159] National Committee on Dust-Related Lung Diseases, *The Law on Occupational Health and Safety in India: Legislations Inadequate*, 5 LAWYERS COLLECTIVE 13, 15 (1990).

[160] Act No. LIII of 1961. It was enacted on 12 December 1961.

[161] Ipseeta Satpathy et al., *An Introspection into Awareness of Maternity Benefit Act 1961 in Semi-Urban Area*, 5(9) INT. J. MANAG. 13 (2014).

[162] A.I.R. 2000 S.C. 1274.

To become a mother is the most natural phenomena in the life of a woman. Whatever is needed to facilitate the birth of child to a woman who is in service, the employer has to be considerate and sympathetic towards her and must realise the physical difficulties which a working woman would face in performing her duties at the work place while carrying a baby in the womb or while rearing up the child after birth. The Maternity Benefit Act, 1961 aims to provide all these facilities to a working woman in a dignified manner so that she may overcome the state of motherhood honourably, peaceably, undeterred by the fear, of being victimised for forced absence during the pre or post-natal period.

Thus, the beneficial schemes under this 1961 Act are available not only to the regular working women or working women on a permanent basis but also to the women employees appointed on a contract basis or on ad hoc or temporary basis.[163] Moreover, the contract which takes away the benefits, as provided under the Maternity Benefit Act, 1961, is void.[164]

ii. Right to Payment of Maternity Benefit

Section 5(1) describes the right of the woman workers to get maternity benefit and also fixes the rate of benefits and the period for which the woman workers is entitled to receive such benefits. Thus, Section 5(1) states:

> Subject to the provisions of this Act, every woman shall be entitled to, and her employer shall be liable for, the payment of maternity benefit at the rate of the average daily wage for the period of her actual absence, that is to say, the period immediately preceding the day of her delivery, the actual day of her delivery and any period immediately following that day.

From the explanation it is clear that the average daily wage means the average of that particular woman's wages payable to her for the days on which she has worked during the period of three calendar months immediately preceding the date from which she absents herself on account of maternity, the minimum rate of wage fixed or revised under

---

[163] *Priyanka Gujarkar Shrivastava v. Registrar General*, 2017 Lab IC 1646; *Neetu Choudhary v. State of Rajasthan*, 2006 (107) F.L.R. 492.

[164] *P. Brinda v. Tamil Nadu, Dr. Ambedkar Law University*, (2020) 5 M.L.J. 396.

the Minimum Wages Act, 1948 or ten rupees a day, whichever is the highest. Thus, the Kerala High Court in *Malayalam Plantations Ltd. v. Inspector of Plantations Mundakayam*,[165] observed that there is nothing to suggest or to infer from Section 5 of the Act that she should be paid by way of maternity benefit anything more than what she would have earned if she had worked during the same period. In other words, the law does not require the employer to treat her differently from a worker on leave with wages. This idea of the Parliament in enacting the law is clear from other provisions as well.

Furthermore, this Section provides that she must be paid at the rate of the average daily wage for the period of her actual absence. The expression 'actual absence' emphasizes the fact that it covers only working days. Nobody will say that a worker is absent on a holiday. That shows that the Legislature intended only to direct the employer to pay maternity benefit at the rate of the average daily wage for the working days absented by the worker. Thus, the Uttrakhand High Court in *Indu Joshi v. State of Uttarakhand*,[166] observed that the benefits under the Act are equally applicable to all the employees. It is also clear that the Maternity Benefit Act makes no difference between the permanent, temporary and contractual employees and all the benefits as envisaged apply to all. The only criteria is that the woman claiming maternity benefit has worked for 80 days in an establishment of the employer in the twelve months immediately preceding the date of her expected delivery.[167] It is interesting to note that earlier it was fixed at 160 days in an establishment. However, through the Amendment Act (Act 61 of 1988) it was decreased to 80 days. Further, Section 12 of the Act protects employment from arbitrary dismissal made by the employer during pregnancy. Thus, any unjust denial of maternity leave and employment, when a woman worker reported to duty, after delivery of a child, is illegal and violative of Articles 14 and 21 of the Constitution of India.[168]

[165] A.I.R. 1975 Ker 86.

[166] 2014 (3) U.C. 1974.

[167] Maternity Benefit Act 1961, Section 5(2).

[168] *L. Kannaki v. Secretary to Government Animal Husbandry and Fisheries Department*, 2012 (133) F.L.R. 48.

Further Section 5(3) describes that 'the maximum period for which any woman shall be entitled to maternity benefit shall be twenty-six weeks of which not more than eight weeks shall precede the date of her expected delivery'. It implies that the leave for the remaining period can be availed after the delivery of the infant. In the case of women having two or more surviving children the period of maternity should be of twelve weeks of which only six weeks is available before the delivery. But, if the woman dies during this period, the maternity benefit shall be payable only for the days she was living which includes the day of her death. The 1961 Act further provides that where a woman, having been delivered a child, dies during her delivery or during the period immediately following the date of her delivery for which she is entitled to the maternity benefit, leaving behind, in either case, the child, the employer shall be liable for the maternity benefit for the entire period but if the child also dies during the said period, then for the days up to and including the day of the death of the child. Thus, the computation of days for maternity benefits totally depends upon the situation of the case and it is different from to case to cases.

iii. Right to Get Other Benefits

In case of the death of the woman before receiving benefits, the employer is bound to pay the same to the nominated person or to the legal representatives.[169] According to Section 8, every woman is also entitled to receive a medical bonus of two-fifty rupees from her employer, if no free-of-charge prenatal confinement and postnatal care is provided by the employer.[170] The Act is also concerned about the health issues of women after miscarriage. The 1961 Act provides that in case of miscarriage the woman is entitled to leave with wages at the rate of maternity benefit for a period of six weeks immediately following the day of her miscarriage.[171] Moreover, the Madras High Court in

---

[169] Maternity Benefit Act 1961, Section 7.

[170] *Snehkiran Raghuvanshi v. V.C. King George's Medical University Gandhi Memorial,* 2020 (4) A.L.J. 53.

[171] Maternity Benefit Act 1961, Section 9.

Management of Kallayar Estate, Jay Shree Tea and Industries Ltd. v. Chief Inspector of Plantations,[172] observed that it is clear from the preamble of the 1961 Act that this Act is a social piece of legislation. When a question of interpretation arises, it has to be decided in favour of the workman since it is the commitment for the State also. This peculiar feature should not be lost sight of at the time of interpreting this Act. On the basis of this reason, the Court held that for the application of Section 9, in case of miscarriage, the prerequisite gave under Section 5, *i.e.*, the woman has to work for a period of not less than 160 days in the 12 months immediately preceding the date of her expected delivery, is not required. The provisions contemplated under Sections 9 and 5 of the 161 Act are independent and not interdependent and they should not be related or combined. If at all Section 9 has got any relation with Section 5 of the Act, the relation is limited in scope *i.e.*, only so far as the rate of benefit is concerned.

Moreover, in case of illness arising out of pregnancy, delivery, premature birth of the child, or miscarriage and on the production of proof of the same, every woman is entitled to additional leave with wages at the rate of maternity benefit for a maximum period of one month.[173] Section 11 of the Act gives a right to enjoy two breaks of the prescribed duration for nursing the child until the child attains the age of fifteen months in addition to the interval for rest allowed to woman in the course of her daily work. Where a woman absents herself from work on the grounds of maternity benefit, it is unlawful for her employer to discharge or dismiss her during or on account of such absence or to vary to her disadvantage any of the conditions of her service.[174] Thus, this provision prohibits the dismissal of a woman employee during or on account of her absence on Maternity Leave. It also ensures that the conditions of her service would not be varied to her disadvantage during her absence.[175]

---

[172] 1999 (81) F.L.R. 639.

[173] Maternity Benefit Act 1961, Section 10.

[174] *Ibid.* Section 12.

[175] *Rachna Chaurasiya v. State of U.P.*, 2017 (11) A.D.J. 399.

G. Unorganized Sectors Worker's Social Security Act, 2008

This 2008 Unorganised Workers' Social Security Act[176] intends to provide social security and welfare to the unorganized workers.[177] A home-based worker, a person engaged in the production of goods or services for an employer in his or her home or in other premises of employer's choice other than the workplace of the employer, for remuneration, irrespective of whether or not the employer provides the equipment, materials or other inputs,[178] self-employed worker or a wage worker in the unorganized sector, including a worker in the organized sector are entitled to the benefits under the 2008 Act. The Central Government is vested with the duty to formulate and notify welfare schemes for unorganized workers on various matters including health and maternity benefits and old age protection. Moreover, the Act empowers the State Government to formulate and notify various welfare schemes for unorganized workers on matters including employment injury benefit, housing, and old age homes.[179] All these matters are directly or indirectly connected with the right to health of the unorganized workers during their employment and even in old age. Further, the above Act provides for the constitution of the National Social Security Board[180] and the State Social Security Board[181] for the proper implantation and working of various social security schemes.

Except for the abovementioned legislations, there are certain other legislations to protect the health of the workers of the specified sector such as the Motor Transport Workers Act, 1961, the Beedi and Cigar Workers (Conditions of Employment) Act, 1966, the Bonded Labour System (Abolition) Act, 1976, the Dock Workers (Safety, Health and Welfare) Act 1986, the Building and Other Construction Workers

---

[176] Act No. XXXIII of 2008. It was enacted on 30 December 2008.

[177] S. Sivakumar, *Central Legislation*, 44 ASIL 723, 739–740 (2008).

[178] Unorganized Sectors Worker's Social Security Act, 2008, Section 2(b).

[179] *Ibid.* Section 3.

[180] *Ibid.* Section 5.

[181] *Ibid.* Section 6.

(Regulations of Employment and Conditions of Service) Act, 1996, etc. Further, the Trade Unions Act, 1926, Minimum Wages Act, 1948 and the Industrial Disputes Act, 1947 also have an impact upon the health right of the workers in general. However, after having all these legislative protections and various implementing authorities, till date, the occupational health of the workers is not in a satisfactory position in India. Lack of awareness, complex mechanisms of implementing authorities, and delay in proceedings are the reasons for such failure.

Conclusion

The right to health is absolutely essential for human existence and, as a result, it acquired global significance.[1] But what exactly is right to health? Is there, as is often asked, really such a thing? We can see the basic concerns behind this articulation by examining not only the contemporary practice of utilizing the concept but also the history of its use over a long period. There are series of ancient Indian authoritative publications, which gave a glimpse of the ancient system of protection of the right to health. For example, the *Kautilya's Arthashastra* described that the doctor was also subject to punishment and fine for not providing proper information to the patient or for committing a mistake and negligent treatment.[2] Within the international legal framework, primarily right to health was located within legal frameworks that focus on civil and political rights. With the development of specific human rights regimes, it was found that the concept of a right to health is more frequently being used to challenge abuses of health by invoking social and economic rights, even though it places the right to health on slippery terrain. As a consequence, the concept of the right to health got its most vivid acknowledgment in the 1966 International Covenant on Economic, Social, and Cultural Rights which secures every individual's right to the highest attainable standard of health. As per these international instruments, the principles of availability, accessibility, acceptability and quality are not only guiding concepts of the right to health but also help to clarify the nature of the responsibility that the states owe for proper realization of it. Thus,

---

[1] Mallika Ramachandran, *The Right to Health and the Indian Constitution*, 1 Delhi L. Rev. 1, 2 (2004).

[2] Amartya Sen, The Idea of Justice 357 (Penguin Books 2009).

by the conceptualization of health in social epidemiology, a rights paradigm explicitly links health with laws, policies and practices that sustain a functional democracy and focuses on accountability. The key rights needed to secure the highest attainable realization of the right to health include (a) right to non-discrimination, (b) right to information and participation, (c) right to privacy, physical integrity and confidentiality, (d) right to education, (e) right to a healthy environment and an adequate standard of living, (f) right to work and to just and favourable conditions of work and (e) right to social security. Hence, as health is a universal concern and the enjoyment of the right to the highest attainable standard of health can only be ensured through international cooperation and transfer of technology. So there should be cooperation between developed and developing countries and the developed countries should provide technical and financial assistance to the developing countries for securing aspects of the right to health.

In this present day, the sphere of the right to health includes the social determinants, relationships among doctors, medical staff, patients, caregivers and healthcare institutions and a right-based approach to the issues. It will not be wrong to say that presently the concept does not solely depend upon the responsibility of the state to secure the health of its citizens, rather it can be claimed by the citizens as a matter of right. This right expands to the right to participate in decisions affecting one's health and therefore links health issues with active social citizenship which ensures equality of access to care and the other preconditions for good health and demands the elimination of systemic discrimination in the realization of the right to health. In India, the right to health is an integral part of the fundamental right to life as recognized under Article 21 of the Constitution of India. Besides Article 21, the right to health has also been recognized in various other provisions of the Constitution of India. Thus, the 'right' approach to a health issue is common and convincing in international as well as domestic legal norms. It was noticed over time that the substantive aspect of the right to health in various legal instruments has been emphasized without evaluating its implementation. Hence, as health is one of the basic human rights and also a fundamental right for every individual, the Constitution of India needed to be amended to insert specific provisions related to the right to health, so that right to health can get an expressed constitutional protection like the right to education.

Moreover, to address the need of the people and to make 'health for all' a reality, a long distance has to be covered. It is important to note that assurance of access to health care in India is very poor. Substantial proportions of the population have limited access to healthcare. The poor persons suffer from a disproportionate burden of disease yet usually have less access to health care and policy benefits. The growth of primary health centres and other healthcare infrastructure in rural India is drastically low in comparison to urban localities. Even the combined growth of healthcare infrastructure in rural and urban areas could match the healthcare need. Thus, the galloping growth in population is the most important determinant, which is tremendously affecting all aspects of national well-being, including health. Hence, the government should take more initiatives in establishing hospitals, dispensaries and primary healthcare centres in the rural areas to secure access to healthcare to the rural people and should encourage private organizations to establish healthcare institutions in the rural and semi-rural areas of India. Along with this, awareness should be built among the general people regarding communicable diseases and the way to combat these diseases. Further, under the human rights approach, social assimilation is an important aspect for addressing the issues relating to people affected with HIV/AIDS. Hence, community programmes and social programmes should be organized to demise the stigma of HIV/AIDS-affected persons and to integrate them with society. More HIV/AIDS intervention programmes should be organized to spread awareness and impart information about the disease along with the effective steps to secure medical care.

Further, implementation of existing legislations is also of major concern for realizing the right to health to its fullest extent. Till now, numerous issues have already been addressed by the legislatures over time. But all these legislations have not achieved their desired goal due to lack of implementation, lack of internal facets disability and functioning issues. Accordingly, the amendment should be made to brand these existing legislations more worthy in protecting the right to health in India. Under the general legislative framework, the Drugs and Magic Remedies (Objectionable Advertisements) Act, 1954, should insert provisions relating to the constitution and functions of the 'Cosmetic Monitoring Authority' to monitor cosmetics advertisements. There should be clear guidelines and specifications regarding the diseases to be incorporated and excluded in the Schedule of the Act. Similarly, the Transplantation of Human Organ Act, 1994, should include a more complete definition of organ transplantation by including organs that could re-grow over a period of time and not immediately like skin within its purview. Further, a specific amount of monetary consideration for a specific organ should be fixed by the Act in case of donation towards the non-relatives which will help to control the commercial exploitation. With regard to the legislative framework relating to the right to health of women and children, the abortion procedure should be more transparent and there should be clear guidelines under the 1971 Medical Termination of Pregnancy Act with regards to the foetus right to born. The Child Labour (Prohibition and Regulation) Act, 1986, should include a specific provision dealing with 'welfare' in parity with the Factories Act, 1948, and should include children working in the unorganized sector within the definition of child labour. Furthermore, under the law relating to disabled people, the Rights of Persons with Disabilities Act, 2016, should insert specific provisions for the infrastructural requirement to secure better access to healthcare institutions such as provisions of lift and wheelchair. Similarly, the Maintenance and Welfare of Parents and Senior Citizens Act, 2007, should include provisions of management and standard of old-age homes within its purview and secures provisions for the availability of basic amenities in those homes.

Moreover, with regard to the law relating to epidemic diseases, a new statute should be enacted by repealing the Epidemic Diseases Act, 1897, with an integrated, comprehensive, actionable and relevant legal provision for the control of disease outbreaks in India. This should be articulated in a rights-based, people-focused and public health-oriented manner. Under the industrial law, the ESI Act should ensure time-bound benefit delivery services and the hospitals and dispensaries established under the ESI scheme should be well equipped with all the facilities and services because a large number of workforces in our country comprises of the employees registered under the 1948 ESI

Act. Moreover, the ESI Corporation should establish hospitals and dispensaries in all states of India. It is also alleged that in most of the cases the regulatory authorities are not working properly and some of them are not existing till now. Even the overburdened situations of judicial implanting mechanisms and lack of specific agencies to deal with health matters are also causing obstacles in the path of securing the right to health to the citizen of India.

Moreover, it is important to note that in 2009 the Parliament took a path-breaking decision when they decided to introduce the National Health Bill. The basic tenets of the Bill include the peoples' right to health and healthcare along with other allied rights, obligations of the governments and private institutions, users' rights, institutional structure for implementation and monitoring and judicial machinery for ensuring health rights for all. The Bill under Section 2 (hh) defines the 'right to health' for the first time under any legislative approach as the right of everyone to a standard of physical and mental health conducive to living a life in dignity. It specifies that central government and the state governments have the obligations to (a) undertake appropriate and adequate budgetary measures, (b) address biomedical determinants as well as the socio-economic, cultural and environmental determinants of health to provide free and universal access to healthcare services and (c) ensure comprehensive involvement of civil society, especially vulnerable or marginalized individuals or groups. But it is unfortunate that till now this bill is pending before the Parliament. Thus, to secure the right to health, this National Health Bill of 2009 should be passed as early as possible by the Parliament, so that people in India can get a better guarantee of their fundamental human right to health.

ABOUT THE AUTHOR

Sougata Talukdar is a teacher-in-charge and assistant professor at Sureswar Dutta Law College, University of Calcutta, West Bengal, India. He completed his LLM, BA LLB (Hons) and PhD from the University of Calcutta. Dr Talukdar was invited by the National Human Rights Commission, New Delhi, to contribute to the prestigious Silver Jubilee Edition of their journal. He has recently worked on a project on police system series as a researcher and coordinator and has served as an editor and contributor for many reputed legal journals. His areas of personal interest and academic expertise are health law, human rights and constitutional law.

INDEX

Other titles in this series:

Law of Business Contracts in India, Sairam Bhat (ed.)

Water and the Laws in India, Ramaswamy R. Iyer (ed.)

Protection of Himalayan Biodiversity: International Environmental Law and a Regional Legal Framework, Ananda Mohan Bhattarai

Social Justice and Labour Jurisprudence, Sharath Babu and Rashmi Shetty

Social Legislation of the East India Company: Public Justice versus Public Instruction, Nancy Gardner Cassels

Natural Resources Conservation Law, Sairam Bhat

Business and Human Rights, Manoj Kumar Sinha (ed.)

Crime and Justice in India, N. Prabha Unnithan (ed.)

In Custody: Law, Impunity and Prisoner Abuse in South Asia, Nitya Ramakrishnan

Law and Economics (*Volume I: Theory* and *Volume II: Practice*), Subhashis Gangopadhyay and V. Santhakumar (eds)

Separated and Divorced Women in India: Economic Rights and Entitlements, Kirti Singh

Women and Law: Critical Feminist Perspectives, Kalpana Kannabiran (ed.)

The Protection of Geographical Indications in India: A New Perspective on the French and European Experience, Delphine Marie-Vivien

Child Sexual Abuse and Protection Laws in India, Debarati Halder